Writing from Home

A Portfolio of Homeschooled Student Writing

by Susan Richman

PA Homeschoolers, R.D. 2 – Box 117

Writing from Home: A Portfolio of Homeschooled Student Writing. Copyright 1990 by Susan P. Richman. All rights reserved.

Printed and Bound in the United States of America

Paperback ISBN 0-929446-03-8
Hardback ISBN 0-929446-02-X

Acknowledgments

Thank you to Valerie Casses and Ann Fisher for help with proof-reading.

Cover picture was a joint effort of Jesse, Jacob, and Molly Richman. Molly did title page, intruduction picture, and page 236. Jacob did pages 20 and 204. Jesse did pages 112 and 132. Samuel Ward did the illustration on page 303.

Thank you to the following authors and their families for permission to include the following works and for help with proof-reading:

Gussie Abrahamse: *A Dilemma*; *Dear Governor-elect Wilder:*; *My Favorite Book*; *Sherlock Holmes Take-off*; *To the Editor*. August Beddingfield: *Ruford*. April Blair: *Roller Skating*; *Snowflakes*; *Woodland Creatures*. Sandra Blair: *Butterfly in the Garden*; *The Red Rose*; *Tulip of the Valley*. Dorien Casses: *Writing Autobiography*; *Impressionism*; *Grasshopper*. Gabriel Chrisman: *Close Call for Mooser*; *How to Buy a Good Car*; *Mad Lib Book Report*; *Nature Notes*; *Town Meeting*. Simon Chrisman: *Chicken Weather Report*; *Chicken News*; *Making Fruit Leather*. Nica Christensen: *Chickadees*; *Fall*; *Fall in Wisconsin*; *The First Wind of Spring*; *Lines to a Crow and a Sumac Bush*; *One Mother Spider*; *Poems*; Review of *Black Star, Bright Dawn*; Review of *The Great Gilly Hopkins*; *Spring*; *Where the Quiet Meets the Waves*. Skye Christensen: *Hazel-Rah*. Sunshine Civatarese: *How I wrote Teeney's Journey*; *Teeney's Journey Through Life*. Meredith Conroy: *My Caterpillar*; *Science Experiment Journal*. Anne Crouthamel: *Jenny's Surprise*. Robbin Crouthamel: *The Surprise in the Field*. Greg Darling: *Trapper, Our Dog*. Keith Darling: *Chitter*. Nicholas Early: *Burying Trammy and Getting a Puppy*; *Traminer's Operation*; *The Time Trammy Bit a Chipmunk*; *Trammy's Bath*; *Trammy's Wishes*; *When We Were Lost in Todd Sanctuary*. Esther Feagan: *Gideon*.

ACKNOWLEDGMENTS

iii

Jeremy Fisher: *The Royal Ranger Museum Tour*; *Where Am I?*. Joshua Fisher: *The Tree*. Matthew Formica: *Beach*; *Once Upon a Fish*. Timothy Formica: *A Day at the Beach*. Kiersten Galazen: *44 Hilarious Homophones*. Jennifer Girten: *The Journey*. Andrew Glendening: *My Dog*; *My Road*. Adam Guida: *King*. Julie Hoerr: *The Strange Surprise*. Lauren Ingram: *The Story about Lady - A Praying Mantis*. Katy Inouye: *Journal Entry - July 8, 1989*; *Journal Entry - July 16, 1989*. Rachel Johnston: *The French and Indian War*; *Our Busy Little Airport*; *Ricker Mountain*; *Thank you, Quentin*. Kristi Kashner: *Christmas*. Jeff Scott Kirkland: *Beethoven*. Tim Kirkland: *Little Brothers*. Emily Kissell: *Sea World*. Nicole Kissell: *It's a Miracle*. Alice Mae Kuehne: *Peter Babysits*. Tracy Kuehne: *City Rain, Country Rain*; *Penn and the Indians*. Elisabeth LaForet: *The Cow that said Quack*; *Where Geese Fly*. Jake LaForet: *The Adventures of James Brustar*; *A Winter Dream*. Mark Lama: *The Case of the Pantry Raider*. Anna Latinette: *Dogs*. Ian Latinette: *Gotcha Basket Company Tour*; *It's a Dog's Life*; *My Bedroom*; *My Road*; *Our Expensive Trip to Sea World*; *The Triumvirate*; *What am I?*. Micah Latinette: *Bear Story*; *My Bedroom*. Heather Leabman: *Why Canaries Make Horrible Pets*. Dory Lerew: *Dory's in the Money - A Dory Story*; *Grammy's Good Glasses*; *Our Family Newsletter*; *The Small Bird will Sing*; *Why I Like to Read*. Jennifer Lerew: *Do Not Eat the Core*; *Will and John*; *Working at the Library*. Shaw Lynds: *The Breeze*. Taryn Lynds: *Mid-Morning Attack*; *Edwina, A Medieval Cat*. Stephanie Maier: *The Best Summer Ever*. Aram Melis: *Snowflake*. Nathan Melis: *Summer*. Rachel Melis: *Archery*; *Poems*; *A Call to the Window*. William Moffat: *My Life as a Goodyear*. Christian Murphy: *Big Choice*; *Poem*. Clare Murphy: *The Kite*; *The Toy Adventure*. Emily Murphy: *The Museum Warehouse*. Mika Perrine: *A Day with Nori Perrine*; *Shadows in the Moonlight*. Teal Perrine: *The Metrodome*. Scott Petersen: *Pet Corner - Hamster's Great Escapes*. Jacob Richman: *A Baby Crime*; *Big Girl*; *House*; *I Can Sing*; *Math Land*; *My Road*; *What am I?*; *What's My Line*; *Why Does it not Come with Me*. Jesse Richman: *Biopoem*; *Book Response*; *Homeschoolers Visit Blind School*; *The King's Closet*; *My Bedroom: Told from the point of view of mice*; *My Road*; *Our Sneaky, Impatient and Guilty House Dog*; *Response to The 21 Balloons*; *Review of Johanna Spyri's Books*; *Surprise in the Woods*; *The Terrible Saga of Bartholimew Squeak*; *This Horrid House*; *Weight Watchers for Dogs*; *What's My Line*. Molly Richman: *Biopoem*; *Highway*; *Mazes*; *Mirror Baby Visits Us*; *My Bedroom 174*; *My Road*; *Pulling Teeth*; *Snow*; *What am I?*; *What's My Line*; *Wind*. Matthew Shultz: *The Grand Prix Race*; *The Time That Couldn't Fly*. Stephanie Shultz: *The Amethyst that Could Not Shine*. Mark Slezak: *Eclipse of the Moon*. Suzanne Slezak: *Journal Entry*. Elizabeth Smith: *Caroleena You Meant So Much to Me*. Emilie Smith: *Jack Almond*; *Speckle Dog Food*. Rebecca Snider: *I'm Blind Now*; *The 4-Her and His Dog*. Noah Snyder: *High St. Detectives - Volume 2*. Autumn Speck: *My Road*; *What am I?*. Laura Speck: *Biopoem*; *My Bedroom*; *What am I?*. Carina Strappello: *Friends*; *Lilly's Trip*; *Your New Kitten*. Jessica Strappello: *Meagan's New Home*; *Meagan and the Joke*; *The Ocean*. Amanda Strunk: *My Father's Hands*; *My Sister Susanna*. Elizabeth Strunk: *The Mysterious Little House*; *A Frightening Visitor and a Squished Loaf of Bread*. Hannah Strunk: *Messy But Fun*. Elesha Taylor: *NASA-Kennedy Space Center*. Sara Taylor: *My Vacation*; *Christmas Lights*. Elizabeth Tisdale: *An Unforgettable Valentine's Day*; *Review of Mildred Taylor's Books*. Mark Tisdale: *Christmas at Our House*. Mary Tisdale: *A Very Sad Christmas*. Holly Tobey: *Snowfall*. Hope Tobey: *The Poor Crow*. Lochlanina Tobey: *Fall's Apparel*. Megan Tobey: *Florence Nightingale of the Ocean*. Daniel Trembula: *Sam Houston*. Jennifer Trynovich: *Winter*. Samuel Ward: *The Tale of Trill*. Nathan Williamson: *Dear Aqua-Air Personnel*. Ryan Williamson: *Journal Entry*; Responses to *Charlotte's Web*. Luke Wilson: *Boston Observer*; Review of *Early Thunder* by Jean Fritz; Review of *Matilda* by Roald Dahl; Review of *The Adventures of Tom Sawyer* by Mark Twain; *Tour-Ed Mine*. Rachel Wilson: *My Idea Sheet*; *Rosebud*. Kirsten Grace Williams Winston: *A Special Birthday Book for Grandpa's Birthday*; *Snow*.

This book is dedicated to my family—

To Howard, my husband, who worked non-stop on all the technical and computer details of pulling this book together, and who was my most important editor, encourager, and helpmate all along the way.

And to my children, Jesse, Jacob, Molly, and Hannah, who all took part in their own ways in the creation of this book, and who have helped me see more clearly how children can grow as writers, and to know how unique each child is.

Table of Contents

Foreword

by Susannah Sheffer
Editor of *Growing Without Schooling*

It's exciting, for several reasons, to see this collection of writing by home–educated children and teenagers.

First it's exciting because the book is more than simply a collection of the young people's finished writing. If that had been all there was to the book, people whose work was not included in it might read it and think, "That's nice, but I could never do that." But Susan Richman has had the opportunity to learn about *how* these children write. She has heard the stories behind the finished work that was submitted, and has included many of these stories here. We hear about how many revisions a published piece had to go through before it was ready to be sent out, or how the writer came to feel comfortable experimenting with this particular form, or how he or she overcame an initial reluctance to write at all. I love hearing about these things because I am interested in how children grow as writers; I also know that this commentary will make this book much more useful to parents and children than it would otherwise be. The book is more than a proud display of accomplishment (although of course it is that too). It is a way for us to begin to understand what makes accomplishment possible.

Second, the book is exciting because it dispels one important myth about home education: that it is done in isolation, depriving the young person of any feeling of community. Some people have trouble imagining how young writers who don't go to school could ever have access to the kind of ongoing audience that children in classrooms have. And yet in this collection we hear about writing clubs that many of the children belong to (which sound very much like the writers' workshops that are so important to adult writers). We hear about the newsletters the children publish, the stories they have traded with other families, and—no less important—the helpful response that they get from their attentive families. Susan Richman says she thought that bringing out this book would be a way of giving the young writers an opportunity for a broader audience. I'm sure the book will do that, but what is also impressive is how many genuine and interested audiences these writers already have.

Third, this collection reminds us—all of us, not just the children among us—of what writing can do for our lives. When children write because they choose to, rather than because a curriculum requires them to, we are able to see *why* children write and, by extension, why anyone chooses to write at all. These children write because they have stories to tell, points to make, observations to record, feelings to express. We see how writing has helped them come to terms with difficult experiences, make sense of something that has confused them, remember something important. Writing is not just a record of something finished—first you think up the story, then you write it down; first you have the thought, then you simply record it. On the contrary, writing is itself a way of thinking, figuring things out, seeing more clearly, and I think that many of the writers in this collection have discovered this for themselves. A young writer and friend of mine said about this: "I write because I love it, of course, but also to communicate something. And when you communicate something, you want to be as clear as you can. And yet, the writing helps me clear up my thoughts, so it's like I rewrite something to make it clearer, and yet the rewriting helps me to see things *more* clearly. So then it has to be rewritten again, because now I understand things better than I did when I started!" Writing can be a way of figuring out what we mean, what we think, what we have seen. It can bring us closer to the world and to our own experience.

Sometimes (and I too am guilty of this) we look at children's writing through a developmental lens only: we are interested in how much the child has learned about the conventions of spelling or punctuation or storytelling, or we read the work and think about how good it is for someone that age. It *is* interesting to think about how writers grow and develop, and even more interesting when we realize that this development never stops and that we can look at our own work through the same lens. But if we look only in this way, we may miss what the writing is trying to say, and how moving or interesting or evocative it is regardless of the age of the writer. Let us also read the work in this collection as I imagine the writers must hope we will read it—as fine examples of just plain good writing.

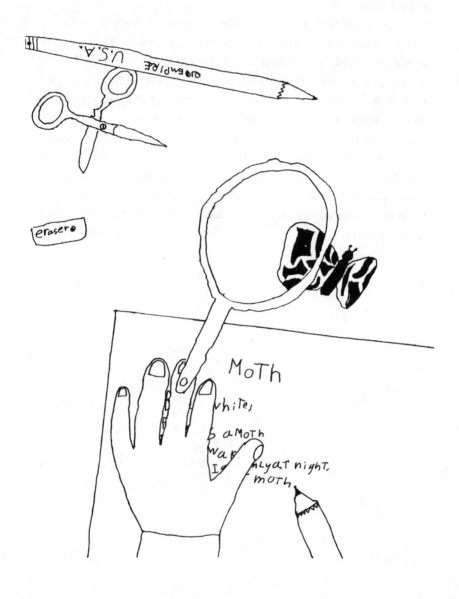

Introduction

This book is first and foremost a celebration of homeschooled student writing. The young writers represented here are primarily taught at home by their own parents. These are families who have made the commitment to be the base for their children's education, families who care a great deal about how their children grow and learn. These are families who are willing to learn with their children, and to learn from their children, families where learning is still an adventure and not drudgery.

The idea for this portfolio of writing took root last spring while I was serving as an evaluator for a number of homeschooling families here in Pennsylvania. Homeschooling families that have filed under our state law are required to assemble a portfolio of samples of their children's work. As an evaluator I had the privilege of looking over many of these portfolios, and I quickly began seeing wonderful writing—vivid writing with a true voice, humor, unique wonder or image. Often I asked the young writers if they'd ever had the chance to have their work published—had they ever sent anything off to a magazine or newsletter that prints children's work? Although a few had entered pieces in various contests, most of the children usually shrugged and said they'd never thought of sending their writing off to anyone. Only their families, or sometimes members of their writing clubs, had seen and appreciated their good work.

I often read these pieces aloud to my own children, who had accompanied me on evaluation trips, and they thoroughly enjoyed hearing these good stories by fellow homeschoolers. The writers glowed at this attention and appreciation, but a nagging thought kept at me. I kept feeling that more people should be able to read and enjoy these stories and poems and essays. Many were too long for the four page children's writing section included in each issue of our quarterly journal, *Pennsylvania Homeschoolers*. Encouraging each child to publish his or her own works individually would not reach a very wide audience. I even thought of starting an official lending library of homeschooled children's self-published books, but saw that still the works would not go far beyond my shelves or my county.

Then the idea hit—my husband and I could publish a book length anthology of this student work ourselves. We publicized the idea in *Pennsylvania Homeschoolers*, and were gratified with an overwhelming response. Children from all across the country, not just children from Pennsylvania, responded with their stories and poems and newspapers and research writing. Parents wrote to say how excited their children were at the prospect of being published in a real book, and that even the experience of looking through their folders of past writing to see what they had already completed that might be appropriate, was instructive and encouraging to them. One mother even wrote to tell me that when she first read about the project, she dismissed it out of hand, thinking they had nothing to contribute since her child did not write "stories"—but she was then sending in her daughter's fourth packet of writings.

We realized right off that the book could have a double audience—both homeschooled students, and their parents. The children could enjoy the stories directly, hopefully receiving inspiration for their own writing, and the parents could gain new ideas for approaches to writing that had worked with other homeschooling families. I wanted to let you in on the process behind these writings as well as sharing the writings themselves, helping you see, when I could, how these pieces began and grew. I didn't want you to shrug the stories off with a discouraged, "But these kids are just talented in writing—my kids just won't write and that's that." I wanted to take you behind the scenes.

A third audience is the wider public—families and children and teachers anywhere who are interested in reading stories and poems and essays that will inspire and delight. If this book can have an effect even beyond the homeschooling community and help children who go to traditional schools find their own writers' voice, then we will feel especially encouraged.

We hope our country's legislators and professional educators will also enjoy taking a look here into the workings of home education, gaining a stronger respect and understanding for this alternative form of education. This work points proudly to the good abilities of both homeschooled children and the parents who have guided them. It is another step in a continuing demonstration that homeschooling works well for many children all across our country.

Just as a portfolio of one homeschooled student's work can demonstrate what an excellent education he or she is receiving, so a broader portfolio such as this book is a way to share how well homeschoolers as a whole are doing. We feel, together with so many educators across the country, that too much reliance is put on standardized test scores. Just as the National Assessment of Educational Progress (NAEP), the "Nation's Report Card," is working on incorporating a portfolio assessment of writing, we are offering here a portfolio of homeschooled student writing for the public to look over and judge. We hope it is a refreshing alternative to the dismal reports which hit the American public so frequently these days—here is a portfolio which clearly demonstrates that a growing number of our children are indeed learning actively and well, and moving eagerly into responsible citizenship in our society.

A note about the structure of the book. The book opens (Chapter 1) with my thoughts on what helps create a positive home environment for writing, based on my own experiences with my own four children, my reading in the field, and what I have heard from many other parents and children. After this overview come the children's work.

It was a tricky task to try to organize the many children's writings that poured in, fitting them into a scheme that would give cohesion and insight into the children's work. I finally settled on the following movement: starting in close to home with observational writing (Chapter 2) and family memories (Chapter 3) and going gradually outward in focus until we end up in other times and imagined worlds (Chapter 11). On intermediate steps along the way the children write about trips and outings beyond their homes (Chapter 4), books they have taken to heart (Chapter 5), and research they've undertaken (Chapter 6). You will read the delightful newsletters many homeschooling families produce (Chapter 7), and you will see the children meeting together for writing clubs and inspiring and learning from each other (Chapter 8). Then you will hear their poets' voices creating new images for their inner and outer worlds (Chapter 9). Next the children spin out fictional stories, starting with realistic pieces (Chapter 10) and moving towards more imaginative tales (Chapter 11).

The book ends with a collection of longer stories, stories that show what young writers can do when they work over long periods of time and are ready for the challenge of a bigger idea (Chapter 12).

1. Creating a Writing Environment

Many parents wonder how to get started in writing with their children. When should they begin, how do they motivate, how should they structure lessons—or should they be structuring lessons at all? What type of environment encourages writing, and what puts the brakes on a child's thoughts and cripples his voice? What does it even mean for a child to find his or her writer's voice? Should the parent just wait for a child to miraculously become "ready" to write, or can a nurturing and aware parent help the process along? I hope this book will gradually offer some answers to these questions and more.

Some young people may wonder what in the world they have to say that is worth writing down. I hope that this collection will help you all realize that all of our lives are full of story possibilities. I would feel happy if some young writers find themselves saying, after browsing about in this collection, "If *that's* writing, then I've got something to say, too." I hope it may make some of you itchy to get out a pencil and begin jotting down your version of life with siblings, or what it's like to be lost, or lose a pet, or even to imagine kings and queens in far away lands.

Although I certainly hope that this book urges all of you to jump in and start exploring the world of writing for yourselves, I do want you to be forewarned. You may hit some rough ground along the way if you're just starting out, and I hope you won't feel discouraged when those times come. The climb is worth it. Sometimes, seeing only these final polished products, you may not realize the work and time and effort that has gone into them.

Some parents may see these pieces as a type of magic that couldn't happen with their own, very normal children who may complain or squirm or worry themselves out of every writing task. In Donald Graves' words, some children just may not be in "shape" for writing when they first start out, just as few people are ready to run a mile, let alone a marathon, the first time they start out to jog. We all need time to warm up and feel in stride with our written voices. Have patience.

Also, do recognize that these pieces have been edited for spelling and grammar and usage. I did not (on purpose!) leave in mistakes, even though some mistakes of young children are definitely cute and charming. I don't have room to show the many rough drafts that some of these pieces went through, but be assured that many went through lots of crumpled paper before they arrived on these pages. Some of the best pieces came to us with still some errors in punctuation or spelling, and I have worked hard to see that *occasion* has two *c's* but only one *s*, I've put quotation marks in the right places and made what I hope are appropriate paragraph breaks where there may have been none for five pages. I'm sure many of the children and their parents also spent a lot of time working at editing and proofing together. Any adult writer needs an editor to help patch up his work and fix the little details that escaped his eye, and I have given the writers in this book that same service. I think our children need us to be both honest with them and supportive as we help them bring their work to publication, and I think that it's proper to offer assistance when a proofreading job would be just too overwhelming.

I also have to admit here that each of my older three children has cried over writing, and more than once. (Hannah, at two and a half, just cries if I make her *stop* writing on something she shouldn't write on...) Sometimes I've been the direct cause of their tears because

I've responded to their gifts of writing with critical eyes that only saw spelling errors or sloppy handwriting or lack of punctuation. None of us are perfect paragons of patience, and none of our children always respond to even our best suggestions in a properly enthusiastic manner. We live and learn with our children and appreciate that we can all bounce back after some rough times.

Jesse, now twelve, has sometimes procrastinated over writing, staring off into space thinking wandering thoughts while the pencil lies on his desk, mute. At times he has needed to be nudged into beginning a writing task, especially when the topic was not self-chosen. But now topics are bursting out of him, and he sometimes writes for as long as an hour or two even on Saturday mornings, side by side with me, each of us at a computer, discussing his new ideas or plans or problems with the story at hand. It's exciting to see him thinking like a writer, making a writer's choices, growing into his own voice. He's knowing that writing takes time and thinking and work in order to give that final delight, and he's willing to put in that time.

Jacob is now nine. He has balked and moaned and stared at blank pieces of paper—and cried. Pencils have fallen out of his hands and handwriting does not come easily or very comfortably, although he's made great progress. But he has also now composed 15 page single spaced stories on our computer, and has known the delight of feeling ideas rushing him along pell-mell. Over time he's learned how to find topics he loves, and also how to find inspiration from others' writing. The fright of blank paper is not so great anymore. He knows he has lots of beginnings to fall back on, and lots of new ideas to move towards.

Molly, now six, was an early and avid reader and writer, but she still has sometimes worried herself into severe writer's block over correct spellings, or written in purposefully jagged and ugly letters because she was angry with me for "making" her write. If she, for whatever reason, hasn't written for a few weeks, it is almost always harder for her to begin. When she writes almost daily, ideas zoom out readily and happily and at all sorts of odd moments. She now often asks me for a pencil and a scrap of paper when we are out driving in the car, so she can catch a thought of a poem right then.

But that is in contrast to the day when I suggested she write something, anything, after a few weeks without much writing, and she balked and stomped and fumed. It seemed all was lost, until I suggested a writing game where we would each write a "riddle" description of something in the room. Neither of us would let the other one know just what it was we were writing about, making our little essays into guessing games. When she saw that I would be in this with her, and that it would be a *game* and not *writing*, her mood abruptly changed and we set to. Forty–five minutes later we were both still having a terrific time together, and her writing block and her irritability had fallen completely away.

I find that my empathy and patience are much greater with my children if I have spent some time writing recently myself. I start watching how I write, and I become more aware of when I'm making just the types of mistakes that my kids make, or having the same types of blocks. Jesse and Jacob have both had special difficulties with spelling. When I'm writing I begin noticing how often I misspell things when I type fast, and often don't catch them until a close look through afterwards. The boys have written huge long sentences that never end for what seem like hundreds of words. When I look dispassionately at my own first drafts, I see that I sometimes write run–on sentences also, with clause after dependent clause strung together. I have to really reshuffle them later to trim them all down to size. Jacob sometimes covers over his paper or the computer screen if I come (in a friendly way, mind you!), to see how he's coming along with his new piece. He's just not ready to have any other eyes on his work yet. When I write I realize how much I hate it when Howard, my husband, does the same thing to me. If busy days have kept the kids from writing for a while, they almost always have a hard time getting going. Words won't come, topics are non-existent. I know that if circumstances have meant I haven't been able to write for a good while, I too feel rusty and awkward and out of practice. Every word then seems like a squawk, out of tune and jarring. All these experiences help me feel more understanding of my children, help me realize the need for the Golden Rule as I respond to their work, as in everything else in our lives. If I can also make these same mistakes, shouldn't my children be expected to? After all, I have many more years of writing experience under my belt than they do, and yet I'm in no way perfect—especially on a first draft.

Being involved in my own writing also somehow lends me credibility with my kids as I offer suggestions to them. They know I'm speaking from my experience and my own struggles, and not just being arbitrarily mean. I also recognize in what areas I don't yet have experience, such as fiction writing, and so I acknowledge that my children are here the experts and I need to learn from them. I know it is also probably true that a child who sees clearly that a parent never writes, may have an especially hard time seeing the whole writing field as worthwhile. Many parents don't have the time or inclination to write regularly, but many of their children may still become excited by writing. It just may take some extra work on the parents' part to maintain an understanding and encouraging attitude. It may mean that these families will want to see that their children have the contact that a homeschoolers' writing club or class can offer, or some on-going project such as a family newsletter.

Many of the parents and children who wrote to tell me about how writing works in their homes told stories that were similar to each other. The children write regularly, sometimes almost every day. I rarely heard from a young person who said, "Oh, I never write at all,

this is my very first piece I've ever completed." Instead I heard from
children who are busy writing sequels to sequels! These children
are in touch with writing ideas partly because they are writing so
much and because writing has in many homes become fully
integrated into their play as well as their more formal schooling
work. Many mentioned that they are encouraged to choose their
own topics much of the time, and many said that on first drafts
correct spelling wasn't imperative—spelling and grammar fix-ups
were usually left to a different day when the time was right for
looking over a piece with a more dispassionate proofreader's eye.
Several told about having unabashed fun with writing, enjoying
making up jokes, having their dolls write miniature newspapers
sharing doll gossip, or writing to penpals all around the world. Ann
Christensen, mother of three, put it very well when she wrote:

> One more thought on kids and writing. I do make my kids write
> every day because I feel it's important to make writing a habit.
> They always write on the subject of their choice and they don't
> have to share it with me if they don't want to. If they can't think
> of something to write about they can always write in their
> journals. Nica's dolls even keep journals! One thing about daily
> writing is that they start to plan out their writing. Sometimes at
> dinner Nica will say, "I think I'm going to write an article on
> *Draw Squad"* or her goose or whatever. This wouldn't happen if
> writing was sporadic.
>
> Another way my kids use writing in play is through
> mailboxes. I'm not sure where they got this idea, but outside
> their doors they each have something representing a mailbox.
> Letters fly back and forth between these mailboxes. Treats,
> notes, bits of fabric, etc., are exchanged. Recently they made a
> pile of mailboxes for their stuffed dogs, and the dogs all
> exchange letters too. For Skye (8), who is very new to the

writing game, this is such a fun, safe way to learn to let the words flow. Even Mariah (5), who is just writing phonetically, writes prolifically and the big kids are very supportive and patient with these unreadable letters.

I've thought about what has helped my own children feel a growing comfort with writing. One of the positives has been to help them feel inspired by good examples of others' writing, especially examples from other children. We collect books by children, both formally published ones and simple home–published works. (Some of our favorites are listed in the "Resources" section in the back of the book.) We have a special shelf in our living room library where all these works by children are kept, a way of recognizing that this is an important category of writings for us. Our own children's works are there also, of course. I've always been amazed that when other kids visit and the whole group seems to need a quiet time of lying back on the sofas and just reading, it's more likely than not the books on that "Written By Children Shelf" are the ones to get picked up and read. We also subscribe to several of the good quality magazines that publish all children's work (see the "Resources" section for a list). And Jesse always grabs *Growing Without Schooling* to read the many interviews and writings of homeschooled students published regularly as an integral part of the magazine. They all enjoy the "BackPack," a children's writing section in our newsletter, especially when they know the writers.

I find other sources of children's writing too. Whenever I've read a book about children's writing (and I read as many as I can, as I need the inspiration too!), I always ask my older children if they would like to hear the examples of children's work included in the book. They've never turned me down on that; they've always wanted to hear what the children have written, and usually what the adult author had to say about the pieces too. We discuss the children's work, we enjoy it, we say what we like and don't like about it, or how we would have changed it if *we* were writing it— and I soon find that what I've read aloud has had a direct impact on Jesse's or Jacob's or Molly's writing. They are trying out that idea, or bouncing off that theme, or incorporating that structure into their own next pieces. They've absorbed the sound and the possibilities of good writing.

For us, keeping children's writing around also means keeping folders of our own children's old writing, rough drafts and all. Just yesterday evening Jesse, our twelve year old, spent a very happy stretch of time going through his "files." He looked over his old handwritten newspaper, *The Pickshur Tavern*, and compared it to his newest laser printed copy of *The Richman Family Observer*. I think it's fair to say he was almost overcome with waves of nostalgia— yes, he remembered writing *that*, oh, and here was *this* piece about Gruff our billy goat! He found he still loves writing about many of the same topics. He found an early draft written when he was nine or so that was told from the viewpoint of a mouse who was almost caught by one of our cats. His current issue of the *Observer* has a similar article, this one much longer, more detailed, more humorous, but still the same basic idea. He had forgotten these "literary antecedents" of his current work, and was delighted to rediscover them. He is right now working at putting up a display on his bulletin board in our dining room showing all his different newspapers, and how they've grown and changed over the years. He also realized how hard it was to read many of his very early "invented" spellings, and he became more aware of how patient I must have been to have taken the time to decipher them. He said that although he's no spelling wonder now, he can see he's certainly come a long way.

Another help to my own children is for them to feel a real audience for their work, someone they are writing for. I remember once hearing John Holt, the educational reformer and late founder of *Growing Without Schooling* magazine, say that he just couldn't write a word on a new book or article unless he could clearly visualize the book as a finished product and imagine *who* would be reading it. He saw his readers maybe laughing aloud over a clever line, or he pictured exactly what types of people would want to buy the book, he'd even imagined where they'd be sitting when reading through it. *Then* he could write. *Then* he could begin and feel it was worthwhile to put in all those hours at crafting draft after draft. My children—and I—feel the same way.

Sometimes we are our own best audience—we laugh over each other's funny pieces, feel moved and appreciative of introspective pieces, and inspire each other with our own different ideas. Molly was beaming and floating a foot off the ground when she came down to tell me that Jesse thought her latest poem, *Wind*, was a real prize winner. We have lots of time to really get to know each others writing voice, and we enjoy seeing each other grow and improve.

Other times, broader publication is a real help, and publication can take many forms. Our own children and many other homeschoolers have taken part in creating family newspapers, sending them off to delighted grandparents and family friends. Jesse and Jacob have both had a profitable time marketing the books that they've published themselves, and Molly is making plans to collect her many poems into a full length book very soon. It's meant a lot to them to be published in our statewide homeschooling newsletter's children's section, the "BackPack," Jesse has had a book review published in *Stone Soup Magazine*, and Jacob has had an essay published in *Growing Without Schooling*.

While thinking of publishing outlets for children, I recently read a charming essay by E.B. White, the author of *Charlotte's Web*. It told how a surprising number of the twentieth century's fine writers all got their start in writing by being published in the *St. Nicholas*

Children's Magazine. He tells how Edna St. Vincent Millay was an honor member of the *St. Nicholas League,* winning numerous gold and silver badges from the magazine throughout her girlhood. Other soon to be notable writers whose prize winning works also appeared in the magazine's pages included Conrad Aiken, Scott Fitzgerald, Stephen Benet, Ringgold Lardner, William Faulkner, Cornelia Otis Skinner, Bennett Cerf, and John C. Farrar. I plan on ferreting out a library that actually still has copies of these turn of the century issues and see if I can find some of E.B. White's early journeys into print. He was a regular contributor and winner, too. Who really knows the effects that early publication can have on a child? It may indeed color a child's view of the task of writing for many, many years to come. How many of us can still remember specific times when we were published as youngsters? I myself was a shy writer who usually kept away from publishing possibilities, but I can still picture the brief essay I wrote on Christopher Columbus that made it into the pages of *The Student Prints,* my middle school's student paper.

Another important encouragement to my children has been their homeschooler's writing club, and we'll share much more about this in a chapter devoted especially to that. Suffice it to say here that we have to admit that sometimes we parents just might not be a very exciting audience. Or we may be a fine audience, but the children may need to be growing beyond just us. Our goal in homeschooling is not, after all, to keep our children with only us as reflectors of their worth and abilities. It is a healthy sign when our children start feeling like stretching and reaching out to others. Writing clubs can provide that appreciative audience, and the discussions that pop up while everyone is sharing their work are instructive and invigorating.

We're interested in figuring out how other writers work, too. Often we take the time to look into the lives of writers whose stories the children love. One of our favorite resources to begin this sort of research is called *Books are by People*, by Lee Bennett Hopkins. It is a collection of essays based on interviews with well–known children's writers. We learned how Robert McCloskey actually had ducks living in his bathtub while working on his Caldecott Award winning book, *Make Way for Ducklings*. Or how H.A. Rey rode out of Paris in World War II on a bicycle, leaving behind almost all of his possessions—except for a manuscript copy of a book about a curious little monkey named *Curious George*. It even helps heal a young person's crushed spirits when the first rejection slip comes in to learn that Wanda G'ag's delightful folktale *Millions of Cats* was initially rejected by publisher after publisher, and G'ag was on the verge of giving it all up.

Another thing we keep coming upon is that many of these children's writers begin by first telling stories to their own children, or to nephews and nieces they see frequently. "Rough drafts" are often honed as these children ask for retellings of their favorite stories—the author-to-be begins to find little ways to improve the stories or add to them or embellish them. Our children have also had the chance to have several adults around them who love to tell them original stories, and who invite them to add their ideas too. One of the boys' favorite play activities is to spin out long (very long!) continuing stories while they milk the goats, hike up a hill, laze around, or play outside, and I can see how this storytelling has a direct impact on their story writing.

We also notice good writing no matter what it is we are reading—maybe a newspaper feature article, or a *Time* magazine essay, or even an autobiographical reporting of the establishment of the original South Pole Station. We feel glad that people of all walks of life are, and can be, writers, and feel buoyed up by a well told story or thought, no matter where it is found. The kids are realizing that "writing" doesn't have to mean writing in some one particular way, but that instead there are many ways to write and share with others in our world. We have tried to give something of that range with this collection of student writings also, although of course some areas may be more represented than others.

Another somewhat surprising thing that has helped my children write better is the notion of deadlines. Adult writers have deadlines all the time—the magazine editor expects the final copy due on the 15th, the letter must be written before the vote is taken in Congress, the book chapter must be finished if you want to be able to set food on the table that month. The letter of condolence or the letter of thanks must be sent out promptly. Though undue stress is, of course, not a help, we've certainly found that similar deadlines for our children have helped them to complete big writing tasks.

My kids have faced deadlines such as these: the contest entry must be mailed by the 8th, the book must be completed and printed up by the Homeschooler's Arts Festival, *Stone Soup* wants the book review by the end of the month, the next issue of the *Richman Family Observer* must be ready by the next writing club, the family book must be ready for the presses by Dec. 20 so we can get it to Grandma by Christmas, and the final proofing of your story must be done by mid–January if you want it included in *Writing from Home*.

I have certainly recognized that for myself, as a writer, deadlines are usually a necessary spur to finishing, or even beginning, a writing task. I find it easy to procrastinate indefinitely unless I realize I have a firm deadline in mind, even one I've self–imposed (such as getting this book out by late spring!). I've seen my kids stretch a writing job out for months without drawing a piece to any sort of closure. We have scads of rough drafts lying about that were never quite brought up to publication partly because there simply didn't seem to be any target deadline date.

Now, I of course recognize that this is probably true of all writers—there are always more rough drafts than finished works, and that's as it should be. These drafts can even give you places to start from when the ideas for new pieces aren't there, as my children have found. And probably not every piece a child writes even *should* be brought to final form. I am only saying that I know that when my children *have* completed a major writing job, a deadline was an important part of the picture. If nothing else, a deadline lets you finally put one piece of writing to bed, and leaves you now fresh to begin on something new. There are always ways to rewrite and rework and sometimes we just need to say, with finality, "it's done." The idea of valid deadlines is probably closely tied to real writing purposes and real audiences. It can't be faked, and is different from our saying arbitrarily, "That story is due in three days."

The computer has also dramatically changed my children's attitudes towards writing. None of us have particularly nice handwriting, and we all feel impatient with the slowness of pencil on paper and the mess of cross-outs and erasures and arrows. Because the children are often now writing for publication, even if it's just their own family newspaper or something to put into their year-end portfolio of work, they realize that they will often want the final copy typed and printed out. They all now usually choose to do even their rough drafts directly on the computer, taking full advantage of the proofreading ease and block move rearranging possibilities.

We actually have two complete PC computers now, and two printers, and even that doesn't seem like quite enough! There is still almost always someone who wants to get on one of the computers to continue some writing project. But then I think of school classrooms that would be lucky to have two or three computers for each group of twenty-five kids, and I realize what ready access my children really have to this very powerful tool. When they use the computer to compose, they don't have artificial time limits put on them; they can write for long uninterrupted stretches, not 10 minute turns. I think I can say without doubt that Jacob's long *Math Land* story included in this portfolio would never have been written if it were not for having a computer. Or at best it certainly would never have been revised or corrected if it were written out long hand. And all my children love the *Spellcheck* feature that comes with our word processing program—it is a lifesaver, and a saver of mother–child relationships also!

I was surprised at the great number of children who submitted works for this anthology that were printed out by computers. Some use their computers only for final drafts, composing first on paper. Others type in directly using a variety of word processing programs. Having a computer is, of course, no guarantee that children will begin writing up a storm, and many long stories were submitted written out neatly in pencil on lined paper. (Many had terrific handwriting, too!) But computers do open up a whole new realm of composing possibilities, and I imagine there are very few serious adult writers who compose mainly by hand on yellow legal pads or on manual or electric typewriters anymore. I know once I, a true–blue computerphobic, found out the ease with which I could change my written ideas, move my thoughts around, erase and blend and reformat my writing, I was sold in a mere three days. I don't care to learn anything about how to program computers (I happily leave that to my husband, Howard, and my nine year old son, Jacob), but I can't go a day without my computer terminal when I have something to write. We go into shock around here on the rare times when all computers are "down."

Most of all, though, we are helped by finding that writing, no matter how we do it, is about sharing with others and being in touch with people. Our whole family has appreciated getting to know other homeschoolers through their writings. We really feel we have good friends all across the country because we've read their stories and poems and newspapers. We've had the chance to laugh with them over funny happenings in their lives, go on trips to places we'll never actually visit, and peek into livingrooms 3,000 miles away. And we know others have felt the same about us.

A final caution here in reading through *Writing from Home*. Remember that no one child wrote all of these pieces. No one child would have the time to! Your child will hopefully develop his or her own writer's voice, but that doesn't mean that he'll come out with products that look just like these. Enjoy the wide variety here, and then enjoy your child's uniqueness. Let the pieces be a source of inspiration but not a threatening sledgehammer.

I remember many years ago when I used to take Jesse to baby swim classes. He loved the water as a baby, and laughed aloud when I'd toss him into the air and let him swoosh into the water as I'd catch him. He was eager to try swimming on his own with a little float on his back. Our enjoyment was hurt, though, when I'd hear other mothers say to their mere toddlers and babies, "Why can't *you* do that too? Just look at him, there, swimming along. Why don't *you* do that? What's the matter with *you*?" Their critical attitude only made their little ones more fearful and sure that they wanted nothing to do with water.

We hope you do not react with that attitude while reading the many fine pieces in this portfolio! We hope instead that you will read with a celebrating attitude, an attitude of wonder that opens you to new possibilities of appreciation and inspiration. Meet these children now, and accept their gift of writing to you.

2. Observing Up Close
—and Writing it Down

"I think I'll draw it and I'll write it all down!" says six year old Molly as she runs to the project room for a pencil and notebook. She's just seen our monarch butterfly hatch out of its chrysalis. She's watched closely and carefully, and now she's going to record what happened. She knows by drawing and writing she'll save her observations, but maybe she doesn't quite realize yet that by doing this she's also sharpening her observations. As she begins to write she continues to watch the butterfly stretch and open its wings, wonders just when it will actually begin flying, and she stretches to describe it as best as she can.

This section shares many writings that show close and regular observation of the world. Several are actual journals, kept regularly over time, giving the writer a long term writing project as well as the regular practice which leads to improvement. I think this is often a good place to begin writing, helping the writer get grounded in rich, concrete detail before zooming off in flights of fancy.

Writing while observing something you care about can help a person feel more deeply and see more deeply than merely looking and *not* writing. Writing down our thoughts keeps vague thoughts from fluttering away—like Adam's butterfly that you'll soon meet. Just as a painter sometimes needs to have his subject in front of him in order to improve his art, so does a writer.

Some background about this first entry. Fullis Conroy had suggested that if her daughter, Meredith, was going to study their newly found caterpillar in depth, then she might as well go all out and keep a real journal record of change and development. Fullis is an avid record keeper herself, and so Meredith also had this example to fall back on. She wrote her observations in pencil in a spiral notebook, making it easy for her to write while actually watching her caterpillar. I think you will be amazed by the close attention to detail and the vivid description.

My Caterpillar
by Meredith Conroy (age 8)

August 7, 1988. Mom found a caterpillar in her herb garden. She picked the stalk of parsley it was on. She put it in a jar that had a lid with holes in it.

Mom looked it up in our two books on butterflies and moths. We found out it was a Swallowtail. It is light green with black stripes and yellow dots on the stripes. It is a fat caterpillar. It is about 1/4 inch at the neck, its widest point. It's about 2 inches long. It's legs look like little bumps. It has three sets of actual legs, not bumps. It has six pairs of bump legs for gripping. The other legs are used for grabbing food.

It has no manners because it eats very fast and it shoves food into its mouth. It shakes its head while it eats. Sometimes it eats fast and sometimes it eats slow. It usually eats for a long time and then it rests for a long time.

August 8, 1988. Mommy fed it last night. Almost all the parsley is gone. It eats fast! It didn't seem to be moving but after watching it for one minute and 26 seconds, he moved a little but not much.

August 10, 1988. Mommy fed it on the 9th. She also cleaned out the jar. She couldn't find it and noticed it was on the lid. It had shrunk but it still looked the same. We looked at it tonight and it has changed. It is upside down and stuck to the lid. I think it is a pupa. It is tannish greenish. Its skin is in a ball at the bottom of the jar. It has stopped feeding (because it can't when it's a pupa). The pupa shakes a little sometimes but not much.

August 15, 1988. It is light green and it has yellow dots on its back. It has three bumps where the neck used to be. And little tiny bumps on the sides. (They look like little ears.)

August 18, 1988. It seems to be falling off. It looks like this [here Meredith entered a small sketch]. It seems to have little light green circles that look like eyeballs. Part of its body is held up by only two threads of silk.

August 21, 1988. It has finally turned into a butterfly. It is a male (I think). He has orange dots with yellow outlines, then some blue purple, then more orange dots, then yellow. It is beautiful. I love him. I am going to be sad when we let him go. His body is dark brown with yellow spots. It took 11 days from the time we noticed it was a pupa.

We let him out but he didn't start flying. He finally flew away.

August 25, 1988. We thought at first he couldn't fly. We thought that he had damaged his wings because we left the old dried parsley in the jar. Then we thought maybe he wasn't ready to come out of the jar. After about an hour on the porch he flew away. Daddy was the first to notice that it had turned into a butterfly.

Homeschoolers seem to really enjoy watching butterflies hatch out. We've raised many monarchs, a swallowtail or two, attempted raising some moths, and we've learned to recognize (and squash!) gypsy moth pupas on sight.

Adam Guida also watched a butterfly emerge and launch off into the world. He had been homeschooling for just three months when he submitted this observational essay. Incidentally, he likes to write directly onto a computer, because it's so much easier to make corrections. He wrote, "I don't like to use a pencil because erasing and writing over is no fun."

King
by Adam Guida (age 12)

King is a monarch butterfly with pretty orange wings that flutter in the wind.

We hatched King from a chrysalis. When we found the chrysalis it was green with gold spots. It looked very fragile and pretty. One morning it hatched into a monarch butterfly. We named him King because monarchs can be kings.

When we thought his wings were dry, we tried to get him to fly. But he couldn't fly. He had a broken wing. So we put him in a terrarium and fed him hummingbird nectar. He was always determined to fly because he flapped his wings. One day when we were feeding him, he started to fly around the room.

We decided to release him outside. We said good–bye and told King to have a safe trip to Mexico because monarch butterflies migrate to Mexico for the winter. He flew very high over the tree tops and out of sight.

I was happy because he flew away. King didn't have to spend all of his life in a terrarium.

In this next piece Keith has really observed his pet raccoon closely. I imagine he'll read books, like *Rascal* by Sterling North, about a boy and raccoon, with special interest since he's not only had some similar experiences, but he's written about them too.

Chitter
by Keith Darling (age 9)

We had a small pet raccoon and his name was Chitter because he always chatted. He used to drink milk out of a bottle. He would climb up on my back and I would get scared. He used to tear our couch up and go to the bathroom under it and we would have to clean it up.

We live across a large pond from our Grandma's house. Chitter would swim over when we'd be visiting our Grandma because he wanted to see us. We would have to take him back over again, but he would always swim back across again and again. It was so funny to see his little dark brown head bobbing up and down across the water.

One day we went to church and we had left Chitter in his house. When we came back he was gone. I miss him.

When I met Lauren Ingram I was impressed with how much she knew about animals and nature. She loves reading nature magazines such as *Ranger Rick*, published by the National Wildlife Federation. Her mother also told me that Lauren loves to make up stories about animals and their friends, then act out the stories. She often puts on "shows" for her family members which usually involve Lauren doing a lecture on a topic which she finds interesting and important—the most recent involved discussing mammals vs. insects vs. reptiles, and how the dinosaurs fit in. Probably the clearly written and detailed articles in Ranger Rick helped her tell about her praying mantis pet in such depth. In fact, often *Ranger Rick* includes observational articles dictated or written by children. Keen observers might want to consider it an outlet for their writings.

The Story about Lady—A Praying Mantis
by Lauren Ingram (age 7)

It began in October, 1989. My Dad brought home a praying mantis. He was riding his bike way up in the Heights when he saw it. Can you guess how he got it to me? He put it in the pouch of his bike and brought it home. I was playing with my friend Eleanor across the street at her house. Mom had to call and call for me to see what Dad had for me. I wondered what it was. My friends and I came running. When we got to the porch, we saw that Dad had put the praying mantis in a plastic box with a white top. The top had a hole punched in it so that she could breathe. The box is round in shape.

I was very excited. I wondered what she would eat. My Dad said that they ate insects. He was right, but it was sure hard to catch them. Dad caught a huge mosquito. She ate it. I tried to catch ants. It didn't work too well. I put honey on the ground and a stick under the honey. I would lift it up when the ants were in a good position to be caught. I would put them in with lady, but she got caught in the honey from the stick. So I helped her out with a clean stick. I cleaned out her cage with an old rag and a few paper towels.

Then I caught a May Fly. She wouldn't eat it. So I started to get her crickets at the pet store. They cost ten cents a piece. I used my very own money that I had been saving. I bought three the first time. The lady at the pet store put the crickets in a plastic bag and then filled it with air. We brought the crickets home and put them all in Lady's cage. I watched. She was sitting on a branch that I had put inside her cage. Just a medium sized branch. She was watching the crickets very carefully. Suddenly she reached out with her front claws and grabbed this cricket and began to eat it like you would eat corn on the cob. It was so neat and I yelled for my Dad. He came downstairs like the wind. When he saw it he said, "I wonder how that creature caught that cricket." And I told him all about it.

Lady would drink water from an eye dropper. One day, she stopped eating and drinking. She didn't eat for about four days. Then one night, I came out to check on her to bring her in from the cold. I saw that she had a present for me. It was eggs in an egg sack. We could actually see her pushing her eggs out. I got my Mom and my sister Erin to come out and watch. My friend Preston was here too. Meghan was out there too, but she didn't understand very well. Then I called my Dad at work and told him about it. He said that he would see it as soon as he got home. Then I called my friend Eleanor. She came over with her friend Kristen and her little sister Becca.

A few days later Lady ate again. I was so glad. I was hoping that she would stay alive until my Grandma Emmie could see her, and that will be tomorrow, November 9, 1989!

We're going to see if the eggs hatch. She laid them on the ceiling of her cage! My friend Ellie loaned her chameleon cage to me to keep Lady in. It was clear plastic with a plastic sliding top. I cleaned out her cage once a week for a few weeks. Then I stopped, and I would clean it only when it needed to be cleaned.

Lady lived for one more week after she laid eggs. I gave her a cricket a day. She would catch it as soon as she saw it and then she would eat it.

When I found her one morning, she was dead. I took her out of the cage. I looked under her wings because I had always wanted to see that part. I found that the wings, when she lifted them, would make a bright color. But when she had them down, she just had a bright green color on the top of her wings. One time when I tried to pick her up, like they say to pick up a mantis in books, she put her claws back. One time she even tweaked me on my finger. After that I knew that I would never pick her up again, because I knew that her claws were sharp. So I looked at her wings, and then I buried her by our big maple tree under the wood chips and dirt.

And now, I am wondering what praying mantis babies look like. As soon as the spring comes, I'll find out! I also wonder why praying mantis mothers are smaller than praying mantis dads. I'll just have to keep reading and find out.

Although my children are not currently keeping regular journals, I certainly take opportunities to suggest they write up their observations, especially about the natural world. Jesse wrote this little piece after a hike in the woods with his brother Jacob.

Surprise in the Woods
by Jesse Richman (age 12)

At first they were only a noise, a noise of leaves being trampled by someone or something. Then the noise makers marched into partial view. At first I thought they were deer, then I realized that they were a flock of wild turkeys. They looked almost like the drawings of turkeys that appear everywhere at Thanksgiving. What a difference from the white turkeys of the turkey farm we visited recently!

Observational writing does not have to be dull and without color or imagery. Children can have as much fun with it as with a more "officially" creative or fictional topic. Enjoy Rachel Johnston's next essay about watching her birds at her feeder, and you'll see what I mean. Her assignment from her mother was to note the differences among the birds, and Rachel has turned this assignment into a delight. We can't look out the window at our feeders now without thinking of her imagery. Children can be helped to think of and develop metaphor in the commonest every day occurrences, and use them in prose as well as poetry.

Our Busy Little Airport
by Rachel Johnston (age 12)

Look outside this window with me; there's a bird feeder, with four perches and lots of bird seed. Then beneath it, there's a sheet of plywood, scattered all over with birdseed. And best of all, are the airplanes flying in and out, all in need of refueling.

Here comes private plane Sparrow 125798. It has just made a long journey, all the way from Locust Tree. It lands, and now it's looking around to see which fuel it'd like. Diesel? No thank you, I don't like the taste of it. How about Unleaded? Yes, that suits me fine.

And here comes another airplane! Oops, never mind, it took off for Pine Tree again, after a low swoop. That one was a Chickadee airline. The identifying mark on their planes is a black cap.

Now here come the Juncos. When they chose their airline name, they made themselves sound like trash. I've heard tell that their motto is, "Let them scold, I'm staying!" They really don't care how much the other pilots try to scare them! They just stay! My, they don't follow safety instructions. While you've been reading all this, six more have landed! But they disperse more to regulation. In fact, they wait around after they've been given permission to take off! Oh well, they only keep Titmouse's airplanes from landing, and cause a tie-up.

Now at last Titmouse's Flight 509 can land. It doesn't need

much fuel, because it only does small flights. Pine Tree to Airport, Plum Tree to Airport, and return flights on both are their only flights.

So that's just one morning in the life of Our Busy Little Airport!

Lochlanina Tobey also used her imagination to help her make a vivid and poetic observation about fall and seasonal change.

Fall's Apparel
by Lochlanina Tobey (age 15)

When Fall falls she tears her skirts and leaves some pieces behind her. She is hurrying to meet the Elven Lords of Winter, to buy from them a soft, white cloak of snow. Yet in the Spring how glad she is to let the old gown go; for then she finds a lighter robe of misty clouds and blossom buds, and slips of palest green—which with time 'comes golden–green trimmed with Summer's rain. But other taste in dress has she, and so with summer flowers in her hair she slips and falls again.

Mark Slezak keeps a journal regularly, including in it observations of special moments he's experienced.

Eclipse of the Moon
by Mark Slezak (age 11)

August 18, 1989—On Wednesday night we watched the eclipse of the moon. It was the most beautiful thing I have ever seen. The whole family watched it, but Joel fell asleep. First there was the full moon, but it was reddish. Then it started getting black on the left and it kept on going across the moon. It was prettiest when it was half covered. When it was totally covered you could not see it.

Mark's younger sister, Suzanne, also keeps a journal. Here is an observation she has made about a strange sight at their pond.

Journal Entry
by Suzanne Slezak (age 8)

March 4, 1989—Yesterday Joel and I were on the driveway and I was looking at the pond and I saw big ripples. We didn't know what was making them. Daddy thought it was a goose and I thought it was a big blue heron, but it was deer that swam across the pond and jumped over the fence and over the blue car and into the woods.

Ryan Williamson has kept a private journal for a good while, nobody reading it except with permission. His mother, Jacque, writes:

> Ryan recently remembered how he'd managed to cook over a dying fire, got out his journal and read it to fellow Boy Scouts. He was obviously proud of his fire technique and a lively discussion followed as others related their experiences with fires in cold, wet weather.

I imagine Ryan was also glad and proud that he'd written his experience up in his journal—he was discovering why people from many different walks of life, not just "official" writers, find keeping journals valuable.

Journal Entry
by Ryan Williamson (age 9)

I watched the birds eating at my bird feeder. Then I made a fire with Nathan. First we cooked noodles, but Nathan put a seasoning pack in that I did not like, so I had to cook my own. I'll tell you how I did it. First I put two logs on the outside of the coals from the fire and put the pot on them. But it spilled and put out half of the fire, so that I only had some coals left. I put a log at one end and blew. But I realized that it was losing all the heat. So I got a piece of aluminum foil and folded three of the four sides down and one up so the heat bounced back down on the coals. I put a pot of water and noodles on the coals. It steamed in about two minutes and boiled in about four minutes. It drizzled the whole time.

Some children even begin keeping journals and writing regularly when they are quite young. Katy Inouye of Hawaii was five years old when she wrote the following journal entries. To give you a feel of what to expect from the actual handwritten work of a young child, I'm including here both Katy's original spellings, and a "transcription" into correct spellings. You might want to see if you can figure out Katy's entries first from just her spellings, as if you were trying to crack a difficult code. I think you'll agree that Katy could never have written these entries if she had felt that every misspelling would be frowned upon. In fact, in this first entry I think she only had a half dozen correct spellings. Also I think you'll see improvement in her spelling ability by the second entry, from just a week later. Like anything we do, we get better at transcribing and spelling the more we do it and work at it. The first entry was written spontaneously upon return from a birthday party, beginning with a listing of the "goodies" received.

Journal Entry—July 8, 1989
by Katy Inouye (age 5)

3 THES TO WAR

1 WADR GAN

3CNS

1 PAD

3 CAD CAS

BALO

iT WAS WALD AT KiL PRT TOH AND HE FAS WR
WALD KiL CiD iN THe Hrs He GAT DRDi AND He CiD
All FVO TiS WiD Di MY HAD CAS AT KiL PRT I WAS
NOT WiD iN SAD I WAS NOT HPY Be CAS TOY WAS
NOT PAY WASTH me BWO OW TiS SRiP iS Ni Le DAN
Wei HAD CAK me AND EMiLY GiT TiS iN BAD BT I
HAD OL ice cem iT WAS GOD THE ANDY iS Ne Le DAN
AND WN We GT HOm we AT TeT

[As read to Mom:]

3 things to wear

1 water gun

3 crayons

1 pad

3 kinds of candy

balloons

*It was wild at Kyle's party. Troy and his friends were wild.
Kyle cried in the house. He got dirty and he cried. All of this
wild did my head crazy at Kyle's party. I was not wild.
Instead I was not happy because Troy was not playing with
me. Boo hoo. This script is nearly done. We had cake. Me
and Emily got things in bags but I had only ice cream. It was
good. The ending is nearly done. And when we got home we
ate treats.*

Journal Entry—July 16, 1989
by Katy Inouye (age 5)

I WAS SIK On SONDAY AND We WNT TO THE
PiCNiC I WAS SAD ATFAD AT THE BECHY BT NOY FR
LOG I MAT A GRL NAD VNASA WE LAf WAN BiG WAS
WT BY AND We LRD HOW TO MAC SAD BLS ME AND
VNSA AND EMIL HD LAS FO FON AT THe BeCH AND
Me VNAS AND EMiLY SAYD AWY no THe SAD iN
VNAS'S RiG We HD LS AND LS AFO FON WE CALAT
RiS AND SIS AND We HD 3 LeS 1 I WAS PTAD TAT iT
WAS A PATL AND THE AR TO LES VNAS AND Me
PeTND TAT iT WAS A WAG AND We PTAD TAT We WR
A SCA SHP AND THe TO WiG WR TO Kep THE HIP UP

*[As read to Mom:] I was sick on Sunday and we went to
the picnic. I was sad at first at the beach but not for long. I
met a girl named Vanessa. We laughed when big waves went
by and we learned how to make sand balls. Me and Vanessa
and Emily had lots of fun at the beach and me, Vanessa, and
Emily sailed away on the sand in Vanessa's ring. We had lots
and lots of fun. We collected rocks and sticks and we had 3
leaves. One I was pretending that it was a paddle and the
other two leaves Vanessa and me pretended that it was a wing,
and we pretended that we were a sinking ship and the two
wings were to keep the ship up.*

Here is another science journal entry from Meredith Conroy, this
one about an experiment she and her dad carried out. Her father has
set a definite time of the week to be home and do science work with
Meredith, realizing that if they just "let it happen whenever it might
happen," it often just won't happen. Meredith is responsible for
keeping ongoing records describing what they are doing.

Science Experiment Journal
by Meredith Conroy (age 9)

October 1, 1989. Dad and I did an experiment. We had three jars of water. Each jar of water had the same amount of water in it at room temperature. I guessed that the sugar, salt, and corn starch that we were going to put in it would dissolve. We put in 2 big teaspoons of each substance into the correct jar (we labeled the jars). I stirred them. Here is a bar graph showing how many times I stirred each one. The corn starch dissolved the fastest, but it didn't really dissolve. I know that because when Dad was talking to me when we were done for about two minutes, it settled down to the bottom. Dad picked it up and looked on the bottom. Even though the water wasn't clear, most of the corn starch was on the bottom. So it really didn't dissolve, it just got mixed in. The salt and sugar really dissolved. Corn starch doesn't really dissolve in water.

November 20, 1989. Dad and I are doing another experiment. We are going to see if algae grows quicker in clear water, soil and fertilizer (in water), or just plain fertilizer in water. To do this we got four jars and filled each one with the same amount of water. Then we put the soil and stuff in the water. We went down to the pond near the horses and got some algae. Right now it's thawing because it was frozen.

November 23, 1989, Day 1. We put the algae in the jars in equal amounts. We took pictures.

November 27, 1989, Day 4. All the algae has settled to the bottom. The algae in the fertilizer is growing the fastest. Dad took a picture. The algae looks like spider legs.

December 4, 1989, Day 9. The fertilizer ... is growing wonderfully!... The soil and fertilizer is not doing so well. The algae won't grow very much and the water is rust color.

December 18, 1989. We're done with the experiment. I found out that algae grows best in the fertilizer and water. The soil and fertilizer didn't do anything. I think the reason [that algae can grow without soil] is that ... dead plants in the pond sort of make a fertilizer and the algae can't reach the soil. The soil and fertilizer is now yellowish. Kind of looks like my yellow visor.

I hope all of these many examples have helped you to realize that we all have many topics from our own lives worth writing about. We can look closely and carefully at our own world and catch meanings and observations that help us to be better thinkers.

3. Saving Special Moments

"Hannah has taken her first steps!!! Hannah just walked *to me!*" calls out my nephew Nathan. We all rush in to see if the feat will be repeated. It is! Eleven month old Hannah toddles, arms outspread, and tumbles laughing and proud into her cousin's arms. It is special to me that I not only have this memory in my mind, but I also have Nathan's written story to look back on. It's taped into Hannah's baby book. Nathan wrote his piece while attending our children's writing club during his summer vacation visit, and I'm so glad to have it. Writing about our families can be one of the most special types of writing. It's definitely the type that has a ready audience, and the type of writing that we all want to save and look back on. We can save the funny and touching and sad or even embarrassing moments that go to make our lives rich and full with love and memories.

In this first piece we meet Mika Perrine's baby sister, Nori, and go through a day with this active 8 month old. I once heard a critic of homeschooling (a teacher who had done some homebound tutoring) say that the home was the worst possible atmosphere for learning, as there were always babies crying in the background or toddlers interrupting everything. What he might not have realized is that these same babies are well loved and enjoyed, if troublesome at times—*and* they can become the topics of delightful essays. Babies give us a life full of surprises, for sure!

A Day with Nori Perrine
by Mika Perrine (age 11)

A screaming baby awakens me. I turn over, looking at the clock—it's 6:00 in the morning. Sighing I stick my head in the pillow case and plug my ears, trying to get back to sleep. But I can't, so I get dressed and go upstairs to see Nori. As I open the door, I realize that she had been standing against it, with it supporting her. She lets out a long scream and starts bawling.

I pick her up and she grabs my hair, yanking as hard as is humanly possible. I holler, "Ouch! Let go, Nori!" as if she understands me.

She lets go when I set her down and immediately crawls out the door I left open.

"Nori!" I scramble out the door and almost trip on her. I pick her up before she dives down the stairs and bring her down. It's time for breakfast, and I set her in her highchair. Then I give her some oatmeal and yogurt and start eating.

After 15 minutes I look up. Nori has smeared yogurt and oatmeal all over her face and is rubbing it into her hair now. As I grab a rag and start a hopeless cleaning job, I notice that half the oatmeal is in her lap. I yell for Mom, who says she needed a bath. She always needs a bath.

I get started on my schoolwork and after a couple of hours, I see someone walking up to our house. It's a friend who got stuck in our driveway. Mom comes up. "Could you keep an eye on Nori while I go help get their car out?"

"Sure. Is she still asleep?"

"Yes. Thanks. I won't be gone long."

So, I continue my science, only to hear the phone ringing. I answer it and as soon as I do, Nori wakes up and begins crying. I finally get done on the phone and run over to Nori.

She's wet through and I begin changing her. She screams the whole time and when I'm just about done, I hear a suspicious dripping. she wet the floor. In despair I finish cleaning her up and putting her diaper on.

Mom comes back and takes her and I scrub the floor.

"How about taking her on a sled ride, kids," Mom says after dressing her in her red snow suit.

"Sure." We head out and Curi holds Nori on her lap while I pull the sled. She loves it, laughing, cooing and smiling the whole time. After awhile, we're getting cold, so we go in and take off our coats. It's time to practice violins.

I'm first, so I get the violin ready and start. Mom comes in after a bit to help me. Fat chance, as Nori begins yelling. Mom puts her on the floor and she crawls over, almost grabbing my violin off my lap. She goes over to my case and seems to be playing quietly, so we finish my lesson.

When I go to put my violin away, I see in horror that she has torn up all my practice charts and stuffed some of them in her mouth. I take them out and, finding them unreadable, I throw them away.

Then I notice Nori has disappeared. Looking frantically for her, I see she's crawled down the back hallway. And then I gasp as I hear a big BUMP! She pulled our big mirror down on top of her. Luckily, both she and the mirror are okay.

We eat supper and read stories. In the middle of *King Arthur*, she starts yelling and crawling around the room like a bulldozer. We take her down to Mark and continue reading. Finally, after brushing our teeth, we are ready for bed. "What a day," I think.

But it's worth all the trouble and running around to have such a cute little sister. I smile as I carry her upstairs to Mom, a cooing little eight month old.

I can see Hannah Strunk's family enjoying reading through this delightful little story about their toddlers for years to come and laughing anew each time. Hannah originally created this as a picture book, complete with a fabric collage cover showing her twin brothers, making it a real family keepsake.

Messy But Fun
by Hannah Strunk (age 6)

My family and I were watching the inauguration of President Bush and Vice President Quayle. When it was almost over, my dad said, "Where are the boys?"

I have triplets in my family. Two of them are identical twin boys. One is a girl. The triplets were almost two when this happened.

I went running into the playroom. Oh no!

The gate was open.

I ran into the schoolroom. No boys.

I ran into the laundry room. No boys.

Then I ran into the bathroom. "Boys!" I cried.

Daddy came running. "Oh, boys, what a mess!" Towels and washcloths were stuffed in the toilet. The rug was shoved in too. The boys were wet from head to toe. The floor was covered with water.

Daddy took the boys upstairs and gave them a bath. Mother cleaned the bathroom.

Two boys in the family may be messy, but they sure are fun.

Hannah's sister Elizabeth can also tell a funny family story, this one about something that happened to her. It's nice when we can look back and laugh at ourselves and the times we haven't quite understood what was going on! See when you can guess what the "little house" really was—and notice how Elizabeth structures her story well so that we don't find out too soon, but are just given little hints.

The Mysterious Little House
by Elizabeth Strunk (age 7)

I went to Grammy and Grandpop's house. It was fun. But something funny happened. I heard Grammy telling my sister, Amanda, something. But I did not know where it was coming from. So I looked and looked. But I did not find Grammy or Amanda. I looked all around.

I walked into a little room. It smelled awful. There was a little bench that had a hole in it. Spiderwebs were all over the room. A roll of toilet paper was laying on the bench. It was moldy and had yellow lines.

Amanda was calling me, "Elizabeth, where are you?"

"Here!" I called back.

Then Grammy said, "Where is she?"

Amanda said, "In there."

Grammy said, "That's the outhouse! Elizabeth, get out of there. It smells!"

"OK," I said. I ran out of there—FAST!

I whispered to Amanda, "What's an outhouse?"

"It's a bathroom outside," Amanda whispered back.

"What are you whispering about?" Grammy asked.

Amanda said, "She wanted to know what she was in." Grammy laughed and laughed.

"Where were YOU?" I asked.

"I was trying to find you," Amanda said.

"We were in the chickenhouse collecting eggs," Grammy said. We all giggled and went back to the house.

Here is another funny and true family story from Elizabeth. Enjoy! Again, think of how special it will be to have these stories saved to read over as all the children grow older.

A Frightening Visitor and a Squished Loaf of Bread
by Elizabeth Strunk (age 8)

I made bread all by myself. I was proud of myself. Mommy always helped me. This time I did it without any help.

We sell bread to the neighbors. We did not have enough bread the day before. One man didn't get his big loaf of bread. Hannah, my six–year–old sister, and I went to see if he wanted it. But he did not buy it. I felt sad.

On our way home, Hannah and I were playing house. Hannah said, "My baby is at home."

I said, "My baby is here."

Hannah said, "I'm blind then."

I said, "Here is my baby."

It was the loaf of bread. I laughed. So did Hannah.

I saw a black and white thing really close to the edge of the trees. I could not believe my eyes.

"A skunk!" I yelled. Hannah began to cry. She was scared.

My friend, Neil, lives nearby. He saw Hannah crying. He asked, "What is wrong?"

Hannah said, "There is a skunk over there!"

Neil's father came over. He saw the skunk. He said, "Move over." The skunk went away.

I looked at Hannah. She had squished the loaf of bread! Neil laughed. He thought the loaf of bread looked funny.

When we got home, we told our mother and father. We told them about the skunk and the loaf of bread. My father was happy because he wanted to eat the loaf of bread.

Writing can also help us make sense of things that seem very hard for us to understand or accept. In the next piece Amanda Strunk, Hannah and Elizabeth's older sister, shares conflicting and torn feelings, and how she came to feel at peace with them. Notice how she takes us right through her experience, letting us feel each new emotion with her by going through each step of that difficult day.

My Sister Susanna
by Amanda Strunk (age 12)

I stood by the living room door. What was Daddy talking about? I knew that I was eavesdropping, but Daddy sounded ready to cry. I knew he was talking to our neighbor but something didn't seem right. I thought that when the triplets were born, everybody would be happy. I was. I had two brothers and one sister: Ezra Stephen Carl, Susanna Darlene, and Benjamin Robert Timothy. Then I heard Daddy say, "Well, Susanna is the one who has a problem. The doctors are pretty sure she has Down's Syndrome." I didn't hear the rest of what my father said. I was already fear-stricken as I ran up the stairs to my bedroom. It was enough that Mommy had had to be on bedrest, but now this! I felt like screaming! I had read a book about Down's Syndrome already, but I didn't think it would happen to me. I hadn't even seen my sister and I was imagining a strange non-human looking one-day old girl. What was Down's Syndrome really?

Suddenly, I heard my father say, "Get your coat on. We are going to see the triplets." As I pulled on my coat, I heard both sets of grandparents talking in the kitchen. "I won't tell anyone," I thought. "It's better to keep things secret."

As we drove to Hershey Medical Center, I overheard a conversation about our dog, Licorice. Both grammies were saying how we should get rid of our dog. Suddenly, before I could catch myself, I angrily said, "I won't let you get rid of our dog. I love her. She belongs to me. You can't take her away."

After my speech, everything was quiet. My sister, Elizabeth, was staring at me, scared. Now I was angry with myself. Hot tears came to my eyes. I wanted my mother. I wanted her warm arms to cuddle me close. I didn't want to be in my grandparents' car. I knew my grandparents would probably not want me to be so upset, but I couldn't help it. I wanted to see my baby sister. I wanted to hold her.

Soon we pulled into Hershey Medical Center Parking Lot. I was the first one out of the car. Running to my father's car, I clung tightly to his hand as we walked into my mother's room.

She was holding Susanna! Before I could catch myself, I ran to her. I looked at my baby sister. My father stood behind me with my other three sisters. Then I really started to cry. I told my mother everything. It felt so good to hold her hand. I looked up into her tired face. She was crying. So was I. She smiled. I kept crying. She knew how I felt.

"She is so cute," I said, looking at my little sister. And I meant it. To me she looked very sweet and pretty.

I said good-bye to my mother, and snatched a peek at Ezra through the nursery window. I wasn't allowed to see Benjamin. He was in the intermediate nursery.

That night, I fell asleep crying. I was happy. I had seen my mother. My sister was very cute. Somehow, I knew Susanna would learn to do things even though she was mentally retarded. I smiled and fell asleep.

I'm sure writing also helped Elizabeth Smith to feel healed and ready to face life again after the sorrow of her almost adopted sister's death. Writing has so often been used by those seeking to reaffirm their faith in God and life.

Caroleena, You Meant So Much to Me
by Elizabeth Joy Smith (age 12)

Saturday, November 11th, Caroleena entered our life. My mother drew me aside and told me that there was a two year old girl who needed a family to love and cherish. She knew that I wanted a sister and had prayed for five years for one. We tried adopting before, but because we were home schooling the agency kept us from doing so.

My mother went on to say that a friend had called and told her that this child's parents were massacred and there were no relatives found. Other Christians from Guatemala were caring for her but they were poor and couldn't have her long. I was excited! "But what if this turns out like the rest did, and falls through?" I asked myself. Every time I was alone I prayed that things would work out for us to adopt.

One big problem was for my brothers to happily agree to having another sister. It was exciting to see how God solved this problem.

On November 15th, I went to spend the day with my Grandma. Before I left my mother told me that she just found out the little girls' name was Caroleena. Later that night, when my Dad came to take me home he brought a picture of Caroleena! Her fair face was embroidered by dark hair, pulled back into a little ponytail. Her arms were held in such a way that she looked like she was ready for a hug anytime. She resembled my Dad, and my brother, Tim, when they were toddlers.

I would have never known that this simple snapshot would

be the key to soften my brothers' hearts. One look at her and they were ready to adopt.

Grandma said she too would be glad to adopt another granddaughter, and, looking up Caroleena's name, she told us it meant "Joyful Strong One."

One night I wrote in my journal, "I have been looking forward to this winter more than any other, and now I know why!"

Everything seemed to go fine until November 21st, when we went to a special meeting on Caroleena. Before it started we had a phone call that Caroleena was near death, and no doctor wanted to treat her because she was an orphan. When we got home we tried to contact missionary friends from Guatemala who would know of a doctor that would help her. We desperately tried for hours to find a doctor. Finally some missionary friends said they would call the organization if they heard any news.

Two days later, Thanksgiving Day, we got a call with tragic news. My parents told me that Caroleena had gone to see Jesus, and her family. I sat dumbfounded. Then it hit me. "She's gone!" I cried the rest of the night. It took a while to heal, and every so often I broke into tears again.

As I look back on it, Caroleena had a purpose to be alive as every child does. First, she broke the wall between my brothers and adoption. Second, I had learned to depend on God more than at any other time. Caroleena will now be with my other sister, Amy Beth, who died six months before being born. Amy Beth would now be sixteen years old, and Caroleena would now be three.

Caroleena, you meant so much to me.

In the following piece by Elizabeth Tisdale, notice how she

carefully constructs suspense—she doesn't "spill the beans" so to speak, right away. I challenge anyone to read the first few paragraphs and not continue! If you've never thought about the literary idea of foreshadowing, this could be a good place to learn about it. I also liked the way Elizabeth rounds out her piece with the contrasting image of Valentine's Day, giving her vivid remembrance even more power.

An Unforgettable Valentine's Day
by Elizabeth Tisdale (age 12)

When most people think of Valentine's Day, they think of hearts and cupids, but when I think of Valentine's Day, an unusual hiking adventure comes to mind. I like adventure to a certain extent, but on that day I sure got more than I wanted!

One Valentine's Day several years ago, my dad, my brother Greg, and I decided to go hiking. We still lived in Wyoming and went to public school. My dad had been promising us a hike, and since school was not going, we decided it would be a good day to go. We went to Wind River Canyon, but because of all the steep cliffs, we had trouble finding a spot to begin climbing.

Many cliffs, mountains, and rocks made up the countryside. There was just enough room for a road and railroad track to go through. On both sides of the road there were high cliffs. The icy cold Wind River raced down through the base of the canyon. Some places had frothy rapids.

When we reached a point where we could climb, my dad cautioned us about making sure we did not step on a rattlesnake. We climbed up and up, always watching where we put our feet. If we were not careful, we could end up stepping on a rattler or slipping and falling down the mountainside to the road below. Soon after, we had climbed high enough so that, when we looked down, the cars looked like dots.

It was fun, stepping over rocks, climbing up so high, and enjoying nature, for an abundance of sagebrush and other smaller plants covered the ground. Trees were few and scattered. I also found it scary being up so high, knowing the road was hundreds of feet below. The thought of tumbling to it by accident was dreadful.

The afternoon was drawing to a close. My dad decided we had climbed far enough and had better start back. Soon, we figured out that we were coming down at a different place than where we had gone up. We just kept descending the mountain, for my dad said we were not far off track.

When we had gone a little ways further, Greg went ahead to see if he could figure out a good way to finish coming down. Just ahead of him was a fifteen foot cliff straight above the highway. He inched toward the edge to look down, but before we knew what had happened, Greg had fallen down the embankment to the barren ground below. Seeing some movement, we knew Greg was still alive even though we could see much blood. What if he was bleeding to death? When we called to him he did not answer.

My father told me to step just where he stepped and to do exactly what he told me. As we descended the mountain, my dad kept calling to Greg, telling him we were coming. Although it was not long, it seemed like an eternity before we reached the base. Much to our horror, we discovered that Greg had landed within inches of a cement chunk. As we drove to the emergency room five miles away, we were silent.

Later, we learned that Greg suffered only from a broken nose and kneecap. His braces had spared him having some teeth knocked out.

An unusual Valentine's Day? Yes, but one not to be easily forgotten. I have always loved adventure, but a "hearts and cupids" kind of day is my preference!

And here is another remembrance of a close call—this time for a loved pet. I particularly enjoyed the opening of this next piece— the juxtaposition in time and place between the author and Mooser. It wasn't a very good night for either of them! I also enjoy Gabriel's fine use of language, such as the line "Mooser was very annoyed by his imprisonment" or the phrase, "the offending bit of metal." This originally appeared in the Chrisman family's "occasional publication," the *Oddfellow Gazette*, a delightful paper that you will read more about in the chapter on family newsletters.

Close Call for Mooser
by Gabriel Chrisman (age 12)

On the night of July 18, 1989, I was lying on a sandstone beach on Patos Island, being drenched by rain. At the same time, back on Bainbridge Island, our cat Mooser (age 7) was being hit by a car. My Mom heard a horrible noise, woke up, and went downstairs to find our cat on the porch with a shattered pelvis. He had dragged himself from the scene of the accident and up three steps with only the use of his front paws.

The next day, when I came back from my trip, we brought Mooser to Dr. Badger. He said he could do an operation to set the bones in place, and put in a pin to hold them together. We agreed to try this instead of "putting him to sleep."

After the three and a half hour operation, he wouldn't eat anything but *Pounce*, an expensive cat treat. Also, he didn't like having a bald patch on his hip. We visited and fed him at the vet's every day.

Soon, though, he came home for "cage rest" in a huge dog carrier which we acquired in Seattle. Mooser was very annoyed about his imprisonment, and was relieved when we let him out for short runs in the living room while we cleaned out his cage. Unfortunately, from moving around so much his pin broke through the skin and he chewed on it! We had to take him back to Dr. Badger, who sawed off the offending bit of metal. Two more times the pin inched its way out, and was sawed off, before the vet decided to take it out. Then Mooser was under sedation for a day so he wouldn't move around. They had to make sure the bones would stay together.

After that his recovery was pretty uneventful, and he can run and climb trees just as well as before. I certainly hope that he never gets hit again!

Carina Strappello owns a kitten, and shares here her advice to other new kitten owners, as well as describing what kittens can be like. She really addresses you, the reader, in this piece. Her mother says that sometimes Carina balks at writing—but just suggest that she write something else about her cat, and Carina is off and running. It's an area of specialty for her, and that's an important thing for young writers to develop.

Your New Kitten
by Carina Strappello (age 9)

I know what it's like to have a kitten because I have a kitten myself. As we all know, kittens are very playful and exciting. But when kittens are asleep they are not playful. When they are sleeping, kittens lie in very funny ways. Sometimes they lie all curled up in a ball and sometimes they lie all stretched out.

When you feed your kitten or cat you should keep a bowl

full of fresh water. Remember, every day empty your kitten's water bowl and fill it full of new, clean water. You also need to buy kitten food.

Cats and kittens are very clean. However, you should still brush them. If you don't have a brush you can use an old toothbrush. Be careful with your kitten. Never hold your kitten or cat by the scruff of its neck. Only its mother does that when it is a baby.

Your kitten needs a litter box. After you get your kitten a litter box, you need to buy some cat litter. If you can't get that, clean sawdust will be fine. Make sure you change the litter box at least once a week. Remember you have to train your kitten to go to the litter box, unless the mother cat has done that. If your kitten goes to the bathroom somewhere else, spank it gently and take it to its litterbox.

Kittens like to scratch furniture. You can make yours a scratching post by covering wood with carpet. Or, you can take it to the vet to be declawed if it will be a house cat. You should go to the vet anyway for its shots so it doesn't catch a disease.

Don't scream too loud. Screaming could hurt your kitten's ears. Try to play with your kitten as much as you can. You should train your cat to do things while it is a kitten. When your kitten goes outside and tries to catch birds and you don't want it to, you can buy a collar and then put a bell on the collar. Put the collar on your cat and every time your cat goes outside, the bell will jingle and the birds will fly away.

So be nice to your cat and listen to it purr!

Many children have written about pets with loving attention and a blind eye to any of the problems associated with total responsibility for this other little creature. Not so with this next humorous essay by Heather Leabman. She has some sharp observations and warnings about pet canaries, and they don't exactly make for a strong advertisement for the bird. Take heed!

Notice also how well structured this essay is, each paragraph persuasively making its point, and all of them adding up to a delightful whole.

Why Canaries Make Horrible Pets
by Heather Leabman (age 14)

An adorable canary swinging on his perch and singing a beautiful song can really win a person over. I know. I speak from experience. I purchased my canary on a whim. He lived one week in my humble home and then was ushered right back to the pet shop. I said "bye, bye birdie" to my bird because he was a hyperactive hopper from perch to perch, his ear-piercing screech (that the shop keeper called "song") had us buying stock in Tylenol, and the incomprehensible mess he created had my mom vacuuming three times daily.

Canaries are small creatures. All small creatures burn energy very quickly. A canary is a nervous, jittery pet. He hops from perch to perch constantly while turning a cage (hanging from a chain) in circles. If you are a nervous type of person a canary is not the pet for you. The sound of small toenails clinking against the bars of a cage or perch every five seconds is enough to make the most serene person go crazy.

Canaries are well known for their beautiful song. Most canaries you would see in a store do not have the voice quality you desire. Many (including mine) have a shrill enough voice to awake the dead! Add that piece of information to the fact that canaries sing about seven hours straight daily. A person who has never had a headache will suddenly develop migraines.

Whenever I see a picture of a canary he is usually sitting in an immaculate cage. You don't see the filthy mess a bird can make. For example: scattered seed on the floor of the cage and the floor beneath the cage, gravel paper soaked with seed and water and even tiny bird droppings. Our wall also had some surprises. The gravel paper became filthy just one hour after putting it in. Vacuuming was done three times daily to prevent the seed from being tracked all over the house. After I'd fill his food, water, and treat cup lovingly, he'd dance in it, even getting the carpet wet.

So, if you're looking for a pet, remember the three reasons not to purchase a canary: hyperactive hopping, ear-piercing screech ("song"), and an unbelievable mess. Don't let a cute canary in a store fool you. Remember, I speak from experience.

Skye Christensen is new to writing, and usually finds it a bit of a difficult chore to get thoughts out onto paper. He is writing daily, and his mother writes that as he's learning to read more smoothly and with less effort, his writing ease is improving also. Finding the right topic is often key in helping a writer feel motivated to take the time to write, and Skye found his in telling about his rabbit. This was his first piece of such length and detail. Skye also immediately had a publishing opportunity, his older sister Nica and her friend Mika Perrine have been publishing the *Neighborhood News* for several years and Skye's essay was included in their most recent issue.

Hazel-Rah
by Skye Christensen (age 8)

Last summer some old women found a rabbit under their car and called us up and asked if she was ours. We said, "No," but we would keep her until we found her owner.

We called up some friends who had rabbits and asked if she was theirs, but they said she was not. Ann said it was my turn to get a pet, so I got "Hazel."

Hazel's name comes from my favorite book, *Watership Down*. It is a fictional story book about rabbits.

After I got Hazel, we didn't have a hutch so we put her in our sauna and covered the floor with grass. She stayed in the sauna until we got a hutch. Donn made a hutch on the ground with wire floor, top and sides for the summer.

One of Nicholas Early's best writing topics for several years has been his experiences with his loved dog Traminer, and we are including here a series of these pieces. I think having all of this writing about Traminer to fall back on as memories must have been important to Nicholas and his family as they had to finally deal with Traminer's death. Writing can be a very meaningful way to help us through grief and give importance to the things we've loved. I remember when our family dog, Nosie, died a number of years ago; we all found it comforting to gather together all of the stories Jesse and Jacob had written or dictated about Nosie, collecting them into a special remembering book. It helped give closure to this part of our lives, and helped us have a way to relive happy times when Nosie had been with us.

Trammy's Wishes
by Nicholas Early (9-29-87)

I wonder
>What Trammy's
>>Wishes are.

I bet
>Trammy wishes
>>That he
>>>Will get
>>>>A hunk
>>>>>of meat
>>>>>>and to
>>>>>>>play ball.

Trammy is a playful dog.
He wants to all the time.

Trammy's Bath
by Nicholas Early (11-20-88)

First we carry Traminer into the green bathroom, and lift him into the bathtub and turn on the faucet. Then we dump water on him with a yogurt cup. Then we get him all soaped up and we don't miss anything! Then we rinse and rinse four times. And then we lift him out of the bathtub and carry him outside to shake! Then we get him in and we ask him, "Do you want to play ball?!"

Then he starts to bark!

The Time Trammy Bit a Chipmunk
by Nicholas Early (6–12–1988)

It started with Traminer wagging his tail at the drainpipe! I noticed and kept on playing in the sandbox. Then Trammy started barking. I finally went over to the drainpipe and punched it, and I saw the chipmunk's tail! I shook his rear end right out of the drainpipe; it climbed right in again. I ran up to the deck and thumped a few times, then ran down again and punched the drainpipe right above the chipmunk, and I saw the chipmunk's tail move. Then Traminer BIT it! But it got away.

Traminer's Operation
by Nicholas Early (12–7–88)

At the very early time of 7:00 we took Traminer to the vet to have some cysts removed. When we came to pick him up after teaching, at about 2:45, he was so groggy that he couldn't stand! Some nice people felt sorry for him, so they opened the door for us. I took him home on my lap. On the way to the vet we were thinking of him and calling him "Groggy Doggy."

He tail was always curled around to the right, it was really strange. What a sweet little doggy. He didn't have control over his legs. I brought his water to him and food to him. After that we watched "Lassie." Whenever I got close to him he stank with the powder on his tail, it smelled sort of flowery.

A couple weeks later we got his stitches out that were on his tail. It was painful for him to go running. But now when we ask him to go running he barks and barks and we get him to roll over.

Burying Trammy and Getting a Puppy
by Nicholas Early (January 1990)

Friday, the 5th, I woke up and I heard Mommy crying. We had decided to put Traminer to sleep. We got Trammy out there to watch his grave being dug, which was under the picnic table because he lay there a lot. We took him on a last tour of the house.

When we got to the vet, someone asked Daddy to sign some papers. After we waited a little while they called us into room number one.

When Dr. Lash came into the room, we said good-bye to Traminer, and he relaxed for the first time in ages. It was so quick. I see why it is called "put to sleep," because his head just suddenly relaxed.

The appointment was at 9:20, before all the other people came, for the sake of the people.

After we placed him in his grave, we wanted to have a picture of him. As I was going up, I couldn't stand not to have a lively little ball of fur that would welcome us home, and that we could play with and pet.

After we took the picture, I went in to look in the classified section of *The Leader Times*, to see if there were any ads for Shelty puppies. I also looked in *The Sunday Press*, but there were none in either.

Daddy got the idea to look in one of the old *Sunday Presses*. There was one!

We hunted all over to find a place where they breed Shelties. Daddy remembered a place that he had seen on the way to Mars, PA. It was called: Shelia Shelties.

When we got there, the dogs were barking like crazy. The person in charge recommended a place by Zelienople. We went there, and now, Tuesday, 1–16–90, we are picking our sable–white puppy up in a week and 5 days.

Teeth and the losing of them is almost always a hot topic for young
child writers. Molly felt fluent and proud as she wrote this piece
about her experience at the oral surgeon's—not the usual way for a
six year old to lose a few teeth!

Pulling Teeth
by Molly Richman (age 6)

I came to the oral surgeon scared but happy. I was going to
have three teeth pulled because I was crowded on the bottom
jaw. First I had to wait what seemed to me to be a long time,
while Mommy had to fill out a form. When she was done, we
went into a room which had a dentist chair in it that I was put
in. Then they gave me some banana flavored stuff that
numbed my lip some, so they could give me the shots of
Novocain. Then after a while they started. There was a
cracking noise and a tooth came out with part of the root still
on it! The oral surgeon had special pliers he did it with. Then
the oral surgeon started on the next and with no crack it came
out too, root and all! Then he started on the last tooth. It came
out with a little crack! If you touched my chin it felt like a ball
of fuzz because it was swollen. And gradually it got better.

Another special thing for young children is visiting grandparents.
Kirsten was able, with her mother's help, to create individual bound
books about these visits, making gifts for her grandparents'
birthdays. With activities like this we are showing our children that
writing can be a way of expressing our love and appreciation—
certainly a major function of written language over all time. The
text that we are recording here was actually handwritten by Kirsten,
I'm sure with some modeling from her mother, and on almost each

facing page in her book she had a charming drawing illustrating her message. Some of these were labeled with captions dictated to her mother. I don't think there's any doubt how Grandpa reacted to this lovingly made gift!

A Special Birthday Book for Grandpa's Birthday
by Kirsten Grace Williams Winston (age 3)

Happy Birthday Grandpa!

I love you Grandpa and Grandma.

Thank you for letting us watch movies at your house.

I like to make cookies with you when I go to grandpa and grandma's house and you watch me.

Ole King Cole is my favorite movie.

I like to read "Sleeping Beauty's" book at your house.

Thank you for letting me help you pull out the weeds.

You know what—one time when we were pulling out weeds we saw a worm. Grandpa put it in the bucket and then took it out because he didn't know it was there. I said, "Look, there is something wiggling in there."

Grandpa said, "Oh, it's a worm. We need to put it back in the ground." So we did.

Writing can also help us put in perspective how we should treat our friends, as this next piece by Carina shows. Remembering this story should help the next time you might be tempted to try to only have your way.

Friends
by Carina Strappello (age 9)

Lynn came to my house to stay overnight. She wanted to play a game inside. I wanted to go outside and ride bikes. I told her since she was at my house she had to do what I wanted to do. We fought and didn't have any fun. We were not treating each other the way we should.

Lynn came to my house again. This time she wanted to go outside and ride bikes and I wanted to stay inside and play a game. I didn't want to do what she wanted to do, but I did anyway. We had lots of fun. We rode bikes first and then we played a game. Now we were treating each other as we should.

We all have memories of times we've gotten lost. Here Nicholas tells of a time when his family got lost when out on a hike.

When We Were Lost in Todd Sanctuary
By Nicholas Early (age 8)
I wish we hadn't gotten lost!

We were planning to go to Todd Sanctuary. It was late afternoon when we started driving there. We spent 20 minutes driving there.

When we got there, we looked at the maps and started hiking. First we saw the cabin, then we saw the trails and we started hiking on them. We hiked around for two hours.

It looked like it wasn't too late to go to the pond, so foolishly we went to it. I went to throw some stones into the water.

Then we decided to go to the car. We started back, but as soon as we got into the hemlocks we couldn't see a thing! We went over a bridge, then we were just walking along. We thought that we were on the trails, but we weren't. We were lost in those thick scratchy hemlocks. I got many scratches. There seemed to be holes all over the place. First we were on the trails then we weren't.

An hour and a half after we got lost, we came to a clearing.

We sat down and Daddy went ahead and we waited and waited for him to come back.

We yelled to him, and he yelled back to us how he'd fingered the letters out that said "Cabin" with an arrow. He called to us and said, "Come!"

We yelled back, "Get the flashlight then come back!" but he didn't hear us. We came as fast as we could. We had a little bit of trouble getting across the stream that was in our way, but we finally got to the car and drove back.

When we got home we had a delicious supper of green rice. And boy, it was good!

Teal Perrine found a subject in seeing a professional sports event. The twist is he's not going to tell you about the game, but instead about the experience of attending the game. For another unusual twist, he writes in the second person, using the pronoun "you" and not "I" or "he," helping us feel even more a part of the scene because it is happening to *us*. Notice how many vivid and telling details and images Teal creates—he doesn't rely on vague words such as "neat" or "fun" or even "awful" or "yucky."

The Metrodome
by Teal Perrine (age 8)

Five thousand screaming fans, pelting the players with hot dog wrappers. The green turf is more like a sea of snickers wrappers. Trying to get a hot dog, you have to yell in the attendant's ear. On the way back you slip on spilled beer, your hot dog zooming down the aisle. Racing after it, you feel peanuts snaking down your shirt. Oh well, so much for the hot dog! Trudging back to your seat, you hear a smoosh and you look at your shoe. You've just stepped on half a Snickers bar. You look at the scoreboard. It's still the first inning!

Gussie's mother writes that they had been reading some essays by E.B. White, the author of *Charlotte's Web*, and others by Andy Rooney, and had been noticing how these writers could make the ordinary seem very special. This inspiration helped Gussie see how she could turn the little events in her own life into similar delightful vignettes. Although Gussie usually chooses to read fiction, most often fantasy at that, she feels most comfortable right now writing non-fiction pieces, and as her mother told me, Gussie says it "feels good to learn that to write doesn't mean that you *have* to create fiction." Instead we can all look to our own lives with a writer's eye and highlight what might have otherwise been unexamined or forgotten. Gussie's mother, Adele, also told me that this was the first time that Gussie had ever used dialogue in her writing. She was pleased that all on her own Gussie had used a variety of "tags" instead of always using "said." Hope you particularly enjoy Gussie's final image, a real stroke of a fine writer.

A Dilemma
by Gussie Abrahamse (age 11)

I know the Bible says, "Honor thy Mother and thy Father." In general, I agree, but sometimes it is not as easy as the Bible makes it seem.

When my dad and I were in Florida, we had a little discussion about a movie we wanted to see on TV. It was called "Dirty Harry." Now if you have seen a Clint Eastwood movie, you know that they are violent. My mom has a rule that I can't watch movies like that. So, we thought it best not to tell Mommy about it, but it slipped out a week later. The incident went something like this:

My mom and I were driving in the car, and I asked her whether or not she would let me watch "Dirty Harry" if it ever came on TV.

"You would have to ask Daddy," she replied. "I don't remember it very well."

"But I want to know your opinion," I ventured.

"I don't really know," she said again. "My guess is that it would be too violent. But why do you want to know?" she asked shrewdly.

"Well... uhm... see... uhm...," I spluttered.

"Gussie, did you watch 'Dirty Harry'?"

"Yes," I replied meekly.

"And Daddy told you not to tell me?" my mother pushed on.

"No," I said, more confidently. "He said, 'We'll not tell anybody about this, will we, Gussie?' But I knew what he meant."

I find that it is best to honor your mother in some circumstances and your father in others, but when it comes to getting approval—be careful! They might ask the wrong question and your secret will leak out like yolk out of a cracked egg.

Enjoy how well Rachel describes her new sport of archery. She doesn't just say "I like it" or "it's so fun"—instead she lets us hear, feel, and imagine along with her as she pulls back her bow. This essay first appeared in the homeschooling newsletter edited by her good friends, Mika Perrine and Nica Christensen.

Archery
by Rachel Melis (age 11)

I love the sound of the twang of the arrow as it zooms off the string, and if it was a good shot, the striking of the target. I can imagine those medieval knights, Robin Hood, King Arthur

and countless men of the longbow. It all comes back with a
flurry at that sound.

When I received five wooden arrows for my birthday (just
what I wanted) my dad was immediately pestered to set up a
target. Of course, I didn't make my first shot, but after a while
I could proudly walk to our stack of hay bales and pull the
arrows out of the bull's-eye.

Every now and then my brothers and I go squirrel hunting.
Our prey always seem to know we won't hit them, at least not
this year. And until we master squirrels how can we even
think of the bold deer that come to eat off of our target for
lunch?

But even in fun you must remember that the bow and
arrow, if used by the cruel or careless, can be very dangerous.

I really like the feel of that slender stick in my hand and the
pull of the bow for hours of fun at our straw target.

4. Meeting the World

"But how are they going to learn about the *real world?*" the doubtful lady at the checkout counter asks when she finds out the children helping their mother with shopping are taught primarily at home.

We've all been asked this question. The writings in this section are one answer—we don't just stay home all the time. We go out to meet the world more often than any school can ever arrange, because it's so convenient and easy to pick up and go out with just your own family. The adventure is often more fun with another homeschooling family along, or even the whole local support group. Many of us expect our children to write up something about some of these outings afterwards as a way of helping everyone see what was learned and gained, a sort of "proof" that we weren't *just* having fun. Also, if you are in a state like Pennsylvania that requires homeschoolers to assemble a portfolio of student work as a main evaluation measure, these essays are very useful to include. I've seen school people pore over these sorts of pieces—they let the school officials know that our children not only can write in an organized manner, but that they also get out and see the "real" world. It's good public relations.

I think you'll agree that these sorts of essays don't have to be dull. Ian Latinette's renditions of family and homeschool outings actually have the delight for me of a *Prairie Home Companion* monologue.

Gotcha Basket Company Tour
by Ian Latinette (age 14)

We were on our way to yet another Homeschoolers Tour. Conditions were normal. The parents were discussing something of obvious great importance in the front seat, which I couldn't hear because I had my head stuck in a pair of earphones, listening to science fiction. The kids in the back seemed to have decided to play "Wild Indian," instead of whatever they were supposed to do, and Jonas was begging for some of Philip's Cherrios.

We drove along in this peaceful and contented manner until we saw a large building, next to which was a large sign: "Gotcha Basket Company." We pulled in, smug in the realization that we were early and that no one else was there yet. So, we waited (and waited and waited). Finally it was almost time for the tour to start. But, unfortunately no one else had showed up. We sent someone in to ask if we were at the right place. We weren't.

We drove down the road another two miles, and there it was. "Gotcha Baskets" proclaimed the sign on the front. We went in to make sure that this was really the right place. It was.

Soon the other (slightly late) homeschoolers had arrived, and the tour was underway. First we visited the large warehouse, where the wood is cut and the loosely woven baskets are stored. The guide explained how they buy two thicknesses of maple veneer wood: thin for the slats and thicker for handles, lids, and rims. He explained how the workers would often take home a trimmed bundle of slats and then weave them into loose baskets. Then, in the back of the smaller building, they would "pull down" the baskets, making them tighter and stronger. Then the rims were riveted on, handles or straps attached, and the completed profit (I mean product) was then sold in the twelve to seventy dollar range.

Along with the basket comes a totally unconditional replacement policy—run over it with a Mack truck, return it and get a new one. The baskets were not the wimpy wicker things you see at craft shows with spray–painted dried flowers in them. These were serious carrying devices. The woven part was double, the rim was double, there were more rivets than were strictly necessary. All of this contributed to the overall strength and durability of these "Gotcha Baskets."

After the tour, the guide said that we could have as many pieces of scrapped weaving material as we wanted. It was hard to squeeze into the car on the way home, and there wasn't any place to put your feet.

Our Expensive Trip to Sea World
from Ian Latinette (age 14)

Several months ago, our family went to Sea World of Ohio. On the way, we got lost, turned around, took a wrong turn, and saw several herons, egrets or other storklike birds in a marsh. When we got there we first decided where we would go and in what order. We went to a killer whale and dolphin show, a waterski exhibition and a "Royal Lippazan Stallion" show, which was the flop of the century. (Of course Micah, our horse person, loved it.) We also visited the seal feeding area and the dolphin petting pool. At both of these places you paid 93 cents for three dead fish in a paper cone to (supposedly) keep the fish juice from running out. Then (if you dared to touch them) you firmly grasped a cold, stiff, dead fish by the tail and fed it to the animals. I found a trick by which I was able to pet the dolphins at least five times. The trick is this: stand next to someone who has at least three cones of fish.

We also visited a dusty aquarium and saw a "tidal pool" with fish, crabs, clams, anemones, and a crashing flow of water every once in a while that made everybody twitch. I rather liked that trip, and I hope we go there again sometime. (When we come back I'm bringing my own fish!)

Here is a field trip review written by Luke Wilson, and I can testify that this piece was read word for word by his school district's assistant superintendent and the district's lawyer at a meeting with the family where I was present as the family's evaluator. They loved it—and again, were probably not only gratified to know that Luke could write so clearly and in such an organized way, but also that he had the opportunity to go out in the world. I think they could see that Luke's field trips were not just lost school days where everyone goofs off and no one listens to the tour guides.

Tour–Ed Mine
by Luke Wilson (age 11)
When we got to Tour–Ed Mine I was pretty excited. We had half an hour before our tour began, so Eden and I looked at the stores and rooms modeled after the way they might have looked in a real mining village a long time ago. There was a barber shop, kitchen, bedroom, country store, pharmacy, dry goods and other rooms you could look at.

Then it was time to go down into the mine. We climbed into these small, enclosed carts that moved along on a track. As we went into the tunnel, I learned what "pitch black" was like! It was so dark I couldn't see my hand in front of my face.

The mini–train stopped and we got out and walked to where the mining machines were set up. The tour guide told us how each machine ran and what it did. Then he turned them on. They were very noisy!

Eventually we all got back into the mini-train and went back up the tunnel to the mine entrance. Our group went into a little shop where a man talked to us about the evolution of the lights the miners used. They started out with just a candle that the miners would put down and start digging. The next type they used was still a candle, but it was attached to the miner's hat. There were several other types and then he showed us the final cap that is used today with a sort of flashlight attached to the miner's hat.

Also, you weren't allowed to use gas power, but only electricity, because the gas could explode. One thing the miners used to detect natural gas in the mine was a canary! When there was gas in the mine, the canary would pass out! One reason there isn't as much coal burning as there used to be, is because when you burn coal the fumes make acid rain.

After this talk, we dug for some bituminous coal with a pickax. That was super neat!

I think you'll be able to tell that eight year old Elesha has really gained a working knowledge of the space program from her essay that follows.

NASA-Kennedy Space Center
by Elesha Taylor (age 8)

My family and I took a two hour tour of NASA-Kennedy Space Center in Florida. I saw seven rockets. Two were small, three were medium, two were big, and two great big rockets. The outdoor Rocket Garden, next to Spaceport Central, features authentic rockets from each stage of America's space program.

On the bus, our first stop was a building that has pieces of equipment they used on the moon. Then we saw a movie that showed us what they do up on the moon.

Next we saw the track which the crawler uses that takes the rockets to the store house. The crawler is as wide as eight lanes of cars. After that we saw the two launch pads where they launch the rockets. Then we came back to the space center. We also went through a nature display. Finally it was time to see the movie about space.

We enjoyed our visit at NASA-Kennedy Space Center.

Jeremy shows he is really in control of organization in his report of a museum trip. And he was only seven years old when he wrote it— when I was typing it up I thought surely it was by his ten year old brother Joshua! I especially enjoyed how Jeremy asks the reader a question at one point; he was writing with an audience in mind.

The Royal Ranger Museum Tour
by Jeremy Fisher (age 7)

First, we got ready for Sunday morning church. When church service was over, all the boys in the group called Royal Rangers got together and we all ate bag lunches. When the church bus got back from taking people home, we got into the bus and a church van. Then, we started off to the Carnegie Museum.

It was terribly noisy the whole way there! It took us about one hour and thirty minutes to get there.

When we got there, we divided into age groups and the tour started. My group went to the "Polar World" exhibit first. We learned that in the North Pole there are no trees and you would need furs to keep you warm, but there is no wood to burn. What do you think they burned? They burned fat. When fat burned it didn't spread much, but that was good or it would melt their igloo.

Then we went on to the Indians. We learned about snake dances of Indians of the desert. They would find as many snakes as they could, then the chief would dance with the snakes, poisonous or not, because they believed snakes would ask their god to send rain for crops. They also believed that snakes were scared of eagles, so there were two Indians behind the chief waving eagle feathers at the snake so he wouldn't bite.

Then, on to the dinosaurs. We learned about the longest dinosaur they had discovered so far, and the meanest dinosaur.

Then the tour was over. We went into a gift shop. I bought a painted seashell and my brother bought a quartz crystal. Then we got into the bus and the van and we started the long trip back.

This next piece, telling about our visit to a school for the blind, was initially hard for Jesse to organize. He had a welter of impressions that were all out of order as he began to jot his ideas down. It was the perfect chance to discuss the benefits of outlining, and because he could use it right away, it all made ready sense. He took a separate page of notebook paper to record each major phase of the outing in proper time sequence, then filled in notes of details he wanted to highlight. The actual writing up then was quick and effortless, as he simply had to flesh out this framework. And I realized that now he'd effectively met a curriculum goal of learning about outlining in a very natural and purposeful way.

Homeschoolers Visit Blind School
by Jesse Richman (age 10)

In September Mommy called the blind school to arrange a tour and they said, "Call back in January." So she called then and they said how about Feb. 23rd. Mommy invited three other families to come and they all did. One of the reasons we went was to find out about how blind children are taught in special schools today. Not that we had not read books on the subject, but we wanted to see it for ourselves.

As we were parking in front of the school we noticed brightly painted play ground swings and monkey bars. We also saw four or five half size school buses with children in wheel chairs being wheeled out of them and into the school. When we went inside we were greeted by a receptionist we think was blind. That was partly because she used a Braille typewriter and had Braille copies of Reader's Digest and Guidepost.

Next we saw a girl going up and down stairs slowly with a classroom aide. She must have had another handicap besides blindness.

Two tour guides took us to a large room and we asked them some questions. Some one asked if they used guide dogs at the school. The guide's answer was, "No, we already have enough trouble in the halls with canes and wheel chairs getting tangled up together. Adding dogs to it would make it much worse and the guide dogs cost $70,000." Then she put on a video tape about the blind school. The tape said the blind school has changed in the past 20 years and now has 130 multiple handicapped children out of its 175 students. The school also has 225 staff members. That is more than one on one. The tape also told us about a very limited print reader, that students can use in a library card catalog. This machine is named the Optigon.

When the film was done we split into two groups and went to some of the classrooms. The first classroom my group visited had children who were in wheel chairs and could do almost nothing for themselves. Not even lifting up their arms.

They were very small for their age. I know because none of them looked like they were over ten but all of them were. One of them was turning on and off a TV with a switch that was mounted on a piece of wood which looked like a plastic panel. He only had to touch the panel and even that was very hard for him. On the door were graphs to show what the children had learned. There were four adults and six children in that classroom.

Then we walked to the reading and writing classroom. On the way I saw a number of boards with rug or foam scraps glued on to them. I asked our guide about them and she said that they were landmarks to help blind children find their way around the school. When we entered the classroom, most of the students were writing on braille computer typewriters. These have 20 letter Braille displays so that they could revise their writing. Then one boy showed us how they use a Braille typewriter that has only six keys, one for each Braille dot. The teacher (who was blind) showed us one normal text book, the same text book in large print, and one of six volumes of the same text book in braille. One girl wrote five lines of Braille with her stylus for us. She wrote it so fast that Mommy thought she was faking it. She was not. She wrote her name, the date and "I love my stylus" and a few lines about her school that I forget.

Then the blind teacher said they had to get to an assembly. But Mommy said that SHE was the assembly because she had offered to do folk singing after the tour.

Then we all went to the room where we had seen the film. Mommy got out her guitar and let the children feel it. Then she sung some songs for them that need audience participation and they were a very responsive group, even when they had to call out color names. They knew the names of colors.

After more folk singing we went home. I felt that I had
learned a lot about how blind and severely handicapped
children are taught today. Now I have seen more of blind
people than a glimpse out of a car window.

After a field trip to Pennsbury Manor, Tracy did some more research
on William Penn's life and his relationship with the native Indian
peoples. She then wrote the following essay from the point of view
of one of the Indians. It is always useful to be able to see someone
else's side of things, to broaden our vision beyond what we narrowly
see, or in this case what the history books might tell us. I'm sure the
experience of writing this piece helped to open Tracy's eyes to new
possibilities, and shows how writing afterwards can be a direct
extension of the learning gained from a field trip.

Penn and the Indians
by Tracy Kuehne (age 11)
Below is an account of one Lenni–Lenape Indians' thoughts
on the Great Treaty with William Penn:

Something very unusual has happened. The Great Spirit has
sent us a man. We call him Onas, which means quill or
pen. His real name is William Penn. Onas would like to be
friends with us Indians, which is mysterious and confusing
to me. Most white men are only interested in stealing
animals and land, not in treating others with respect and
kindness as Onas has.

He signed a treaty with us two moons ago. We had a
great feast. Onas talked about his plans and dreams for the
colony. He sat with us young men. The roasted hominy
tasted better than usual.

Then some braves set up some races and obstacle

courses and started showing off for Onas, but he jumped up and beat even the fastest braves! No white man has come even close to winning the chiefs' hearts as Onas has. His skill greatly impressed them.

Then came the solemn part of the affair. We all sat around and Penn told us if we followed our part of the treaty, he would do his part and we would have more fun times similar to the one we just had. I do not know of one brave who did not sign the Great Treaty that day.

Signed, White Feather

Sometime later a visitor, one of Penn's friends, was surprised to see some of Penn's Indian friends squatting at the table and pointing to whatever they wanted to eat.

Penn's influence on the colony was big to the Indians. He was a great and unusual man who wanted peace and friendship with all men. Most men at that time did not feel that way.

Later, after Onas went to the happy hunting grounds, the Indians honored him as a true and loyal friend.

Field trips also give our children an opportunity to show their gratefulness by composing thank you letters once they are home. As homeschooling mother Adele Abrahamse writes:

Yesterday Gussie wrote another one to *Bodo's Bagels*, after a field trip there. There was a picture of a bagel on the front and this line, "Thanks a *hole* lot for the tour." Inside she wrote, "Even though I've learned how to make bagels, I'm still going to leave the job to you." Here was an example of a note that used humor, and gave us an opportunity to talk about homonyms and the fun you can have with them.

Another homeschooler in Gussie's Homeschooler's Support Group wrote the following thank you note, asking further questions about the topics presented:

Dear Aqua–Air Personnel,
   Your precise and detailed descriptions of experiments made this field trip one of my favorites. I was really amazed at all of the tests you do in such a small space. I was stunned at all of the test tubes and flasks. I'm also glad that we don't have to wash our dishes so thoroughly as you clean your glassware.
   I helped at a pool this summer. I used a color test pH meter and never thought there was any other way to test pH. Your meter was convenient, decently accurate and speedy.
   After weighing my signature on the analytical balance, I wondered how much weight difference there is between an ink pen signature and a pencil signature.
   Here are some questions I wished I had asked you:
   1. Has your place ever been broken into? The neighborhood looked risky.
   2. Where do you buy all your equipment?
   3. Have you ever had any water damage?
   4. How long have you had the lab there?
   5. Why did you get into water testing in the first place?
   Thanks a lot for your valuable time spent on us and for the Petri dishes that I plan to use with my science project.
Sincerely yours,
Nathan Williamson (age 12)

Jacque Williamson, Nathan's mother, writes:

This was written after a terrific homeschool support group field trip. Nathan was so impressed with how much personal attention each staff member had given that he wanted to make his thank you more personal than usual. We discussed what flavor he wanted his letter to convey and then, to keep that flavor, he dictated to me (unlike all his other writing which he writes himself). The dictation allowed us to discuss and weigh ideas as we went along, allowing for a more fluid letter.

As he was dictating, he suddenly said, "I wished I'd asked them if they'd had any break-ins." I noted it down and later we talked about other questions he'd had after the visit. We decided to add the questions to let the staff know what he'd been thinking. The next day he got the nicest phone call about his letter and they offered him lots of test tubes *free!*

Emily Kissell's letter shows how a trip can be followed up on later when a child has a growing interest in what was experienced on the outing. Emily knew where she could turn for more information on her chosen topic, and incidentally learned more about the proper format of a business request letter through her writing. Think how different this is from the school English textbook assignment that might have had a child write a *pretend* letter of this sort, regardless of the child's real interests and aspirations. They might look the same superficially, but which one carries real learning?

Sea World
Director of Public Relations
7007 Sea World Drive
Orlando, FL 32819

Dear Sir,
    My name is Emily and I am in fifth grade. I would like to train animals when I grow up. I have been to Sea World and I would like to know how the trainers are hired. What are the

requirements to be a trainer? Are there colleges that offer this kind of training? Do you have a trainer who would be interested in writing to me to tell me about their jobs? Please send me any information you can.

Sincerely,
Emily Kissell (age 10)

These next two letters really have nothing to do with outings or trips, but everything to do with using letter writing to share point of view and make a difference in the world. They are letters that Gussie Abrahamse wrote in response to the recent gubernatorial elections in her home state of Virginia. Gussie didn't just sit back and figure that since she was too young to vote it made no difference to her. Instead she was right in there having her letter to the editor published in the Charlottesville *Daily Progress* and afterwards writing a letter to the winner, Governor-elect Wilder.

To the Editor:

Have you ever gone to the supermarket to get bananas, and some were really, really green, and others were so ripe that they were bruised and mushy? I would have a hard time choosing. Well, that's the way I felt when I watched the gubernatorial debate on television on Oct. 9.

First there was Marshall Coleman. He would not answer practically any questions that either Douglas Wilder or the press people asked him. When Wilder asked about not having a negative campaign, he would get around the question by getting back to a negative thought about Wilder.

Then there was Wilder. His record shows that every bill that would enforce the death penalty, he voted against. Criminals are out of jail so quickly that sometimes I feel they have more rights than the average person.

Patrick Henry is top banana in my book, but if I can't have him for governor, I guess I'll take Wilder.

Sincerely,
Gussie Abrahamse (age 11)

Gussie's mother told me that at times Gussie balks at writing. The suggestion to write to Governor-elect Wilder when he had won though was met with immediate enthusiasm, as Gussie is so very interested in the world of politics.

Dear Governor-elect Wilder:
I think it is really really great that you won—especially since you are going to be the first black Governor elected in America, and in a state that seceded from the Union too. I really think that is special.

I am an official member of the Democratic party. I'm not sure how *that* happened because I am just eleven.

I home school. I hear that you don't really like home schooling. I can understand why, but I hope you won't change any laws about home schooling because public schools work for some people and not others. I would have been labeled, "learning disabled" because I didn't learn how to read until age eight. But then I read *The Lord of the Rings*, by J.R.R. Tolkien at age ten.

Congratulations, and have fun.

Sincerely,
Gussie Abrahamse (age 11)

Any outing can be an inspiration for writing—it does not have to be an official "educational" field trip with obvious "learning objectives." The rich and diverse family outings we take can open up many new writing topics, and help sharpen observational skills.

Writing can help hold a special day in our memories, often better even than a photograph of the event. By looking back later at what we've written we can relive what we felt and experienced, not just what we looked like as we smiled at the camera.

In the next pieces we have two brothers both describing the same impromptu fall day at the beach. Timothy typed his up with his family's word processor computer program, printed it out with very large letters, added a computer illustration, and gave it to his grandfather as a present. Our relatives are certainly another built in and readily enthusiastic audience, and what a good way to keep them up to date on what everyone is doing.

The Day at the Beach
by Timothy Formica (age 8)

It was a long journey to the beach. On the way we saw beautiful trees. When we got there, the seagulls were all about us. The wind was blowing. The sea was splashing. It was wonderful.

We set up camp on the sand. Matt and I started to make a sand castle. Peter and I were getting buckets of sand.

After a while, the tide came in. We tried to keep the tide from coming in the sand castle, and breaking it down. It was getting late, and the sun was beautiful. It was time to go, but we had fun!

Beach
by Matthew Formica (age 11)

As the waves crept closer to our sand castle, Timothy, Peter and I worked with more vigor. We had been working on it for over an hour and a half and it was eight inches high and two feet wide!

In order to resist the tide, our castle would have to be wide and strong. We put lots of dry sand and sea shells on it. Also, there was a trench for water drainage and a line of interlocking shells in a row in front of the castle.

We had to run back and forth to the dry sand as the tide lapped at the base and sides of our castle.

The beautiful trench that I had made was washed away. Once, the waves washed over the top of the castle!

The sun was setting and our castle was still standing firm. I got one last look at the castle before we left the beach.

Jessica Strappello also had the opportunity to go to the ocean and observe and experience the world of waves and salt spray. She wrote this description while actually sitting on a beach on Maine's rocky coast while on a family vacation trip. I think you'll be able to tell by the lucid and telling images that this is no vague memory, but actual living experience.

The Ocean
by Jessica Strappello (age 12)

It sparkles, it shines in the bright, bright sun. Now it moves quietly and peacefully. Then the waves begin to form and crash against the rocks. Salty spray lands on your lips. The waves rant and rave in frustration—the ungiving rocks blocking their way. A seagull screams. A little ship tosses to and fro waiting for calm. Now silent, now noisy. It is either crashing like thunder or rippling along like a bubbling brook.

Sara Taylor wrote a very long and detailed piece about her family's summer vacation camping. We all know that summer doesn't end the learning for our children, and writing a piece like this certainly shows that to everyone else too. I certainly hope Sara's grandparents saw a copy of this report, as they were able to be part of the outing too. Notice the many references made to family history and experiences of grandparents and parents when they were young. Our homeschooled students have a unique opportunity to feel in tune with different generations, not separate and disconnected from the continuity of their family's life.

My Vacation
by Sara Taylor (age 9)

The warm water felt good as I jumped into the campground pool in Mercer, Pennsylvania. We had arrived the 25th of August. We had pitched the tent and laid out the sleeping bags. Now our vacation had really begun.

When we got back from the pool, my grandma was making fried chicken for dinner. While my mom made potato salad, Laurel, Emery and I collected firewood. By the time we had enough wood, dinner was ready. As we ate the delicious chicken and the scrumptious potato salad, we talked about our day. That night we slept soundly.

The next morning we woke up bright and early. When we went to the bathroom to wash up for the day, we discovered that there would be an Amish bake sale that very morning. When we got back, we waited for my dad to return to watch Emery, so we could go to the bake sale. We planned to buy a raspberry pie to surprise my dad. Then we saw him walking up the road carrying a package. It was a raspberry pie! He had already been there and gotten his own pie! We had a delicious breakfast anyway.

After breakfast we went to Pymatuning. Pymatuning is a lake where there are carp, ducks, and seagulls. We threw in some bread. All of a sudden, all the carp and ducks were jumping and tumbling over to get the bread. The seagulls were circling overhead, waiting for a chance to dive in and grab it. Finally, one of the carp caught the bread and swallowed it. They looked like greedy little two-year-olds, grabbing and fighting.

We found a picnic area near Pymatuning. It felt good to eat lunch after the long morning. We ate chicken and ham with the home-made bread from the bake sale.

Then after lunch we packed our things and left the picnic area. We were going to Conneaut Lake Amusement Park! When we got there, Emery had fallen asleep. It was pretty hard trying to wake him up.

As we walked down the street, we heard the music of the merry-go-round. It was eighty-nine years old but still as bright and colorful as it had been in the olden days. My mom and grandma had ridden on it as girls. When my dad had gotten the tickets, we climbed on. I chose one of the old horses with a real horse-hair mane and tail. Around the top there were pictures of the old Conneaut Lake Park of long ago. A little pipe organ played "Old MacDonald Had a Farm," as the merry-go-round began to move.

After the ride we went to get cotton candy. As we watched, the lady in the booth twirled the fluffy, pink cotton candy around the stick. It was fun to watch, but when she had finished, it was bigger than my head! We couldn't even eat it all.

We went to look for a map. After we had found a map and decided where to go next, we found we had lost Emery, who is only three. My mom, dad, and grandma went looking for him, while we waited with Grandpa. Finally my mom found him. He had made his way back to the cotton candy stand. From then on, we kept an eye on him.

Holding Emery firmly by the hand, we walked down toward the shore, where a paddle-wheel boat was docked. We had decided to go on a cruise around Conneaut Lake. As we stood in line waiting for tickets, we heard the big horn blow. We found our seats, and the boat started to move. After a while, Laurel and I climbed up the steep steps to the upper deck.

There we could see everything. On the shore were beautiful houses. My favorite was a big, old, blue house with a lacy iron balcony. The pilot in the wheelhouse said that people rent the big houses for the summer and go back to their own houses in the winter. We saw lots of people playing in the sand and swimming in the lake. We waved to them, and they waved back.

After the cruise, we had ice cream. While we ate, my dad looked at how many tickets we had left. There were enough to go on the merry–go–round again. After our last ride, we headed back to the campground and went to bed.

The next day was Sunday. We decided to go to church in Meadville. My grandparents were the first members in that congregation nearly forty years ago. There weren't many people there, but most of them remembered my grandparents.

After we had eaten lunch, we went to the house where my grandparents lived when my mother was born. In the back there was a small forest and a pond. There were lots of frogs in the pond. After we had finished at the old house, we started for Lake Erie.

At Lake Erie we found a nice beach and got our things laid out. Then we went swimming. After that I went exploring. I found lots of driftwood, sand, and rocks. Then we spotted a big ship out on the lake. We watched it until it was out of sight. The interesting thing about it was you could see that the earth curves. When the ship first reached the horizon, the bottom disappeared first. Then the middle dropped out of sight and finally the smokestacks.

That night was our last night at the campground. The next morning we took our tent down and packed our things in the car, but our vacation wasn't completely over yet. We had decided to stop at Cook Forest on the way home.

At Cook Forest we ate lunch. Then we hiked on a mountain trail. Soon we came to a tree that had fallen down. Emery, Laurel, and I were allowed to walk along the trunk. It seemed half a mile long. When we got back on the trail, my mom told us about Cook Forest. She said that some of the trees were just saplings when the Pilgrims came to America. That was when a forest fire had destroyed most of the forest. The trees had been growing undisturbed since then. It is the only place in Pennsylvania that is still virgin forest. Then we came to an ancient tree that was very thick. My mom, my sister, and I tried holding hands around the trunk. Our fingertips barely touched.

After we had gotten off the mountain trail, my grandparents started for home, but we stayed to take a canoe trip down the Clarion River. We picked out our life jackets and rode on a pickup truck that would take us to the launching place. After we got our canoe in the water, my mom found that my dad wasn't very experienced. We kept hitting rocks. One time we got caught in such a swift current with so many rocks we had to carry the canoe to deeper water.

A little way on, we saw some people looking for something. We asked what they were looking for. They said their canoe had tipped over and they had lost their video camera and one of the man's shoes. We said that if we saw a shoe or video camera floating down the river, we would tell them. We were all very relieved when we reached the landing spot.

We changed out of our wet clothes, had a hot supper at MacDonald's and drove home to Grandma's. At Grandma's we told everyone about our canoe ride. Grandma said she was glad she didn't come along. That night we slept peacefully in real beds.

That was the end of our vacation, but I felt that we had a very successful time and that we learned a lot.

This last evocative piece was written after Rachel and her family hiked up Ricker Mountain, and saw the remains of a now-long-dead town scattered along the old roadway. I think it is a very moving statement about life and death and how closely a person can feel into a situation that speaks of the past.

Ricker Mountain
by Rachel Johnston (age 13)

The green mountain rises against the blue sky. Today we plan to climb that mountain. An old community stands there, or rather the foundations of their homes, barns, and out-buildings stand there. They have weathered many storms since they were built in the 1800's.

As we hike up the mountain trail, the beauty of the trees is striking. Under the canopy of trees, sometimes to the right and sometimes to the left, run old stone walls. And every once in a while, we leave the road to look at the foundations of some building, with the grass growing between the field-stone cellar walls.

Here is a public graveyard: in fact, the only one on Ricker Mountain. The stones, some of them field-stones, some otherwise, are hard to read, if they have inscriptions at all. A road runs through one corner of this quiet place. I can picture children running along the road, hurrying to get to school on time. Here comes a wagon, going the other way, with its owner on the front seat. Let's follow him. He proceeds back outside the walls surrounding the solitary burial place, and down the road. Aha! it's a farmer taking his corn crop to his nearby barn. He drives around the barn, to the back, then in. As he unloads his corn, to be used during the winter to feed his animals, I can hear the animals munching on some hay—but no, I don't hear anything any more. The farmer is fading; he is gone. Just the mossy cellar hole of his barn remains.

Oh, there, across from the man's barn I see some steps. Up the steps lies the Ricker private cemetery. Generations of Rickers are buried here. A wagon creaks to a stop, and a man jumps off the seat. He and some other men, all bare-headed, sadly bear a box, a casket, from the back of the wagon. Gideon Ricker has died. The founder of Ricker Mountain is now gone. One man furtively wipes his eyes. "A righteous man," he says softly. Another says, "Well, now the man can rest beside his wife at last. No more hard work for him." But—where'd they go? Poor Gideon's gravestone, now nearly illegible, bears silent witness to the fact that only God remembers the righteous through the years.

Further along the road we come to William Clossey's field. The guide book reads:

Jack Cameron, a westerner, bought this land, sight-unseen, from William Clossey in the 1890's. He was unable to make a living on this unyielding land, and died a poor and homesick man. He was cremated and his widow buried his ashes at the corner of the stone wall, north-east of the homesite. A small ring of stones marks the spot.

Standing by the cellar hole, we can see the steps, now more

like a ramp, leading down to the dirt cellar floor. I can almost see Jack Cameron's widow, coming back from having her late husband cremated, up the road, crying as she comes. She enters the house, sits down at the rough–hewn table, sets the small box containing the ashes before her, and begins to sob, for her husband is gone. Presently, she arouses herself, goes down into the cellar to get the shovel, returns for her precious box, then walks to the corner of the stone wall, thinking all the while of her husband's last request: that he should be buried on the Oklahoma plains, where he had been raised. He had not realized how impractical it was for a penniless, heartbroken widow to travel hundreds of miles to bury a dead husband where he was raised. When she reaches the spot, blinded with tears, she digs a small hole, and gently, lovingly, places her box in the hole, after giving it one last kiss. Breaking down, she cries as hard as ever over the one she loved so much, quite oblivious to the things around her. Then, remembering her job, she fills in the hole. Because she cannot afford a gravestone, she carefully encircles the place with stones, so she can remember where it is. Then, she picks up the shovel, and walks slowly back to her house, thinking of her husband as he had been.

Then she is gone, and only a small, lonely ring of stones remains.

5. Loving Books Means Sharing Books

"It's one of the best books I've ever read! But I guess that every book I read is. Get Jacob to read it—I think he could. It's great!"

This is my son Jesse talking to me, but not out loud in a conversation. He's writing in his reading log, telling me about the latest book he's read, *The Sword in the Stone*, about King Arthur's early education with Merlin. I answer him in writing also, saying, "Wow! Another book that you've loved. I'm so glad you enjoyed it! We'll have to thank Ian Latinette for recommending it. And I will recommend it to Jacob."

Book recommendations often fly back and forth between homeschooled children. "Have you read *Mrs. Frisby and the Rats of NIMH?* You should, it's really terrific, especially if you liked *Charlotte's Web*."

And when homeschooled children find they have a loved book in common, they really get talking—about favorite parts, favorite characters, how they felt about sad or happy endings. Books are often a common experience for our children, helping them feel closer to their friends.

I remember last year Jesse worked for a week or so writing a review of a number of Johanna Spyri's books that he'd enjoyed, comparing and contrasting them with each other. He knew that I wanted his review to be included in our newsletter, *Pennsylvania Homeschoolers*, in response to a reader who was asking for reviews of wholesome children's books. Jesse knew he had an audience—and a deadline. The act of writing down his thoughts made him think much more closely about the books, made him come to generalizations and realizations and understandings about themes and characters that he never would have come to by just reading. He also realized he wanted to say something about Johanna Spyri's life in his review, and so we looked for biographical essays about her and read and discussed them. I doubt if he would have done that bit of research if it were not for the book review project.

Just reading can become a bit passive for children, something they drink in and enjoy, but very different from the hard work of original thinking and problem solving that have to go into every writing act, no matter what the topic. Jesse noticed this himself as he got into the project, began saying aloud that he appreciated this way of thinking about the books, began saying that he hadn't thought about all these things before he needed to sort them out through writing. Here is his review.

Review of Johanna Spyri's Books
by Jesse Richman (age 11)

Almost everyone knows about Johanna Spyri's book *Heidi*, but she has written some other very good books that are also about orphans or children who lost one of their parents and live in the Alps.

Johanna Spyri was born in Switzerland and grew up in the Alps. Her father was a doctor and she may have often seen invalids in his office. After her marriage she had a little boy who had bad health. Perhaps that is the cause of the presence of invalids in *Heidi*, in *Rico and Stineli*, and in *Cornelli*. She used to tell her son stories, however she did not turn to writing them down until after her son's death.

Summary of Books by Johanna Spyri:
Cornelli is a greatly moving book about a motherless child

whose father goes on a business trip, leaving her at the mercy of her aunt who wants to turn her into a lady. I think this, not *Heidi*, is Johanna Spyri's best book.

Dora is a story of how a girl loses her father, moves into her aunt's house and finally ends up in the Alps. Dora helps to make the family run better and benefits and encourages all of the children. Unlike some of Spyri's books, this book has bushels of humor.

How Wettsel was Provided For is about how a girl, whose mother has died, came to live at the house of Andrew the carpenter, her mother's true love, and so after much turmoil gets provided for.

Rico and Stinelli is different from the others in a number of ways. First, it has a boy as the main character. Also Rico and Stinelli do not end up in the Swiss Alps, but in Italy.

So if you have read and enjoyed *Heidi* I sincerely recommend that you go to your library today and borrow other books by Johanna Spyri!

Jesse was gratified to hear that several folks actually did go out and look for these little known gems. He could see that his writing act extended beyond his desk and could actually influence others.

Many times homeschooled children feel more motivated to write book reviews if they know they serve this sort of real purpose. Perhaps the review will be submitted to a magazine or newsletter they subscribe to, such as *Stone Soup*, *Cobblestone*, or a local or statewide homeschooling newsletter. We have been including more and more book reviews from students in the "BackPack" children's writing section of our *Pennsylvania Homeschoolers* newsletter, and the writing has an authentic ring to it. The children know they are writing *to* someone, and that because of their review another child might meet a very good book.

Jesse had a book review published in *Stone Soup* magazine a year ago, even receiving a surprise payment for it. I found that once Jesse viewed himself as a potential reviewer for *that* particular publication, he found it much more interesting to read the other student reviews in *Stone Soup*. Before, they were not of particular interest, but now they were eagerly read, as he identified with the reviewer's role. We spent a good bit of time discussing how the children structured their reviews, what sort of opening leads they used, what questions Jesse wished they had answered that they hadn't, how engagingly written they were, and more.

The following is a detailed review which really shows that Nica loved the book she was writing about. She originally published it in the *Neighborhood News*, the monthly newspaper Nica and her good friend, homeschooler Mika Perrine, publish monthly. Again, this gave Nica the realization that her words were really going to communicate to a valued audience. Can you resist going down to your library and finding a copy?

Black Star, Bright Dawn by Scott O'Dell
Review by Nica Christensen (age 11)

Bright Dawn was not like any of the other Eskimo children in Womengo, a small Eskimo village on the Gulf of Alaska. She was brave and knew many of the old Eskimo ways. She was very skillful at hunting and fishing and she always drove her father's sled with him down to the ice near Norton Sound where the fish were plentiful.

But one day something awful happens to her father. The family moves to Ikuma, a town with more Whites than Eskimos. Bright Dawn must learn the language of the white man and make many changes in her life.

Dogsled racing is a popular sport in Ikuma and soon Bright

Dawn finds herself racing with the other children. At first her father is upset. Dogs are for work, not for racing! But before he had lived long in Ikuma he was racing too! And winning almost all of the races!

In Bright Dawn's team there was one special dog. It was Black Star. He was the lead dog, and he was Bright Dawn's favorite. His coat was a beautiful snow white and on his head was a black star. But the most beautiful thing about him was his eyes. They were ice blue and they seemed to look right through you. But they were friendly eyes and even though the dog was mostly wolf, he was gentle and generous to the other dogs.

In spite of an accident on the ice, Bright Dawn's father was soon the fastest musher around. And soon people were asking him if he would like to run the Iditarod, the famous sled dog race from Anchorage to Nome.

He decides he'll do it and training starts at once. But when the sled hits a tree and he breaks his arm, Bright Dawn finds herself going to race the Iditarod.

This is a very moving story and I definitely recommend it!

Here is another review written by Nica. I especially enjoyed how she opened her review. This is indeed a book I've always seen, but never read—now we will! Once again, Nica first published this in the *Neighborhood News.*

The Great Gilly Hopkins by Katherine Paterson
Review by Nica Christensen (age 10)

Please, my dear reader, don't just look over this review. I know what you're thinking. "I've seen that book one hundred times at the library and it looks just boring!" That's just what I thought when my Mom brought it home. But... when I started reading it, I couldn't put it down.

The Great Gilly Hopkins is about an average, bratty eleven year old. Both her parents have left her and so most of her life she's been moved around from house to house. Of course, no one wants to keep her for long, so when she ends up at the junky, smelly, old house of Maimi Trotter's, she doesn't expect to stay for long. But as Trotter says, "There's no kid who didn't make friends with me." And before Gilly knows it, she's liking her new family.

Next door lives an old black man who's blind and always comes to dinner at Trotter's. Then there's the school and all the strange and funny things that happen there. And, oh, how can I forget William Ernest, Gilly's adopted brother who gets to be her one and only best friend!

I could go on with all that happens! But you'll have to read it for yourself. I loved this book and I hope you'll read it.

Elizabeth Tisdale has reached many people with this review, as it was printed in both *Pennsylvania Homeschoolers* and in her own family's newsletter, *Agape Learning Lab News*. I like how she gives us the basic outlines of each book's theme and plot, but doesn't give away the whole story. She has given us just enough to make us want to find the book to fill in the details through our own reading. Elizabeth has also had a book review accepted for the children's magazine, *Stone Soup*.

Review of Mildred Taylor's Books
by Elizabeth Tisdale (age 12)

Mildred Taylor, perhaps a less well-known author, has written three moving books: *Song of the Trees; Roll of Thunder, Hear My Cry*; and *Let the Circle be Unbroken*. They are some of the best books I have ever read.

The stories center around a Black family, the Logans. One sees the events through Cassie's eyes, the main character. She has three brothers, Stacey, Christopher John, and Little Man. The setting is Mississippi at the time of the Depression.

Song of the Trees is the first book of the series. Papa is away working on the railroad. Big Ma, Cassie's Grandmother, has an important decision to make. In the end Papa is forced to make a quick trip home. Dramatic measures are taken to save the tree's song.

Roll of Thunder, Hear My Cry was about the year of the night riders and burnings. It was the year Cassie was humiliated in public simply because she was Black. During this year she learned a valuable lesson.

I feel that the final book by Mildred Taylor was the most thought provoking. *Let the Circle Be Unbroken* dramatically illustrated what the law was for Blacks. I learned even though the Blacks had the right to vote, they had a heavy price to pay if they wanted to try. Stacey also learned the cruelties of the work world on a Southern sugar cane plantation. I hope you enjoy these books as much as our family did.

Contests offer another avenue for book reviews. I think it's safe to say that the book responses and reviews which follow probably wouldn't have been written unless the contest, with its constraints, real audience, and possible awards or rewards, had been presented to the child.

Gussie Abrahamse wrote the following review as part of the *Motts' Apple Awards* annual contest. Because she knew it would be judged, she had the sure incentive to rewrite her piece several times to get it just how she wanted it. She also had the chance to share first drafts with her local homeschoolers writing club and get feedback from them on ways to improve it.

My Favorite Book
by Gussie Abrahamse (age 11)

You have asked me to write about my favorite book. It would be easy to pick a book and tell how exciting, sad, or fanciful it makes me feel. The tough question is—what is my favorite book?

My favorite *type* of book is fantasy. How excited I get when a warrior is in combat with an evil sorcerer! My favorite book? Now that is a hard question.

The Lord of the Rings, a trilogy by J.R.R. Tolkien, is one of my favorite books because it makes me feel so adventuresome. The contrast to the nine characters out in the snow, struggling up a mountain, and me, safe in bed, under two or three blankets, gives me a secure feeling.

I was sad when it ended, not because the story was sad, but because I thought that it was the only fantasy book in existence.

Little did I know about the books of Anne McCaffrey, Lloyd Alexander, Tamora Pierce, and Robin McKinley. These books also make me feel adventuresome, but in their own special way.

The Lord of the Rings was the book that unlocked the door of fantasy for me, and for that I will always be grateful.

Luke Wilson entered the *Cobblestone History Magazine* book review contest, where he had to write a review of his favorite American history book, fiction or non-fiction. Beyond winning or losing, I think Luke benefited from the experience, focusing his thinking and coming up with an excellent review. Makes me want to look this book up!

Early Thunder by Jean Fritz
Review by Luke Wilson (age 11)

My favorite American history book is *Early Thunder* by Jean Fritz, an author whose writings I enjoy reading very much. This historical novel is set in the Revolutionary War period, when whole towns, families and friendships experienced an ever growing rivalry between the Whigs and Tories. People remaining loyal to the king of England were called Tories and people who wanted independence were called Whigs. It's my favorite book because the story is shown through the eyes of thirteen year old Daniel West.

I felt as if I was Daniel in the town of Salem, Massachusetts as the story unfolded with all the conflicts that were part of this colonial period. I could relate to Daniel's struggle of being in the position to appreciate two opposing points of view. The author brings the story to an exciting climax when Daniel makes a difficult choice, earning the respect of others and gaining new self-confidence.

Sometimes a contest's form and length requirements may force a person into condensing his thoughts, squeezing them into a much smaller space than seemed possible at first. This experience in crystalizing can, ironically, be a stretching experience.

The following little essay was written by Dory Lerew for a local Walden Book Store contest, and *won* as their "best entry." Dory won a $5.00 gift certificate for her good effort, and I'm sure had no trouble picking out a good book to adventure into.

Why I Like to Read
by Dory Lerew (age 9)

Reading helps your imagination go Wacko. For instance, if you are reading an exciting jungle book, all of a sudden PLOP you are in it. You get to ride on an elephant's back, play with a lion, and eat with a giraffe. What a way to spend a day!

Some homeschooled children are beginning to keep book logs or journals, where brief responses to the books they've read can be kept together. I've found with my own children that if I respond in writing, in a dialogue or written discussion about the book, that they are more eager to write and think and stretch. Just be prepared for occasional responses like this first example! I remember reading in one book on the reading and writing connection that responding to a book by wanting to read another book should always be considered appropriate!

Book Response
by Jesse Richman (age 11)
Instead of writing this book review I would rather be reading *The Prince and the Pauper*, finish it today, and go on to *Huckleberry Finn*. Yesterday I finished *Tom Sawyer* after three days.

Some students write responses to each section of a book they read, such as Ryan Williamson, age 8, does in the following responses to *Charlotte's Web*, by E.B. White. As Ryan's mother Jacque wrote:

Ryan was 8 when he wrote these reading log entries. The boys were past the stage of reading to me and I felt a need to keep in touch with their reading. Each had a reading log notebook. Inside the front cover was pasted:

Each day write the following in your reading log:
A) Table of Contents entry for today.
B) Then on your log page for today:

1) date
2) name of book and author
3) pages read
4) write about one of the following:
    a) predict what will happen next
    b) quote some words, phrases, or sentences you
    really liked for the way the author said them.
    c) tell your reactions to what you read today
    d) Why do you think the author wrote what
    happened today? How does it fit in with what has
    happened so far?
    e) If you are confused about some part, write
    questions you would like to ask the author.
    f) Does the author have a strong belief that shows in
    the book? What is it, and where in the book does it
    show?"

Daily reading log entries proved too tedious at this age, so we later did them only occasionally. Two years later we try to do one every week, and now they are 75–100 words long. It's never been a favorite writing activity for Ryan, in part, I think, because he views it for me and not him, and in part because he is not a very verbal child and this critical thinking on paper is tough. He'd be happy to draw about it! This is very different from a book review, which he finds easier to write. I plan to begin making written comments to Ryan after log entries to encourage more exchange, hoping to make it more personal for him.

Responses to *Charlotte's Web*
by Ryan Williamson (age 8)

    November 2. He describes a lot of realistic things that people do to pigs, like this: make them eat bad leftovers, and make them sleep in mud piles.

November 3. I like stories about animals. Here are my favorite authors: best is E.B. White, second best is Robert Lawson. I love their stories!

November 4. I like the way Charlotte was introduced in the book. It was like this: in the middle of the night Charlotte said, "I'll be a friend to you," cause that night he wanted a friend.

November 5. I think the author is a great author because he describes so much that you know everything that he is trying to tell you and I want to know the author and read all of his books so much.

November 6. I've read two of E.B. White's books and I am on my third one and E.B. White only wrote three books. I know we have all of the E.B. White books.

I found, like Jacque, that Jesse was viewing his reading log as a chore that I was requiring, something to zip through as fast as possible—or put off as long as possible. Since I have begun responding in writing to his entries, really discussing them with him, things are going much better. Jesse is actually now enjoying rereading his entries.

Response to *The 21 Balloons*
by Jesse Richman (age 12)

The 21 Balloons is a good book but not the best one I've ever read. This delightful tale goes full circle and lets Professor Watermen keep his dream while running him through some marvelous adventures. It will be next on Daddy's list! In the book Professor Waterman sets out in a balloon, and is forced to land on the volcanic island of Krakatoa where he meets the citizens, and becomes a share holder in the diamond mines. He escapes with islanders by the help of 20 balloons when the island blows up, and goes around the world in 40 days.

I responded to this entry by writing:

> Jesse, you've really told me a lot about this story! I get a feel for the whole movement of the plot, and what the major conflicts are. Around the world in 40 days! He beat Nellie Bly, huh! Are the citizens of Krakatoa local native peoples, or colonists from some European country? Sounds like Columbus might have liked that island with its diamonds, do you think? Thanks for writing!

For his tenth birthday, Carol Wilson gave her son a nicely bound blank book that was designed for recording thoughts about favorite books. Luke has enjoyed rereading his responses, remembering his favorite characters and books.

The Adventures of Tom Sawyer by **Mark Twain**
Reviewed by Luke Wilson (age 10)
I especially like the part where Tom and Becky are trapped in the cave and Injun Joe climbs up over the rock and Tom scared him away. I wish I was him and did the things he did. Although he was always getting into trouble, I think he would have been a good friend.

Matilda by **Roald Dahl**
Reviewed by Luke Wilson (age 10)
Funny story about a girl genius who has magical powers. The story also includes the meanest headmistress in the world! In addition to that there's the most wonderful, loving teacher

that helps Matilda every step of the way.

This year Luke, now 11, responded to a favorite book, *Johnny Tremain*, by Esther Forbes, in a very different way. He used the background gained in the book, and in other readings of early Revolutionary Boston, to compose newspaper articles for the *Boston Observer* as they might have appeared in pre-Revolutionary days. This was a direct offshoot of the book, since Johnny Tremain becomes involved in the newspaper, as well as the events. Luke did quite a bit of studying to see how newspaper articles are constructed, what style of writing is required, and checking out details of events in other source materials. I don't think there's any doubt that Luke really understands these events, and feels more like he has lived through them after writing these mock articles.

Our family has always enjoyed a book of "newspaper" articles of just this type, following America's history from it's early discovery to near present. We have also loved pouring over old reprints of Civil War newspapers. Newspapers can truly turn the past into present and bring us right into events. Sometimes it is eye-opening just to realize that the newspapers of any time cannot see into the future and guess the outcome of actions and events, just as Luke is careful not to mention any notions of independence or revolution or new governments in his following articles.

Boston Observer, March 6, 1770
by Luke Wilson (age 10)

For eighteen months the town of Boston has endured increasing numbers of British soldiers sent to enforce the King's rule and keep the peace. Bostonians have grown more and more uneasy with the "lobster backs" presence, especially since the soldiers began pitching their tents on the Boston Common. Last evening the tensions finally boiled over. A small crowd began throwing snowballs at the redcoats. As the snowballing became more intense, some rocks were reportedly thrown as well. At some point during the skirmish a British soldier fired a shot, more followed. When the smoke cleared, 5 colonists lay dead. The British authorities claimed that no orders had been given to fire upon the crowd. The angry colonists are already calling this act of violence the "Boston Massacre."

Boston Observer, **December 17, 1773**
by Luke Wilson (age 10)
　　Last night at the harbor in Boston, Massachusetts, anywhere from fifty to seventy-five men dressed as Mohawk Indians boarded three English ships and dumped the ship's cargo of 340 chests of tea into the sea. One of the organizers, who wishes to remain anonymous, claims this was a protest against the taxes on tea and other goods sold in the colonies. The British can't put a finger on anybody because it was so well organized. The Whigs consider it a great triumph and the Tories are furious. There is considerable discussion throughout Boston about what the British government will do next.

Boston Observer, **April 19, 1775**
by Luke Wilson (age 10)
　　Last night in Boston, Massachusetts, General Thomas Gage sent 700 British soldiers to capture Sam Adams and John Hancock, two prominent, outspoken Whigs, and to destroy a major colonist's supply depot. General Gage had picked up the information about the stores from his spies. The General and his men marched to Lexington where they met a group of 38 farmers and townspeople. Shots were exchanged, eight

colonists died and nine were wounded.

The colonists were prepared because they had been warned by three men whose names are not known. These men rode from Boston to Concord to warn the people. One man was taken prisoner, but he quickly escaped. Although the "lobster backs"—as they are sometimes called—destroyed the stores of ammunition in Concord, the British met fierce resistance at the Old North Bridge and suffered 14 casualties. But the worst was yet to come for the British.

By then, word had spread through the countryside, and angry colonists shot at the British from all sides on their return march to Boston. Two hundred and forty-seven soldiers were killed or wounded for the British and eighty-eight for the colonists. It is clear from the results of this encounter that the British are facing a formidable foe and will have no easy time enforcing the Crown's policies.

Responding to what we read can also take the form of writing a new fictional piece directly inspired by another writer. In this way we can not only feel the setting and characters and conflicts found in the original book more, but we can see more clearly all the imagining, work, and research that goes to make up a full book. Jennifer Girten wrote this next story as a response to *On to Oregon*, which made a great impression on her. She is in her fourth year of home education, and besides being a fine reader, she also enjoys the outdoor life of camping and horseback riding.

The Journey
by Jennifer Girten (age 8)

Sara and Davie lived with their mother and father. They were good little children. They obeyed their mother and father.

Sara lived on a farm in Wisconsin. Every morning Sara

helped with the morning chores.

One night when Sara was in bed, she heard her parents talking about this place called "Oregon." It sounded so strange to her because she wished Wisconsin would have more flowers than clover.

The next morning at the breakfast table Pa told the family about leaving Wisconsin. Pa said that there were all kinds of different flowers in Oregon.

So Sara helped Ma pack and Davie helped Pa hitch up the horses. Sara and Davie wanted to sit at the back of the wagon and watch the rest of Wisconsin go by.

Soon Wisconsin was out of sight. Sara knew she would miss Wisconsin but she was going to Oregon.

Soon it grew dark and Pa stopped the horses. Ma took out some bread and corn. After they ate they went to bed.

The next morning Sara could smell cooking outside. Ma was making a special breakfast for everyone. Pancakes! The family enjoyed the delicious breakfast.

Soon the horses were hitched once again for the long journey to Oregon. The scenery was beautiful to look at. They were in Idaho and soon they would be in Oregon. On the long journey they saw buffalo, sheep, turkeys, wild cattle, goats, and lots of mountains.

Finally they were in Oregon. They were tired. They built a house and lived happily ever after. Soon Sara's dream came true. She walked to a field and there were thousands of flowers. She didn't see any clover at all.

Gussie Abrahamse is part of a Sherlock Holmes club in her area, attended mostly by adults. A club activity one evening was for the members to share their own creative efforts, writing in the style of a Sherlock Holmes mystery. All the pieces were to be published in a club collection of activities. The specific motivation was a bit of a news article that Watson shows to Mrs. Hudson, who "showing unusual perceptiveness, explains all." Playfulness was encouraged in the responses. The chance to try to mimic another writer's style is one to take—it enhances your feel for what that author goes through while creating.

Sherlock Holmes Take-off
by Gussie Abrahamse age 11

Oh, my dear! Dr. Watson, I thought you had more sense of deduction than that! Obviously, the man was going to commit a crime. He wore the one shoe because that was what he would carry the stolen object in. In his haste, he forgot to put on his other shoe.

He did remember, however, to shell a last peanut so it would appear the peanut vendor committed the crime. He also remembered to check the dog hole by the front door where he was going to bury the booty. Finally, he raised his umbrella so he wouldn't be recognized as easily.

Now, wasn't that obvious? Go check with Mr. Holmes and I'm sure he will tell you the same thing.

Last year we had just finished reading an excellent biography of Elizabeth Blackwell, the first woman doctor in America. We didn't usually do "projects" after reading books, but we by accident came upon a grand writing idea that all three kids dove into with excitement and delight. Even Jacob, who often grumbled at that time about writing, was a ready participant. We'd read in the book *Teaching Critical Reading with Children's Literature*, by Nancy Polette, about an idea to use with any biography. In a nutshell the idea is to write a script similar to the old TV show "What's My Line" or "To Tell the Truth." Each of three "guests" claims to be the famous person you have just read about. The moderator poses questions to test each person's truthfulness. At the end the "audience" is invited to vote, and of course you announce who is really who. The book contains a sample show script, which happened to be about Florence Nightengale and so quite close to our Elizabeth Blackwell, and the kids thought it was hysterical and were dancing about in their seats ready to start. Coming up with the "phony" answers from the impostor Elizabeth Blackwells was a delight!

What's My Line
by Jesse (A), Jacob (B), and Molly (C),
and Susan Richman (Moderator)

Moderator: What is your name please?
  A: My name is Elizabeth Blackwell.
  B: My name is Elizabeth Blackwell.
  C: My name is Elizabeth Blackwell.
Moderator: What was your childhood like?
  A: I was born in Los Angeles. My father was a prominent doctor of the big city. He took great pride in our educations. Every night he used to take me and my three brothers and sisters up to his study. There we spent many happy hours. I learned so much in those years that I could do almost as much as my father before I went to medical school!
  B: I was born in 1821, and my father was a cotton farmer in the South and had lots of slaves. They were very nice to me.
  C: I lived in England at first, then I moved to America.
Moderator: How easy was it to get into medical school?
  A: Oh, it was a breeze! I just looked a medical school up in the phone book, called and was immediately accepted.

They said it was a great idea having women as doctors and threw out half of the male students.

B: Very easy. A medical school in Philadelphia gave me a scholarship.

C: Oh, very hard. They (the men at the school) voted about if I should be able to get in the medical school and there was only only one "nea." I fear it was only a joke.

Moderator: What was your first hospital experience like?

A: I found some comfortable work at a very clean exclusive hospital. I was treated as I wished to be, which was as a fine lady. There were not enough days in the year for all of my dates.

B: I was at a very clean hospital. They washed the place every day. I almost fainted the first time I saw surgery.

C: It was in Paris. It was filthy, it was very bad, for me and the people I was working for. They only let me work for women.

Moderator: Did the women feel positive about coming to a woman doctor?

A: Yes! Every woman who I ever saw as a patient thought I was a great doctor, none had any suspicions.

B: Oh, yes! All the women went to me. They were sure I would do a better job.

C: No. that's NO with a capital N and O! They would not let me touch them. Oh, that hospital was horrible.

Moderator: Did you ever want to specialize in any one type of medical practice?

A: At first I wanted to be a surgeon, but after a minor attack of ship's fever that lost me the sight of one eye, I was forced to give it up.

B: I always wanted to be a nurse but too many men had already taken that job, so because they had taken the job I had wanted, I took the more respectable job of being a doctor.

C: I wanted to be a surgeon. I had already dissected a dead person, and I had observed surgery too. But a baby who had a very bad sickness which had some kind of fluid in the eyes—well, I got some of the fluid in MY eye, and it takes TWO eyes to be a surgeon and I got blinded in one eye, I could not be a surgeon.

Moderator: Did you ever wish to marry and raise a family?

A: Of course. Why not? There was really no place for an un-married woman in my time period. At first I tried to resist but it was no good, I got married.

B: Yes, I married and I had a large family and after I married I stopped being a doctor.

C: Yes, I did, but I had no time, and I was going to America, and my love stayed in France. When I got the fluid in my eyes, he was the first one to help me. Later on I did adopt a little girl from the orphanage.

Moderator: And now, which do YOU think is the real Elizabeth Blackwell? It is now your time to vote for your choice! We'll let you compare your own research on this matter and see if you can tell who was an impostor and who is the actual first American woman physician.

Another format that the children in our writing club have enjoyed is to create "biopoems" about favorite characters in books they've read—an idea I first read about in the excellent book, *Plain Talk About Learning and Writing across the Curriculum*, published by the Virginia Department of Education. This seemingly simple exercise helped them think more closely about their chosen book characters. After reading through these examples, see if you can discover the basic format of a "biopoem."

Biopoem
by Jesse Richman (age 12)

Anne
Brave, lonely, courageous, in hiding,
Daughter of Otto Frank,
Lover of Nature, freedom, and life,
Who feels lonely, desserted, and hopeful,
Who needs love, understanding, and a friend,
Who fears the Gestapo, the Germans, and loneliness,
Who gives love, companionship, and stories,
Who would like to see the Germans leave and freedom and
    justice rein,
Resident of Amsterdam,
Frank.

Biopoem
by Molly Richman (age 6)

Wilbur,
Fat, radiant, famous, funny,
Son of pigs,
Lover of Charlotte, Fern, and Charlotte's Web,
Who feels happy, sad, and friendless,
Who fears death, loneliness, and bacon,
Who gives fame, love, and spiders,
Who would like to see outside, the woods, and Fern,
Resident of Henry Zuckerman's barn,
Wilbur.

Biopoem
by Laura Speck (age 12)

Hildy,
Skinny, has long brown hair, always in braids, dresses like a
    boy half the time,
Daughter of a man named Willy M., her mother died and she
    has a stepmother,
Lover of her dream to get her family back together,
Who feels that nothing in life goes right for her and that she
    will never give up trying to put her family together as
    hard as it gets,
Who needs her friend Ruby and her family, along with God,
Who fears a man named Vester, her grandmother who sends
    Vester after her and takes her from her family,
Who gives her life to find her family and her home and a
    Grandma,
Who would like to see her family back together in California,
Resident of many journeys,
Hildy.

Now, one last idea for an instant book report—and hopefully some
good laughs for all of you, too!

Mad Lib Book Report
by Gabriel Chrisman (age 12)
    This   __(adjective)__   book,   ALL   ABOUT
__(plural noun)__ tells how to __(verb)__ __(plural noun)__
and __(verb)__ __(adjective)__ __(plural noun)__ . It even
tells you how to drink __(liquid noun)__ . The characters in
this   book   are   __(name)__ ,   __(name)__   and
__(famous person)__ . In all, it was a __(adjective)__ book.

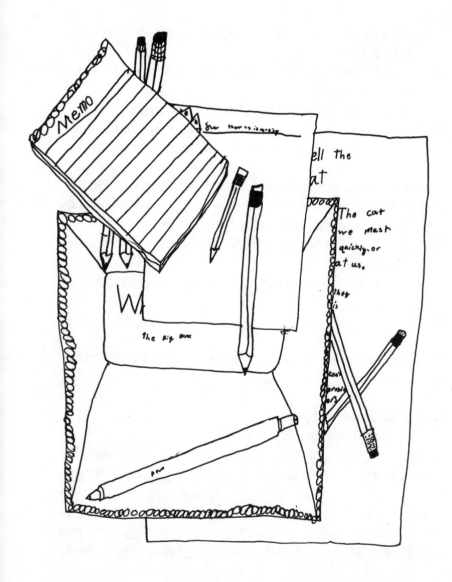

6. Reporting Research

I remember many years ago a young 9 year old neighbor came up to visit at our house, a borrowed from school encyclopedia under his arm. He told me he had to write a "report" for school, and it was to be about the Kremlin. The encyclopedia was appropriately *Volume K*. On talking more with the boy, I gradually became aware of something shocking—he actually believed that the teacher *wanted* him to copy verbatim the encyclopedia entry on the Kremlin. He thought that's what writing a report meant—copying the dry words somebody else (an anonymous someone at that) had already written. He had no notion of the wrongs of plagiarism, that stealing someone else's words and passing them off as your own was very wrong. And he had even less notion that the goal probably was that he actually learn something about his topic. The Kremlin meant nothing to him at that point, and I'm sure it didn't mean much more once he'd finished his "report."

It is refreshing to see how some homeschoolers are changing this notion of the report. They are making it a writing form to really explore other times and places and events, an opportunity to do research and reading in a wide variety of sources, and a way to help them see how they fit in with the bigger world. The world is a fascinating place for homeschooled students who go beyond school textbooks and encyclopedias, useful as these may be, and launch into reading full biographies and in−depth historical writings. It is a world full of great people who we can learn from and emulate and appreciate.

Some of these next pieces even bridge fiction writing with research reporting, letting us know that the students have really felt deeply about their subject.

I especially enjoy the way Nicole opens her biographical sketch of Edward Jenner—she brings us right into the central question in his life immediately, and lets us feel the human dimension of his searching. How much better than an opening that dryly states that Jenner was a great medical doctor who discovered a smallpox vaccine in the year such and such. This is no encyclopedia clone!

It's a Miracle
by Nicole Kissell (age 12)

"Dr. Hunter, do you know what cowpox is?" The question was asked by a young man in his twenties named Edward Jenner. The question he asked had taken his teacher by surprise! But, yes, John Hunter had heard of cowpox. Jenner went on to tell him of the legend that if a person had had cowpox, they were immune to smallpox. Smallpox, a horrible disease! Even when the victim lived through it, there were scars and sometimes blindness or insanity as the result of it.

If the legend was true, could it be used by deliberately using cowpox to protect against smallpox? This question took over twenty years to answer, but, yes, it was possible! Dr. Edward Jenner found the way.

In these twenty years there were many interruptions. There was his marriage to Catherine Kingscote and the birth of his first son, Edward, as well as research in other areas. There was also the death of his teacher and friend, Dr. John Hunter.

On May 14, 1796, in a small cottage near his home in Berkeley, Edward Jenner started his greatest test. It was on that date that Dr. Jenner inoculated James Phipps with cowpox venom. It was not until several months later that Jenner tested his vaccine. He needed to confirm that cowpox was smallpox in cows and that it could be used as a safe vaccine. In July, Jenner finally forced himself to find out. He found out that all the years of hard work had paid off.

It was another ten years before he could convince the world that his vaccine really worked. Finally, he won that battle too. Edward Jenner died having given a great gift to the world, the gift to be free of one of the most terrible diseases of his time.

In reading this next research and biographical essay on Mary Patten, I thought readers should know something special about Megan Tobey's family. In August of 1989 her father was the victim of a reckless driver, and was left severely brain–damaged and partially paralyzed. After being hospitalized for almost half a year, he came home to be with his family, and they are seeing miracles taking place daily as he progresses far more than any doctor said would be possible. Just as in Mary Patten's brave life, here is another example of loving courage that carries us beyond what we think we are capable of. I also think that it must have been healing for Megan to learn about and then write about a person who had been through struggles so similar to her own family's. The experience probably helped her to gain the courage and fortitude she and all of her family have so needed.

Florence Nightingale of the Ocean
by Megan Tobey (age 14)

Mary Patten was described as "A girl of medium height with lustrous eyes and very pleasing features," who at sixteen had married Captain Joshua Patten of Boston.

In 1854 Captain Patten assumed command of the clipper *Neptune's Car*, and along with Mary set sail for exotic ports. During these voyages, Mary seized the opportunity to learn the art of navigation.

With a new charter they set sail again from New York on July 1, 1856, bound for San Francisco via Cape Horn. Extreme weather conditions had forced other vessels to turn back from this route and to complicate matters for Captain Patten, he found the first mate asleep during his watch. A struggle ensued, amid which Patten received a severe blow to the head. Subsequently, the first mate was thrown into the brig for conspiring to mutiny, and Captain Patten collapsed from stress and the blow to his head.

These harsh circumstances induced the crew to turn back, however the second mate did not know how to navigate. Summoning great courage, Mary assumed the role of Captain, determined not to turn back. She performed the navigation, kept a log, and tended her ailing husband.

Exhausted, Mary managed to keep on course, through sheer will power, even though more experienced Captains had turned back. At a point when anyone might break from the strain, the first mate petitioned her for release. Her principled reply was that if her husband saw him unfit for duty, so did she. Maddened, he stirred the crew to mutiny. Gathering her wits and courage, she addressed the crew and persuaded them to keep going.

For fifty–six days Mary had neither slept nor changed her clothes in fear of rape. Barely twenty years old, she had dealt with hazardous weather, mutiny, navigation, a severely ill husband, and pregnancy. She possessed stamina, courage, wit, forethought, not to mention love, and tender devotion toward her husband.

The clipper arrived at the port of San Francisco on November 15, 1856—a full ten days before scheduled. This young heroine returned home with her invalid husband, where she continued to tend him, bore him a son on March 10th, and buried him four months later.

Mary received great notoriety for having saved the clipper, and received a large sum of money from the insurance company for her effort. To this she modestly responded, "I have endeavored to perform that which seemed the plain duty of a wife towards a good husband... I am at the same time seriously embarrassed by the fear that you may have overestimated the value of those services."

Less than four years after her ordeal, Mary died of tuberculosis. Dedicated to her memory is Patten Hospital in Kingsport, New York. Mary had unintentionally aided the Women's Movement by showing that a woman could perform a man's job. More importantly to me, she proved that people can accomplish far more than they can imagine. I hope I will be strong and courageous, yet as humble as "The Nightingale of the Ocean."

Next is another biographical essay, this time describing Beethoven's life. At times, writings like this can have a real purpose and direct audience. I remember when Jesse was having a special piano recital for completing his second book. His teacher asked him and his partner to write short biographical essays on each of the composers whose works they would be playing. This involved researching in several sources, and then doing the difficult job of deciding just what to include and what to leave out in a brief sketch of the person's life. Makes a person more aware of the hard sorting and interpreting work any biographer must do.

Beethoven
by Jeff Scott Kirkland (age 13)

Beethoven as a boy was often more interested in watching the ships on the Rhine than in practicing his music. Only the harsh voice of his father would make seven year old Beethoven sit down and practice more. Often, after long hours at the local tavern, Beethoven's father would come home with his friends at midnight, and make him play music until morning.

Ludwig had a very unhappy childhood with his two brothers and their shiftless father. Their mother was the only one who bestowed love upon the boys. When he was seven, he could play the piano, and he was learning how to play the organ and the violin. At age 11, he played all 3 instruments so well that he sometimes played in the orchestra.

Beethoven's first pieces of music that he had written were published in 1783, when he was 13. He went on to write 32 other masterpieces, unsurpassed in the field of music. Beethoven eagerly studied the works of Bach and Mozart, trying to learn as much as he could about music. His dream was to travel to Vienna to study with the great Mozart. The Prince, hearing about the little musician's plight, sent him a great sum of money, making his dream come true.

In 1787, he went to Vienna, the center of music. His stay in Vienna lasted only a couple weeks, for he received word his mother was dying. It was four years before he was able to return to Vienna, but he stayed there the rest of his life.

Beethoven was a true genius, and music masterpieces flowed from his pen like magic. Beethoven then wrote his only piece of music for violin and orchestra, which has become the most popular violin piece ever written. Archduke Rudolph, of Austria, became Beethoven's friend as his fame spread. Even the Imperial Highness, as he took piano lessons from Beethoven, was often rebuked when his lessons were not ready. Wealth and power never impressed the young composer.

Whenever Beethoven appeared on stage, he received a rousing ovation. His bold new music excited the listeners. Although some people declared his music too modern, Beethoven's music is still enjoyed today, and he is one of the greatest composers in the world. At the age of 40, the great Beethoven went deaf. But even this did not stop him. While deaf, he created some of his greatest music. Beethoven was truly a genius, to create such great and stunning music while stone deaf.

Sometimes report writing doesn't seem like report writing, because you know so much about your topic from your own experience. Rebecca almost apologized for this piece, saying:

> I think the reason I like to write about the 4–H Puppy Club and 4–H puppies is because I don't have to look up anything at all, it's all in my head. I know that's lazy, but it sure is *easy*. Another reason is because I like raising puppies so much that I want to tell everybody about it.

I don't think Rebecca is taking the easy way out—I think sharing what we really know and care about is probably the secret of making our writing vivid and concrete.

The 4–Her and His Dog
by Rebecca Snider (age 12)

This story is dedicated to Czar and Quentin (my Seeing Eye puppies) and my parents and sister, who put up with their

messes. And also to Donna Boyd, my 4–H leader, who was
dedicated to her 4–Hers and their dogs...

The Seeing Eye is an organization that uses 4–Hers to raise
Seeing Eye puppies to become guide dogs.

The 4–Her receives the puppy when it is about eight weeks
old. Then it returns to the Seeing Eye to receive formal
training. Before it returns to the Seeing Eye, the 4–Her has to
housebreak the puppy and teach it six basic commands; come,
sit, stand, forward, rest, and down. These commands will help
the dog when it returns to the Seeing Eye.

Before I got my first puppy, I did not realize how hard it
would be to train him. For one thing these dogs are strong.
They weigh anywhere from 70 to 95 pounds, when they are
full grown. Now that I'm on my second puppy I've gotten
stronger and more able to handle my puppies.

First of all, when we get our puppies we keep them in a
confined area so the pup does not go all over the house.

Most 4–Hers use the kitchen by putting a gate across the
doorway. We keep them in there until they are housebroken
with short excursions to the rest of the house on leash.

We do *not* let them chew old shoes, because then they
won't be able to tell the difference between "their shoes" and
ours. But you can give them Rawhide bones and balls; they
love them. Also you cannot feed them table scraps or
anything but puppy chow.

When you get your puppy, you also get a few things to help
you train your pup; you get a brush, leash, and bed chain
because your puppy sleeps tied to your bed. Plus you get your
worm pills, vitamins, a 4–H guide, collar, and a 50 pound bag
of puppy chow. The Seeing Eye sends you money, dog food,
and pays all vet bills. There are also monthly meetings to

attend where the 4–H leader has a training session for the puppy and his 4–Her.

Only people in eastern Pennsylvania, New Jersey, and northern Delaware are able to raise Seeing Eye puppies because the people from Seeing Eye want to be able to visit puppy raisers and help them with their pups. The Seeing Eye, Inc., is located in Morristown, New Jersey.

Even if I have to get up early in the morning and take a puppy out, or clean up his everlasting messes, I still like doing this project because raising these puppies has taught me lots of self–discipline and a stick–to–it attitude.

Rebecca has learned how report writing can extend into fiction when you really know about your topic. She has also learned how writing can be a help when a person is getting over a loss. Writing can be a fitting way for us to keep something we've loved in memory and in our heart.

I'm Blind Now
by Rebecca Snider (age 12)

Czar was my eleven month old German Shepherd puppy, and my first puppy I was raising for Seeing Eye. On February 1, '89, Czar ran out in front of a pick–up truck and was killed. This story is in memory of him...

When I was blinded in a car accident, the shock was overwhelming. I didn't know where to start. Since I had been lying in the hospital those long hours, I had time to think. I had heard of Seeing Eye Dogs, who guide blind men and women. Did I want a dog or not? It would be better than walking around wondering if I was going to run into something. Plus, I had a job in the Harrisburg Capitol; I would need something or someone to get me around. Finally, after thinking on this subject for quite a while, I came up with my answer—I would request a dog.

First of all, I would need to contact the Seeing Eye in Morristown, New Jersey.

When I called, they arranged for me to come the next week. I was happy I could get a dog so soon. But what I didn't know was that I would not have a dog for about 2–3 months. Just like the dogs, I had to be trained to handle one.

When I arrived in Morristown, they told me I would be starting my training the next day.

My trainer's name was Joyce Thompson. She said we were going to take a "Juno Walk." A "Juno Walk" is when the trainer acts as the dog, to help the blind person get used to handling a dog.

I was only in training with Joyce for about a month, but had to wait for a dog longer.

After waiting for about 2 months, Joyce told me my dog was ready. He was a male German Shepherd named Czar. He was black, with white and gold feet, legs, neck, and shoulders. He was the nicest dog I ever met.

I'm still at the Capitol in Harrisburg. There are even other guide dogs here. I love it here. With Czar, he makes it so enjoyable. I think every person who is blind should have a guide dog.

However, there are problems in having a Seeing Eye dog.

One day, walking down the street, Czar didn't stop when we came to a change of ground surface. So I had to give him a hard leash command, which is jerking him with the leash. It does not hurt the dog, but, if I didn't do that I could be hurt. Well, there were some ladies behind me who thought I was being cruel to Czar. After I was done correcting him, I turned to them and explained about what I was doing.

Most people think that blind people don't have any trouble getting into stores and public places with our guide dogs, but we do.

One time, I went into a clothing store and a guard tried to throw me out because he thought I was not blind. (I don't look blind.) The best thing to do is to leave calmly and not stir up any trouble.

My eyes, Czar, and me are best friends; I would never hurt Czar for anything. After all, I LOVE MY EYES!!

Rachel Johnston knows the French and Indian War. She has read extensively about the time period, much more than most adults, but she's done even more than that. She and her father participate in a military reenactment unit that marches on Sundays in the summer months at Fort Pitt in Pittsburgh. She has literally dressed for the part of a fife player and marched with the troops. We only had room to print this excerpt from Rachel's very complete twelve page research report, but I think it will give you a good feel for the depth of her knowledge and understanding. Rachel wrote this paper as part of her project in the first Western Pennsylvania History and Science Fair, and perhaps needless to say, she won first place. Following this is Rachel's fictional story based on what she knows about the wartime way of life—you'll see that she at times really feels herself living back in the 18th century!

The French and Indian War
by Rachel Johnston (age 12)

Many years of hostility came before the French and Indian War proper. During this time, the French were making ties with the Indians. The Indians were raiding towns, and in the new world generally, friction was building. The French and

English would declare war in Europe, and it would spread all through the British and French "Empires." That included Canada and America, so the French and French Indians would make more raids, and there would be fighting generally. During one of these, the French decided on building Louisbourg.

After several French strikes out of Louisbourg, the New Englanders became indignant. The governor of Massachusetts, William Shirley, got up the wildest most unpractical plan of battle the Londoners had ever seen. He decided to get the New Englanders together to capture Louisbourg with no help from their mother country. William Shirley was popular, and after the New Englanders got used to the idea, they latched on, and the militia began to grow. Massachusetts gave 3,300 men, Connecticut 516 men, New Hampshire 454 men, and Rhode Island gave one boat.

Their idea of capturing Louisbourg was ridiculously innocent. When asked what he would do about the French's superior battery of cannon, Governor Shirley said merely that he would capture some of the cannon from the French. Perhaps he had some notion that when the French saw him coming, they would flee, leaving their cannon behind, or perhaps the Lord had told him to take along all the powder and shot he took, telling him to take it to fit the French cannon. Maybe he was as confused about it as anyone else. But certainly it came into use very early in the battle.

On March 24, 1745, the fleet of some ninety transports left the Boston Harbor. Only a short while afterwards, they ran into a northeast wind. Nearly all the soldiers soon wished they had never even heard of Louisbourg because of the terrible seasickness. After two weeks of sailing and three weeks of waiting for the ice to break up, they sailed for Flat Point.

There Duchambon, with 24 French regulars and 50 militia-men awaited them. But after getting fairly close to the shore, the boats swerved and began to sail toward Freshwater Cove. It was a hard race, but at least seventeen men were ready with their muskets when Duchambon and his men arrived. Six French were captured, six were killed, and the rest fled. Before evening, 2,000 men were on shore. Only two had been wounded; none had been killed. The rest landed the following morning, and on the next day, Colonel Vaughan took a scouting party to the Royal Battery. On arriving, he found a cluster of storehouses behind the stone walls. He set fire to these, and soon the whole Grand Battery was covered with thick, acrid smoke.

Early the next morning, on passing the Royal Battery, Vaughan noticed that the flagstaff was bare. Fearing the French were lying within, he sent one of the Indians of his party in. But when the brave climbed in through a gunport, he found that the French had indeed fled. What the reason was, Vaughan didn't take time to ponder, but instead moved into the Royal Battery. As Vaughan looked over the cannon, William Tufts shinnied up the flagstaff, and hung his coat in place of a flag. The Island Battery replied to this taunt with a few ineffectual shots, but then they realized their mistake at leaving the Royal Battery empty, and at once sent boats to try to recapture their property. Unfortunately for them, and very fortunately for the British, Vaughan managed to hold out until reinforcements arrived. The English had captured what William Shirley had correctly seen as the key to Louisbourg. And indeed, from there, as happens when you have the key to a place, the rest was comparatively easy. They brought their own cannon on shore, and set up almost an encirclement of batteries around Louisbourg, and slowly pounded down the walls.

On June 15, 1745, the French surrendered. The capture of Louisbourg was the pride of New England. Of the "soldiers" who set out, only a fourth were killed at Louisbourg, a great number to plague. Only about one hundred died in battle. At the end of King George's war, the war in which this battle was fought, when peace was signed in 1748, the New Englander's pride, Louisbourg, was traded back to the French for Madras, India! The people who had paid blood for Louisbourg felt it as a slap in the face. It was their first realization that England's interests were not always New England's interests. Then too, the New Englanders had learned that they could fight just as well as regulars, a lesson they remembered when the Revolution was brewing....

Thank you, Quentin
by Rachel A. Johnston (age 13)

Now don't say, "Oh," and put this story down when you find out it's about time travel. I believe it's unique all the same. So sit back and enjoy the following adventure...

I wonder what Mother is doing. She must be terribly concerned about where I am. Home, running water, Father— is he still in Germany, or has he come home? Even Scott. I always considered him a pain, but I miss his spoiled self now! What wouldn't I give to have him with me... and along with him would come his crying... I would love that racket. And I hate being 16—it doesn't suit me. All my modern clothes are completely gone. I miss my soft bed: the ground is so hard in comparison. I went to sleep on my 1989 bed, and woke up on this 1758 wool blanket. I've been here 2 days now, and it's night again. I can't seem to realize all that's happened. I used to be Lucy Maude Gailberth. Now I'm Rebecca Anne. I still haven't found out my last name. I'm the daughter of a soldier in His Majesty the King's 60th Regiment of Foote. I'm 16, soon to be married to an 18–year–old soldier. In my old life I had Mommy and Daddy, and I was only 12! I wonder whether the real Rebecca Anne is in my position. At least I don't have a version of her Quentin for her to marry.

All my efforts to explain have been taken as a childish story. I've blundered through it all, and faked my way, 'till I now know the routine...

"Come help get breakfast for the men, Rebecca!" that's Rebecca's mother.

"Coming!" It seems that mealtimes come at least 6 times a day. Oh well. After breakfast, I'll have an hour or so to do as I wish. I just hope Quentin doesn't come and ruin it. I want to have some time to myself to try to know what has happened, and to learn to accept it. But Quentin usually finds me, no matter where I hide. Maybe he won't if I hide in one of the fort's many rooms...

Freedom at last. I'll go find some empty room. I'll look in one of these rooms that's in the far row of buildings. No, on second thought, I've noticed that no one ever goes over to that building in the corner. I'll go there.

...Oh my! This room is deserted and it has books. The first I've seen in a long time. I'll just go see what they are.

Here's a book that looks interesting. I'll take it over to that table.

I've a part of the story that I read. I found it in the Carnegie Library in Pittsburgh, Pennsylvania, but only a very small portion of it. Two entries made up all of the material included in what I read. But, here they are:

> *February 10, 1757.* I've started on the work set before me... . I've ordered everyone on the march. The part I found roughest was getting going.... Everyone seemed to me to be slovenly. It took 2 hours to take down camp and prepare to leave.... But at least that's all over. We're on the march....

> *February 28, 1757.* We've reached Fort—

At this point we go back to my story, as this is the point when the next event happened...

Why is the room so dark all of a sudden? Oh no! There's someone coming in!

"Excuse me, I'll be going now." There! That was easy. Now I'll leave. Oh dear, I'm blushing terribly.

"But you haven't built the fire yet!" he surprised me with that! Another duty I didn't know about.

"Yes, sir," maybe if I'm very cooperative, he'll let me read more of his books. My, this is harder than it looks when I watch Rebecca's mother do it! There. How do you light it? Oh yes, there's the tinder box.

"When it's lit, you can come over here and have a seat on my bed." No wonder he made himself at home! This is his private quarters. Oh my, I'm really in trouble.

At the end of half and hour I had told the man everything about the life I'm finally back to. I knew everything about him except his name. During the interview, he had carefully kept it a secret, so naturally I was very surprised when he said, "I see you've been reading my journal." I was surprised only because the title was "Colonel Henry Bouquet's Journal." But I survived (without my mouth gaping) until the end of my free time. Then I explained why I had to go, and then left. Before I went, he told me I was welcome anytime.

"Go get water from the well, Rebecca."
"Yes, Mother," I have to go the long way around because the short way is blocked by a locked gate.

It was amazing that I met the Colonel today. I'm proud to have talked to him. I'm glad I've finally made a friend. He was so kind to me. I would enjoy chatting with him about—
"Hello, Rebecca."
"Oh, hello, Quentin. I'm off for water."
"Care if I come along?"
"No." I do, but I must lie sometimes to get along here in 1758. I'll just ignore him. At least he's not talking much.
"Rebecca, you've been avoiding me the past 3 days. Don't you love me anymore?"

I didn't expect this. He won't believe me, but I'll tell him the truth.
"Quentin, I'm not Rebecca. I have my place in 1989, and my name is Lucy Maude Gailberth. I'm 12-years-old. I went to sleep in my bed, and woke up here as Rebecca. Please believe me, because it's true. You're a nice person, but I don't care to marry at the age or 12, no matter *how* old Rebecca is!" Quentin, believe me, please do.

"I'll believe you. It's an impossible story, but those eyes of yours (or rather, Rebecca's eyes which you're borrowing) are transparent enough to tell me you're not lying. You may be mad, most likely are, but you're telling the truth in your crazed mind.

"Tell me more about how the change happened. What were you doing?"

"I was writing a story set in 1758, and I fell asleep doing it."

"Maybe if you write a story about the year you're really from, you'll go there, and my Rebecca will be back."

"All right. Tomorrow I'll ask the Colonel to lend me paper and a pen. But you'll have to return it the next day. Okay?"

"Fine."

"Rebecca Anne, why would you want them? Can you write?" What should I tell him?

"Yes. I want to write a story set in 1989. Quentin will return the rest of the paper, the rest of the ink, and the quill tomorrow, I hope."

"Who's Quentin?"

"My fiance."

"All right, you may take them when you leave."

"Thank you."

It's night, at last. Now to try the experiment.

A Shot in the Dark
by Lucy Maude Gailberth

Mother, father, and I are going to a movie tonight. I'm so happy! We're going to see Cinderella. And I found my first 1989 penny today, too! It's always a big deal when that happens.

"Lucy come get in the car!" I've got to go, so I'll see you at the movies. Bonjour!"

"Hello! I'm so glad you could co—"

My, I'm nice and toasty warm! I'll try to pry my eyes open
long enough to see whether Rebecca's mother is up yet...
It worked!
I'm in my own room again! I'll hop out of bed and...
wait—what's that on the floor written in Old English:

My Quentin
by Rebecca Anne

Dear, I miss you. It's not my fault I'm gone. Don't think
I wanted to get into this mess! All I did was fall asleep
writing a story about 1989, and when I woke up, I was
someplace I'd never seen before! Believe me.

Thanks, Quentin!

7. Creating Family Newsletters

"Hey, kids! We just got another issue of the *Oddfellow Gazette!*" I call out while sorting through the day's mail.

Everyone comes racing in. "Read it aloud at lunch! We want to hear it right away! Please!!!" So between bites of peanut butter and jelly, I read through this loved publication. Wondering what this is? It's not a commercial production, not something you'd get a fancy advertising brochure about in the mail. It's another homeschooling family's own newspaper, published about monthly. We've never met this family—they live 3000 miles away—but we're getting to know them well through their writing and feel like whenever we do meet it will be like meeting old friends.

A growing number of homeschooling families are finding that putting out their own family newspaper is motivating, fun for all involved, and even great PR with the relatives. The children come to feel there really *is* an audience for their writing, a reason to write up something about what they have been doing or observing, and in the end there is a real product to hold in the hands after all their work. The joint effort involved helps the newspaper "staff" realize the value of family cooperation—everyone is pulling together towards a goal, rather than competitively fighting against each other. Why, Jesse is even willing to help proofread Jacob's and Molly's first drafts when they are close to press time.

Some of these newspapers, such as the Lerew family's *ABC News*, have been going for years on a monthly basis. Others are one shot affairs or at best semi-annual events. Whatever, the experience is a great one, and the involvement it usually lively. Sometimes parents take an active role in guiding the effort and setting up regular "deadlines" (yep, these are probably the ones that in fact do come out regularly) and in other families the kids do it all and when the spirit moves them (and like in our family, these may be your more irregular publications).

Some actually have paying subscribers and are learning about the business end of running a publication, sending out their newsletters to sixty or more families. Mika Perrine and Nica Christensen, who both have a number of pieces throughout this book, have been co-editing the *Neighborhood News* for over 29 issues now. What an accomplishment!

All of these newspapers give their creators a place to publish their poetry and articles and book reviews, a place to try out new ideas and share with other people they know and care for. This format often gives kids a chance to be playful with words and just have a good time with writing.

Our own kids decided to try putting out their own paper one day last winter when I was knee deep in computer print-outs and scissors and glue, working on the layout of our next issue of *Pennsylvania Homeschoolers*. I first knew something was afoot when Jesse kept very politely and evasively just not hearing me during his math lesson time in the morning. He was busy surreptitiously writing something on a scrap of paper under his desk top. He finally admitted that he was writing notes to Jacob and Molly, inviting them to a meeting to begin a new newspaper. He would be editor and publisher. I discreetly left to go wash the dishes, the notes were properly delivered, and the cub reporters gathered around the chief editor's desk. The assignments were handed out and discussed, soon all were at work, and the *Richman Family Observer* was launched. Although they usually include a "serious" piece or two, such as a straight book review, they are mostly interested in humor and helping the various animals and creatures and babies around the place have a say. The following pieces all first appeared in the *Richman Family Observer*

This Horrid House
By Candy, our most honorable dog
(Jesse Richman, age 11)

I was sitting, or rather lying, on my rugs under the piano, when Jesse came in with a look of purpose in his eye. "Candy, come Candy," he said. I knew it would be hopeless to resist. First he would prod me, then he would shove me, then I would be lifted off of the ground and plopped down outside on the cold wet ground. So, I resigned my self to my fate and slowly marched out.

Weight Watchers for Dogs
By Candy
(Jesse Richman, age 12)

Dear Foxie,

I must take a moment to pour out my heart about something I did recently. I have joined a Weight Watchers group, and I've already won a certificate. The certificate is for the most overweight member, and I had fasted for a whole day before the meeting. At the weigh–in my weight was 40 pounds, and I made a perfectly splendid confession. I was encouraged to set a goal for how many pounds to lose. My goal is 4 pounds by the meeting next month. I am trying to get more exercise than I have been getting by taking walks up to the strip mine with Jesse and Jacob, and I can hardly wait for the meeting so that I can tell everyone about my rabbit chase (see "The Story of a Rabbit Chase: Two Views" in this issue). I am a grossly

overweight dog but I CAN, and will improve.
Yours Truly,
Your Overweight Friend, Candy.

This correspondence was between Candy and Grandma's dog Foxie, and was printed with the permission of both dogs. Foxie, like Candy, is overweight, and she was the first dog that Candy wanted to write to, to announce her joining of a Weight Watchers group for dogs. I hope you liked her letter, we thought it was great.

The Terrible Saga of Bartholimew Squeak
(Jesse Richman, age 12)

This is an exerpt from *Mouse Magazine* published every Sunday by the *Mouse Times* a Mouse Safety Association subsidy...

Ladies and gentlemice, hark your ears for the terrible saga of our beloved friend, Bartholimew Squeak. Early on the morning of the 13th, Mr. Squeak left the tunnel to find some food. After leaving the tunnels myself, I saw Bartholimew begin the climb in the the compost pot. Bartholimew emerged from the pot a few minutes later grumbling about poor pickings and climbed onto the counter. The pickings must not have been good there either because in a short, too short time, he stuck his nose down over the edge and called to me that he would be going over to the drain board of the sink. Soon I could hear him rustling around in the little compost holder up there. Suddenly, in a way foreign to his usual actions, Bartholimew ran down off of the sink and back towards the hole, shouting, "I smell cheese! I smell cheese! I smell cheese! I smell cheese! I found some chee—" His sentence was then broken off by a ringing, banging sound as a trap caught him. Bartholimew was one of our brightest young mice, yet he fell for the trap. Do NOT think that just because you are smart and young you will not fall for the traps. If this continues, we may even have to give up our love of cheese if we want to live. We have a lesson to learn from Bartholimews fate. It is: think before you eat.

Thank You.

This speech was presented by Mr. MicMouse at Thursday night's meeting of The Mouse Safety Association, or MSA, which he is the president of. Mr. MicMouse was on a tour of the house when the incident happened and was probably the last mouse to see Bartholimew alive.

Jacob's favorite topic of all time is to write as if he is Hannah, seeing the world through her eyes. Some of you may have read his earlier book, *A Baby Learns What is What*. He has not tired of the subject, and Hannah is just as interesting now, even more so.

???????BIG GIRL???????
By Hannah Richman age 20 months
(Jacob Richman, age 8)

I am very proud of myself. Now I can answer questions people ask me. If I am asked, "Do you like Jacob?" I simply answer "no", or if I am asked "Do you like Mommy?" I answer "no." Before I could not answer questions; I could only answer "ahadg" to questions. So now I am surely a big girl!

Why Does it not Come with Me
By Hannah Richman age 20 months
(Jacob Richman, age 8)

I go to the table because supper is starting to smell good.
To get up I say "Uw uwuw," and someone puts me in my
highchair. I wait for a long time and finally we have supper. I
started to pour the white stuff in a white bottle. After I have
poured half a cup of the white stuff, Daddy saw me and
snatched the bottle from me and took my bowl and threw the
contents away. Why did he throw it away? Why did he? He
said it was salt. They put it in their soup, so why can't I? I
cried.

I Can Sing
By Hannah, age 20 months
(Jacob Richman, age 8)

NOW I can sing like everyone else. I can sing "Mary had a
Little Lamb." They always cheer for me, so I keep on singing
and singing, until they tell me I must stop and that I have sung
too much. I have made a shortened version of "Mary had a
Little Lamb" so they will clap for me more because it will take
me less time to sing.

A Baby Crime
By Hannah, age 20 months
(Jacob Richman age 8)

I was having lots of fun playing "it" tag. Then they started
playing a game of cards with 9, 5, 3, 2, 8, and lots of cards
with kings and Jacks and Jokers. They shuffled the cards and
then they started to throw the cards around. So I joined in and
threw the cards around too. They stopped me and said "no-
no." Then Daddy got out some ice cream. They gave me an

ice cream cone, and then gave Jacob the box with what was left over of the ice cream in it. They started playing with the cards. I decided to take Jacob's ice cream, because I was done with mine. So, I made a dash for his ice cream, and snatched it. But, before I had eaten one bite, he caught me. Why didn't he thank me for eating part of his ice cream for him?

Molly has now gotten the idea of describing what Hannah does, too, for the newspaper.

Mirror Baby Visits Us
by Molly Richman (age 6)

I heard Hannah, my little sister who is two, talking to SOMEBODY in the bathroom. I wondered who she was talking to. I ran into the bathroom. And there she was sitting on the toilet, happily just talking!!! But I still did not know what I wanted to know. Who was Hannah talking to? Then I got an idea. I asked her, "Hannah, are you talking to the mirror baby?" She said, "Uh huh," and I knew I was right. I said "Hannah, do you want the mirror baby to come out of the mirror?" Again Hannah's answer was "Uh huh," which I knew meant yes. So, I was right again! I went to tell my mom. "Hannah wants the mirror baby to come out of the mirror!" She laughed when I told her that. I laughed too.

The *Oddfellow Gazette* is put out by the Chrisman family of Bainbridge Island, Washington (just a ferry ride away from Seattle). Barbara Chrisman wrote to give me some background about their writing work:

I'm *so* pleased that you enjoy our newsletter! Last year, our first year of homeschooling, writing was a problem for us. That is, we did not write much and it was not "engaging." I've never taught, or even taken an education course, and writing has never been something my boys did spontaneously. They read often and by choice, math is easy for them and they clearly see the need to "progress" in it on an annual basis. Science, geography, all those subjects seemed to come up naturally, and my mother–in–law (an historian) sends us a history–unit–in–a–box periodically. The kids enjoy that partly because it's good stuff, partly because it's a link with "Gogi." But writing—"Mom, don't worry, we already *know* how to write!" (Linsey, age 5, on the other hand is burying us in pages of phonetic spelling: "The cat wuz hape. He hopt on u plan to hawie.")

Over the summer I spent a lot of time thinking and reading about writing. *Write from the Start* and *Writing: Teachers and Children at Work*, both by Donald Graves, and the Lucy Calkins book, *The Art of Teaching Writing*, really impressed me. When we started in September, I gave each of the boys a folder with pockets. I also poured out on them all the enthusiasm I had built up over the summer, and talked about "real" outlets for pieces. Using an idea from *Writing*, the pieces the kids are working on are listed on the cover, an editing checklist is on the left inside cover, and ideas for new pieces (as they occur through conversation or shared writing) are on the right inside cover. Simon's checklist right now includes:

1. Check for capitals and periods (or !?).
2. Underline words you think may be spelled wrong.
3. Is anyone speaking? Use quotes.
4. Are there words you'd like to change to make a sentence more interesting?
5. Watch out for run–on sentences.

Gabriel's checklist includes spelling, almost all punctuation, and paragraphs.

We all write something about four days a week. I try not to be too involved with the beginning stages, unless the writer needs to bounce around ideas for a topic. We just write in pencil on paper (and all have *rotten* handwriting, another whole can of worms!). I am finding that writing is fiercely demanding work, and I need frequent breaks! Sometimes pieces just get "dumped" (in the "done" file) because they're not working out. Simon has a "dumb detective" story that never got off the ground, and they *both* found it impossible to match Tolkein in a "quest" format and have littered the autumn with attempts.

If a piece has potential, sometimes it only needs to be finished and edited—first by the writer, and then "in conference" with me. If it is in progress on Tuesday, it usually gets read to our homeschooling group that meets weekly to share writing and an activity. There are three boys Simon's age (9) and they have been very inspiring to each other. Simon sometimes reads his own pieces with them in mind: "Oh, I bet Nathan will tell me I started too many sentences with *he*." There is no one Gabriel's age, which has been a problem, but he's gotten some feedback too.

We've taken here excerpts from several issues of the Chrisman's newsletter, The *Oddfellow Gazette* (they live on Oddfellow), and I think you'll agree it's a delight to read.

First, how about a weather report, such as all newspapers have. I love the touch of good humor in this piece, and the close observations of detail. Notice the delightful catalog of characteristics of the day—it isn't *just* rainy, but "miserable, wet, soaking, horrible, muddy, misty" too.

Chicken Weather Report
by Simon Chrisman (age 9)

Gabriel and I slipped and slid down the path to the chicken house to let the chickens out. We refilled their food and opened their door. They rushed out, only to find that it was a miserable, wet, soaking, horrible, muddy, misty, rainy day! They marched back in single file, fluffed themselves up, and jumped on the perches looking very annoyed, glaring at us as if it was our fault. The long, wet winter has begun.

Here is Simon's latest "Chicken News" feature, this time discussing egg sitting habits. Be ready for a treat!

Chicken News
by Simon Chrisman (age 9)

Our chickens are organizing egg sitting like a business! The broody banties, Phil and Wrennie, usually start by laying their own egg or by finding someone else's. Then, they lay or collect more and make what we call a clutch. The only problem is that they can not get up to eat or walk around without letting the eggs get cold. So, they "hire" (we don't know what they pay!) another chicken to sit on the clutch while they go about their business, then they come back to sit some more. The babysitter has a short job compared to Phil and Wrennie, as they spend most of their day spread out like a pancake over a pile of eggs! Unfortunately, all this work is in vain since Mario is not doing his job and, as far as we can tell, none of the eggs are fertile. Gabriel and I have the nasty job of sneaking eggs out from under the banties before they rot. So you can see they have an endless task. I wonder what keeps them at it?

The Chrisman *Oddfellow Gazette* always has a section of Classified Ads, and they are some of the most delightful and telling parts of the newsletter. The kids have certainly absorbed the feel of how to write an ad, but have of course translated it into their own fun.

Classifieds
from the *Oddfellow Gazette*

Porch Pals in need of a maid. Gertrude, Corny, and Blackie are exercising their bodily functions on the deck. If interested, call CHI–CKEN.

Live fleas. We have a good supply of live fleas for sale! Purchase by the pound. Call quick, these should go fast.

Babysitter for hire. Excellent at read–alouds and block building. $1.50 per hour. Call Gabriel at 842–5165

Wanted: one time machine in good working order. Reasonable.

Reward for information leading to the apprehension and conviction of a dog who attacked our goats on the night of November 26. Tail had a torn trachea and many other puncture wounds. This dog was large, black and short–haired.

Notice: The house next door to us will be for sale soon. Anyone who wants to live in an old farmhouse on Bainbridge Island, and can tolerate living next to US, please apply for details.

Each issue I've seen of the *Oddfellow Gazette* has a "Nature Notes" feature, written by Gabriel. He is quite an adept observer, and he never writes in a boring fashion. He might have written, "We drove to the beach at night and it was fun. We saw lots of sea animals. They were nice. Then we drove home and stopped for ice cream and went to bed. I liked our trip." *But* that's not Gabriel—you're in for a treat and a *real* taste of ocean life here!

Nature Notes
by Gabriel Chrisman (age 12)

On the night of November 13 at 10:45 p.m., Simon, Nick and I went to the community beach to observe the −3 tide. This is an extremely low tide that comes only a few times a year. It was dark, but we could see a little on account of the full moon. We stirred up a lot of action crunching over the beach in our boots. A Geoduck squirted us and we saw a lot of other geysers. There was Bull Kelp all over, and floating on the water we saw some weird luminescent (or phosphorescent—we don't know which) seaweed. But the weirdest discovery was a soft thing like a slug, but a foot long, and close to a foot wide. I think it was a Gum Boot Chiton eating a Moon Snail, but we couldn't clearly identify the victim or its attacker, or even know for sure which was which. There were some large sea anemones that were eating little animals, and one almost got Simon's finger! We also heard something scuttling across the rocks, and we assumed it was a crab. We saw a lot, but I think we'd have seen more if we'd brought a flashlight.

Another fun feature of one *Oddfellow Gazette* was a "Mad Lib" written by Gabriel. Many of you may know this paper and pencil game, available in most card stores, where you have to supply the missing words for the story without seeing what the story is about.

Someone else just tells you that now a "plural noun" is needed, now an "adjective," now a "verb." The completed story is then read aloud, to howls and laughs from the audience. It's certainly a terrific way to help kids realize that different words have different functions in sentences, and realize how it can indeed be entertaining and useful to know the basic parts of speech. I can imagine many homeschooled children having fun coming up with their own "Mad Lib" stories, and hope Gabriel inspires you to give it a try.

How to Buy a Good Car
A Mad Lib
by Gabriel Chrisman (age 12)

The first time you meet the __(adjective)__ salesman say, "You look __(exclamation)__!" Then shake __(plural noun)__ and look at the __(adjective)__ __(plural noun)__. If you see a __(favorite color)__ __(singular noun)__, test drive it for __(number)__ minutes. If it goes __(speed)__, then check the price. If it is above __(amount of money)__, don't buy it. Sit in the waiting room and look at the __(plural noun)__ until you can see more. Never give the salesman __(plural noun)__ unless he __(action)__.

Even descriptions of making new types of food treats make it into the *Oddfellows Gazette*—I think this one by Simon is so clearly written that you could try it out yourself, and I'll bet you'd enjoy the results as much as the Chrismans did.

Making Fruit Leather
by Simon Chrisman (age 9)

Late in August we went down past the orchard and into the upper pasture to pick plums for fruit leather. After we picked the plums we dumped them into boiling water until they turned from purple to red (about two minutes). We cut them in half and took the pits out. Next, we got out the blender and ground the plums. They were nearly liquid when we finished. Then we set up the dehydrator and poured the plum mush onto one of the layers in it. The next morning we got out the spatulas and attacked! It was hard work but finally we were done. Delicious!

Gabriel has now also tried his hand at serious reporting of news events, as shown in this description of a Town Meeting he and his family attended concerning the drug problems of the suburbs. Many homeschooling families consider the drug situation in making their homeschooling decisions, and I think Gabriel's piece shows just why homeschooled students aren't as likely to take drugs. They take responsibility for their actions and actually *think*. And they have a close and respectful relationship with their parents.

Town Meeting
by Gabriel Chrisman (age 12)

On Sunday, January 21, my family went to the live broadcast of Town Meeting, a TV show where the audience is asked to give their opinion on the subject of the week. The show was filmed in the lunchroom of Commodore Middle School on Bainbridge Island. This time, because of an article that came out in the Wall Street Journal about Bainbridge, the subject was drugs invading our suburban areas.

The producer coached us to clap loudly each time the host reappeared after a commercial break, and not to say anything "we couldn't say to a nun."

Professor Moss, who had said in the Journal article that drug education programs are useless, was thoroughly criticized. One person actually stood up and said, "I think he's an IDIOT!" Other young people stood up and spoke in atrocious language, for instance, "If we woulda known... we wouldn'ta took 'em." Plus, these same speakers admitted to not listening to, let alone respecting, parents and teachers! The host, who was trying to get them to claim some responsibility for their choices, was rewarded with blank stares.

Professor Moss, after forty-five minutes of being constantly asked, "If drug programs don't work, what will?" finally burst out with "It's a case of incompetent parenting!" The woman next to us nearly blew up and muttered "Ooooooh, I'm furious!" However, the host ignored her, as he did most of the other parents. He mainly focused on angry young people who only whined and put the blame on anyone but themselves. It did not make for a very uplifting show.

The Lerew girls have been publishing a family newsletter for years and years, and it comes out faithfully almost every month. This is used as their main writing and language arts tool, and the girls have learned to take over more and more of the actual work. They know about planning what stories they'll write, writing rough drafts, proof-reading and editing, typing into their home computer, laying it all out, and taking it to a quick copy shop for final printing.

The girls especially enjoy telling about their large extended family. I can imagine all the relatives got a kick out of Jenny's detailed descriptions of two young cousins in this next piece.

Will and John
by Jennifer Lerew (age 11)

I have nine cousins. One of them is two. His name is Will. Another one is John. He is a little older than 4 months. Will can talk. He says "Hi" to everyone. He can say everyone's names. Mine sounds like "Denny." This summer he learned "lay off", "hey dude", "awesome", and "cool." He can almost say sentences, but he leaves out "the", "and", and "it's." I put him to bed two times. He is really cute. His younger brother John is cute too. He is strong. He can stand up when someone's holding him and he can roll over from his stomach to his back and almost from his back to his stomach. He is big for 4 months old, but the smallest in our family. He is so cute! I changed both of their diapers two times. I rocked John to sleep twice. A lot of the time I sit down with John and play with him for hours. Anne, their mom, wants me to go home with her! She says there's so many people here to keep them busy. I was real sad when they left. I'm going to miss them. But it was fun while they were here!

Dory Lerew often has fun composing "Dory Stories," where she talks about herself in the third person, a new slant on things.

Dory's in the Money
A Dory Story
by Dory Lerew (age 9)

Once there was a girl named Dory. She was nine years old, she liked to draw pictures, read books, and eat. Her dad was a farmer and her mom was a housewife. One day her dad came home from work and said, "Would you like to come and pick up all the apples that are on the ground?"

"Sure!" they said.

So the next day they went to their dad's work and picked up drops. They picked and picked and picked. They had picked up three bins. Dory's back hurt. The next day when her dad came home he said that they had gotten 165 dollars for picking the apples! Dory was happy and she said she would pick apples any time.

Jennifer often writes about what she's doing in the community, especially the library, one of her favorite places. She has already been helping out for several years with preschool story hour, preparing props and finger plays and lap puppet theaters and carefully choosing her stories around a theme for the day. In the next article she tells about her latest work for the library.

Working at the Library
by Jennifer Lerew (age 11)

One Friday afternoon I went into the library and I asked if the librarian needed any help. She said she did, so I started to work. It was fun. What I did is I took out all the books one at a time and make sure the right card is in it and that there is only one card in it. The next time I did the same thing, but I also stamped some things she wanted stamped. The next time Dory came too, and we did the same thing I did the first time. The next time Dory came again and we stamped and did the same thing with the books. I've only gone four times but they've been fun every time. The librarian says it's a real help. I would like to work there for a very long time!

Dory also wrote an essay about how the family works on their newsletter. It has been published in the "BackPack" children's section of *Pennsylvania Homeschoolers*, and was also entered in an essay contest to choose student speakers at a homeschooling legislative breakfast.

Our Family Newsletter
by Dory Lerew (age 8)

Hello! My name is Dory Lerew. I live in Dillsburg, Pennsylvania, and I am eight years old. I'm here today to tell you about my family's newsletter. We've been doing our newsletter every month for about three years now. We started doing it because we homeschool and we wanted the rest of our family to know what we were doing. At first we just sent it to a few people but now we send it to fifty-five people all over the United States and my mother's aunt in Peru, South America.

I would like to tell you all the steps we do when we make our newsletter. First we make a list of all the things we could write about, like "Reading at the Library," or "The Homeschoolers Field Trip to Fort Hunter." You pick one and think it over. You have to remember how you were feeling at the time and write it all down on a piece of paper. We usually each do three or four. Then we go to our computer and type it up using a disc called "Magic Slate." When it looks the way we want it to, we print it on the printer. Then we cut the stories and get four or six pieces of paper and move the articles around on the paper until we get them how we want them. Then we paste them down. We take them to our church where we make sixty copies of each sheet, back and front. Then Annie staples them together and folds them. Jenny and I address all the envelopes. It is sometimes boring to address envelopes but Mommy says she'll show us a way to use the copier for those when we want. You can't do the whole newsletter in one day—it usually takes us about three days.

I'd like to tell you about some of the things that have happened because we write our newsletter. It's helped my to read and write. When I was learning to read I liked trying to read it because it was in big print and because I already knew what the stories were about. Other people have told us that their kids like to practice reading with it, too. It's helped with my writing, too. When I was little I had to dictate all my articles to my mother. Now I write almost all my articles by myself. It's also helped us to learn how to do everything you have to do to make a newsletter. One time we did everything completely by ourselves. Jenny even wrote down and typed up what Annie dictated to our tape recorder. The only thing Mommy did was to add a line at the top saying we had done it by ourselves.

We have gotten a lot of letters from people we send it to. There's a homeschooling family in northern Michigan that wrote to ask us how we do ours and now they send us theirs every month. Once we got a letter from Susannah Sheffer who edits *Growing Without Schooling*. She said she liked the way I wrote about how my snowpants made little squeaks when we were trying to walk quietly. We also send our newsletter to the *Pennsylvania Homeschoolers* and some of our articles have been in its "BackPack." I like getting comments and nice letters from people who read our newsletter. It makes me want to keep doing it.

The Murphy children, Emily, Christian, and Clare, enjoyed putting out their first issue of *The Murphy Spectator*. Clare describes a wonderful kite flying day as one of the headline articles on page one.

The Kite
by Clare Murphy (age 10)
Today Emily, Christian, and I flew our kites. I was out first. I got mine up really high. By this time Christian had

come out and got his up as high as mine. But it came down in a tree and he couldn't get it up again. Emily had come out and got HERS as high as mine. Emily's and mine stayed up the whole time. At the end it was hard getting it down. It was like playing tug-of-war with a kite. But I did it!!

Clare also reports on one of those hard decisions that all kids sometimes face—trying to decide what to buy at a toy store.

The Toy Adventure
by Clare Murphy (age 10)

On Friday I went to the toy store. I was planning on getting a stuffed animal, but all the stuffed animals were too expensive. So I was disappointed. I felt like a pickle. We had to hurry, so Mom helped me. We looked at the models. We found a model I liked but it was not really what I wanted. Then I saw... these animals that you make out of plaster. There were three molds: a lion, a kangaroo, and a panda. This was what I wanted. It was $7.00. I bought it. I have made all the animals. The kangaroo's head kept coming off, but I got it. I just had to take the mold off slowly. I also made a zoo with cages. Now I am glad I didn't get a stuffed animal!!!!!!!!

In the same issue Christian shares a shopping dilemma he encountered—trying to decide which violin was just the right one for him.

Big Choice
by Christian Murphy (age 13)

I was carefully opening my last birthday present. I got the wrapping paper off and found a shoe box. I opened it and inside was..... a stuffed sock in the shape of a violin with toothpicks for tuning pegs and yarn for strings. I thought, "Oh, that's nice." But when one of my parents (I can't remember which) said, "That signifies the full size violin from Shar Products" (which is a violin that I thought I would not be able to get) I was ecstatic, overjoyed, extremely happy, etc.

A few days later the UPS guy stopped at our door with two large packages. They were of course my violin and bows. The violin did not sound as good as I thought it would and I wasn't thrilled, so we kept looking for a violin.

We had heard about a person in Philadelphia who sold violins. So we decided to try him. He said he would have four violins ready when we came, but when we got there he had seven violins. Then we started trying them out. I played the violins through, but I still didn't have any opinion on which one I should get. There was one that I really liked the look of but didn't think the sound was loud enough. I finally got tired of playing after one and a half frustrating hours in a sweltering room in which we made no progress. Then we had David (the person who was selling the violins) come in and play. After that we made progress! We nominated two violins immediately and David said if we could eliminate one more we could take the rest home.

For the next week whenever I would practice, I would try and decide which violin I liked the best. A lot hinged on what my teacher thought of the violins. I had picked out two that I liked and one of those I really liked. But that one I really liked didn't sound as loud as the other ones and you want to have the violin sound as loud as possible. Even though it was not as loud as the other violins it sounded better than the other ones. It is also 100 years old and I like old violins because they have a history, they are "wise" and they have the songs of their previous owners in them. It also had three cracks, but they weren't in crucial places.

When my teacher looked at and played the violins she eliminated all but three. We finally decided on (drum roll please) the 100 year old one. Now all we have to do is find a case and a bow.

The Tisdale children have also put out several issues of a family newsletter, called the *Agape Learning Lab News* or *A.L.L. News*. They also accept submissions from their readers and encourage their readers to take part in their newsletter. The girl's longer pieces, which appear in other sections of this book, first appeared in the *A.L.L. News*. Mark, their younger brother, also wrote a wonderful and detailed piece describing how the family celebrates Christmas. Mark's mother worked cooperatively with him on this essay, helping him jog his memory and organize his thoughts. The Tisdales chose to photocopy Mark's own handwritten copy of his piece, instead of retyping it for him, and I'm sure this must have helped motivate him to work hard to make it so neat and readable. This story will be such a special way of remembering the family's unique Christmas traditions as the years go by. I can even imagine Mark reading it aloud to his own children one day, helping build a bridge between his childhood and theirs.

Christmas at Our House
by Mark Tisdale (age 8)

We do many things to celebrate Christmas. My favorite part of Christmas is the Christmas Eve Children's Program. Before church for supper, our family has black bean soup. I like having my own part to say in the program. We sing Christmas carols. My favorite song is "Away in a Manger." We come home and have our Christmas pictures taken and then enjoy hot punch and a dried fruit plate.

After Dad's birthday December 10, the Christmas tree is decorated. I like to put on the ornaments. Each of us has some special ornaments. One of my favorite ornaments is Mary's—Baby Jesus in the manger. While we are decorating the tree, we play Handel's "Messiah." My favorite songs are the "Hallelujah Chorus" and "I Know that My Redeemer Liveth."

During the month of December special cookies are baked. the sugar cookies are my favorite. I like to help cut them out and sugar them. Dad's favorite are the date pinwheels. We also enjoy gingerbread cookies.

After many preparations Christmas arrives. Elizabeth and Mary wear candle crowns and serve Mom breakfast in bed, a custom from Sweden when St. Lucia buns are served by the oldest daughter to the family celebrating the Festival of Lights. When Mom finishes, we get our stockings, and Mom snaps our pictures. A delicious breakfast follows with Christmas stollen, hard-boiled eggs, and juice. Then it's time for church and brunch.

Afterwards we come home and open our gifts. Christmas is just our family. Our [foster] babies remind me of when baby Jesus was born. We think they are our special gift. Before supper we read, "Mr. Edwards Meets Santa Claus" by Laura Ingalls Wilder.

Christmas evening we have a delicious supper. Turkey, twice-baked potatoes, green beans or squash with cranberries, molded cranberry jello salad, and home-made rolls are the main course. For dessert we have mock plum pudding with lemon sauce. Christmas candy is our final treat. Until bedtime we play with our gifts and enjoy the lighted tree.

Some homeschooled children put out their own individual

newsletters. In the Smith family, Ben is hard at work on a Civil War newsletter, and his younger sister Emilie has just finished her first issue of *The Animal Times*, this issue focusing on dogs. The paper is xeroxed from Emilie's hand written work, encouraging her to work for neatness and legibility in her cursive script. Here is the feature story, a delightful and imaginative little piece.

Speckle Dog Food
by Emilie Smith (age 7)

There was a puppy named Speckle. When she was still a puppy she decided that there were not enough dogfood plants. So one day, when her master fed her, with a can on her head and her food dish in her mouth, she marched through her land, scattering dogfood. The dogfood soon grew into dogfood plants and Speckle became famous. Everywhere she went she filled dogs' dishes. One day Speckle grew very sick. She stayed at a dog's house and there she died. A puppy lived there, so he took the can off Speckle's head and put it on his head, then he picked up his dish.......

Daniel Trembula is also the editor and author of his own newsletter, and it's devoted to his true love—frontier life. He is usually seen in coonskin caps, and is full of imaginings of escapades into the woods and living in the wild and recreating the life of Daniel Boone. His issue #4 was very well designed, with a table of contents and a wide variety of features, even original pioneer recipes and jokes and word–finds. Here's his longest article, telling about the life of Sam Houston.

Sam Houston
by Daniel Trembula (age 9)

Sam Houston led the military force that overthrew the

Mexicans in the War for Texan Independence. He helped Texas become independent as a country. Later he became the first governor of Texas.

Sam Houston was born in Virginia. His father fought under Dan Morgen in the Revolutionary War (see *Frontier Special* Volume '89 issue 3). Sam's father planned to move to Tennessee and sold their plantation in Virginia. But his father died on his way back from resigning from the army. His mother moved the 8 children to Tennessee in two covered wagons.

Sam did not like farming or working in a store. He went and lived with the Indians. Then he taught school for a few months before enlisting in the army. He fought under General Jackson in the War of 1812. He was the first soldier to get over the creek's barricade alive at the Battle of Horseshoe Bend. Even when wounded he continued to fight and lead his men.

After the War of 1812 Sam Houston went into politics. He became a lawyer. He was a representative from Tennessee. He was even a governor of Tennessee for a short time. Then he went to live with the Indians again. He tried to get Andrew Jackson to help the Indians.

Andrew Jackson sent Sam to Texas to make deals with the Indians to protect Americans living there. Texas was still part of Mexico. There were Americans settling Texas at that time. The Americans in Texas wanted independence from Mexico. Sam Houston eventually became commander in chief of the small and disorganized forces of Texas. At San Jacinto, Sam Houston and his men defeated Santa Anna and his men. Sam Houston went on and became President of the Republic of Texas and when it joined the Union in 1845, he became the first Governor.

Sam tried to keep Texas from joining the Confederacy but he could not. He died in 1863. He was a brave leader.

A growing number of homeschooled children are also editing full scale neighborhood papers, with paid subscribers and other children contributing articles and poems. Scott Petersen, age 11, is in complete charge of the publication *LIFT*, which stands for *Learning in Families Times*. He figures costs, edits, types, lays out copy, and sees to the photocopying. From the issue I saw, I can see he is receiving many fine contributions from the homeschoolers who live near him. Here is an article Scott wrote, telling about life with his pet hamster—it was a follow up to an article about his escaping goldfish! Through the example of his own well-organized and humorous essay, Scott is showing others the types of pieces they too might write.

Pet Corner—Hamster's Great Escapes
by Scott Petersen (age 11)

Hamsters are very different from gerbils. Having gerbils before, I have noticed a significant difference with hamsters. HAMSTERS CAN CLIMB! My hamster's name is Columbine, but we call her Ham. She has escaped three times and that is not good, because we have two cats.

Once Ham climbed out of her cage because the lid was off. She was gone for two days. I found her climbing down the steps. The second time, she climbed up her water bottle and pushed her way out under the lid. We set a trap this time. We put wild bird seed in a smooth metal bucket propped against a step. In the middle of the night, my Mom heard a noise. IT WAS HAM. She was in the bottom of the bucket, having eaten her fill!

We got a locking lid for the aquarium and she STILL got

out one more time. I left the little door in the middle open. We have a metal wheel in Ham's cage. She jammed the wheel with pine chips and climbed out through the door. This time we caught her in about 20 minutes under my chest of drawers.

If your hamster or gerbil or other rodent gets loose and you have other pets like dogs or cats, first check a room thoroughly for your rodent then use that room to lock up your cats or dogs. Rodents tend to run around the perimeter of a room, so check under furniture and in cold weather check under heat vents. Put water and food in bowls in several places just to keep them alive. Once in a while check your bowls to see if food is missing, then use that room for our bucket trap. The bucket makes sure that they can't get loose again. Tip it against a stack of blocks or books that the hamster can climb.

Scott has accepted many poetry contributions for his newsletter also. One of the most delightful is this picture of a cat by Esther Feagan. She has really captured the personality of a feline!

Gideon
by Esther Feagan (age 12)

The yellow cat stalks,
His white, soft streaks are silent.
He spots a moving leaf.
Swiftly, silently he crouches.
It quivers.
Pounce!
He tears his prey apart,
And stalks off with dignity.

Mika Perrine and Nica Christensen are co-editors of the longrunning *Neighborhood News*. Many of their homeschooling friends also contribute, especially those they meet with regularly at their classes at the Penokee Mountain Co-op School, a resource center for homeschooling families. Many of the girls' poems and essays appear in other parts of this anthology, and all were first printed in their sixteen page newsletter. The whole newsletter is chock full of variety and fun, even including a section called "Rte. 1 Rumors" to keep everyone up to date with the doings of all the neighbors. Here is one funny story from a contributor who found homophones to be great (or is it grate?) fun.

44 Hilarious Homophones
by Kiersten Galazen (age 9)

Wood ewe like two come four a walk with me? Yes, eye wood like two dew that. Wear should wee go? Let's go into the woulds. Grate idea! Due ewe sea that flour, what a wonderful cent it has. I here a noise down buy the creak. I'll beet you their! Weight fore me. Bea quiet, it mite be a dear oar a bare.

We silently maid hour weigh down the path. We saw shoo prince in the mud, they had a strange ark too them. There stood my hoarse, it must have come down the rode. We road it bearback up two the barn. We gave her a carat and a pale of water. We combed her hare and thanked her four the ride back home.

8. Writing Together

Picture this: a group of homeschooled children are all crowded around our big dining room table, laughing and clapping, maybe even cheering and calling out, "Read more! Read more!" Then excited discussion begins. "I liked where he gave the genie the name of Fred—not what you'd expect for an exotic being!" "I think it's even funnier than the last chapter." "I like the part where the dragon coughs them up and the characters are just called 'itches' for a while." There are six-year-olds on up to fourteen-year-olds, boys and girls, and a few toddlers playing in the background for good measure.

Soon another child begins reading her poem about snow aloud to the group, and her unique images are appreciated by everyone. A discussion of rhyme and its uses and abuses in poetry begins, with different kids expressing their own views.

Another girl begins reading her new fictional story aloud, and gets some valuable feedback on what time frame to set her story in—it had been confusing at first to figure if it were set in modern times or the last century. The writer says that she'd been confused by that too while she was writing, that she just hadn't been sure herself which she wanted to do. By the next meeting she decides to opt for Civil War times, opening whole new story lines, conflicts and characters.

A six year old girl reads a short piece about losing teeth and everyone jumps in to share their own best lost tooth memories. Maybe some will choose to write about them later on.

The group appreciates how one boy has taken the risk of fiction writing for the first time, and how another boy can make even the reporting of a homeschool field trip a humorous delight. Others share book reviews, short essays on whale research, personal observations, and more. As usual, there is an amazing variety to the children's work, and plenty to discuss and think about. Topics talked about range from deciding what *person* to write in, and how this affects the mood and style of the piece; how kids get ideas for fictional stories and characters; how they create suspense or write from a unique viewpoint; to how in the world you wind up and finish a long piece.

What's happening here? It's a meeting of our Homeschoolers Writing Club. Actually the meetings sometimes even get going before the meeting. I remember one day I drove three families of kids over to the meeting location in my huge van, and right on the ride the kids all were beginning to talk about their stories and wondering what new chapters others had added to their longer fairy tales. They talked about possible topics to use for our writing "game" afterwards.

These are not necessarily kids who loved to write and so decided that it would be neat to start their own club to share their work with others. As parents we created this interest by setting up the regular meetings every two weeks and making sure our kids all wrote at home in between times so that they'd have something to share. Some of the kids in the group originally hated writing, and did as little of it as they could get by with. Ian Latinette, whose marvelous *Triumvirate* story is included in this anthology, was one of the most vociferous writing haters, even though he read everything in sight. The writing club experience has played a major role in helping him change his view of writing.

Some homeschooling families find that their children are reluctant to write when the main audience is only the family. We have found that being part of a homeschoolers' writing club can be a real help here, providing regular input and appreciation and suggestions from others. Our children enjoy the regular times to see their friends, and I can see how all the children involved have grown as writers over time. Other writing clubs have also sprung up all over the state of Pennsylvania, and across the country. It's a natural extension of homeschooling, and well worth the time and effort involved.

But how should a writing club be organized? How to get started? Every group will probably find its own personality and way of operating that suits them best, but I can share some things that seem to have worked well with our group.

Our group tries to meet every two weeks, although I know some groups happily meet weekly, and others only get together monthly. For us, every two weeks is a good balance—it usually gives enough time for the kids to really work on their writing at home in between times, and yet doesn't make us all feel that we were constantly racing off to yet another outside activity. The kids are expected to bring some writing from home to share with the group, and it's rare that anyone comes without a contribution.

Our group currently has eleven children participating, although not all are able to come each session because of travel distances. The kids were, by and large, friends before the writing club began, but are certainly much closer now because of the experience of working together so regularly (not to mention the much appreciated playtime *after* the writing club part is over!). We have little sisters who are six-years-old, on up to big brothers of fourteen and no one has ever complained about the wide age spread. At one point I thought maybe we should divide the group in two, as it sometimes took a long time to get around the table to hear everyone's work, but I realized that the younger ones offered a refreshing enthusiastic presence that we don't want to lose. They are often the first to jump in with positive comments, boosting everyone's feelings. And they've become good writers in their own right, fully taking in all the discussion that goes on about the lengthy pieces the older ones are writing. They have never asked to leave the table early because of boredom with the talk.

In thinking about the mix of kids who might come to your own group, I think it's important to look at the balance of personalities, and see how each has an important role to play. One boy, new to homeschooling this year and new to our group, is just beginning to find his writer's voice, and his pieces are usually short and he doesn't yet feel they are particularly inspiring to the others. But he immediately began taking another very positive role—a very enthusiastic appreciator. He was the one who immediately remembered where fourteen–year–old Ian had left off in his long chapter story about a king and his cohorts—"You were right at the part where the genie is just about to tell his life story! That was really funny. I can't wait to hear the next part today!" Who doesn't enjoy having someone around who really listens and remembers and cares?

Some of the children are naturally shy and quiet, and having someone read their pieces for them is a must most of the time. Writing gives them a chance to be heard saying what they never could have spoken out loud. We have a special opportunity to join in their worlds a bit through their writing. Although an entire group made up of very quiet children might never get off the ground, these children can still offer a lot to a supportive group.

Other students inspire us by the quality of their writing or uniqueness of their approaches. Jesse's long *King's Closet* story was directly inspired by Ian Latinette's *Triumvirate* story, as was Jacob's long *Math Land* story. Jesse and Jacob had never tried writing in a folk tale style before, and both found they thoroughly enjoyed the change. Through discussions at the writing club they shared how they thought up their ideas and developed their characters. For many, including most of us mothers, it was a revelation to hear that these students often began a story without a sure direction of what would eventually happen. Instead, characters were created who by their very uniqueness inevitably set the action going. Perhaps funny names were thought up, and basic personalities fleshed out. Endings came later, and then the earlier parts could be reworked for inner consistency and flow. The writers often shared what the feeling was like to be really following hot on an idea, writing fast and fluently and feeling the ideas just zipping out. By the next session often several more kids would decide to begin long fictional pieces too.

Writing clubs can also be just the support a person needs to be able to really complete a long work. It is easy to get discouraged when working on a long story. It is easy to just put it on the back burner or toss it in the wastebasket and give up—and sometimes that's even the proper thing to do if it really is a dead-end piece going nowhere. But if you know that at your next writing club meeting everyone is going to be asking what has happened next, you know you can't let them down! Although it was always fun to hear something different (and quick!) that one of the older writers had worked on during a break from their long work, we certainly all played a role in keeping the writers going on their long pieces.

Sometimes we set different ways to decide who will read their piece next—picking numbers or alphabet letters out of a hat, going in certain zigzagging patterns around the table, or going from youngest to oldest. The kids find the variety fun, and also they know that they don't have the option of hanging back indefinitely or pushing in "me first" style. Everyone will get their turn, and somehow for the shier kids I think it is actually comforting to know that they don't have to make the decision on when their turn will be. It just comes up and they share what they have.

Kids can read their piece themselves or have an adult or other child read their piece. Sometimes it is best for an adult to read a piece if the child isn't yet an expressive oral reader, but sometimes knowing they will be reading to everyone at writing club has inspired my kids to actually practice reading their pieces aloud at home before hand.

One small thing we do that seems to set an appreciative tone and break any possible ice before it forms, is to always clap when anyone is done with reading their work aloud. This gives the reader the good feeling that their piece has been heartily accepted and respected and enjoyed. Many of the kids are Suzuki music students and are well used to clapping after anyone's performance. This small break of time also gives the listeners time to get their thoughts together so that they can be more ready to respond to the writer. There aren't the awkward pauses that might let the writer worry that nobody liked his piece.

We occasionally have reminder discussions about how we might respond to each others' writing, maybe generating a listing of possible comments to make or questions to ask. Over time lists have included such things as:

—I really liked where you wrote that...
—I liked your choice of words when you said...
—Your story reminds me of when I...
—I was confused at the part when...happened. Did you really mean...?
—Is your story true or fiction, or fiction based on something that really happened?
—How did you get the idea for that piece?
—Where are you going with this piece? Do you know what will happen next, or how you'll finish it up?
—How was this writing a new experience for you?
—Did you get your idea from any book or story you'd read?

—Your piece reminds of a book I read called... because...

—What was hardest about this piece for you?

—How long did it take you to work on this piece? Did you work several days, or all at once?

—What's different about typing, using a computer, writing by hand, or dictating? Advantages or disadvantages of each?

—What are you going to do with it now that it's finished? Bind it into a book and publish it? Send it off to a magazine or newsletter? Frame it? Submit it to *Writing from Home*?

—I think your piece would be even better if you maybe considered...

I let the kids know that we are not there to tear each other's pieces down with criticism, but to support each other as writers, and create a time and place where we can all enjoy sharing our pieces together. We look for growing and moving towards more versatility and uniqueness as writers, and towards pieces that ring true with an authentic voice. I remember here one homeschooling mother telling me about the dreadful adult writers' workshop she had participated in a few years back. Everyone attending seemed to feel the format gave them license to be as nit-picky and mean-spirited as possible, and my friend was devastated by the incessant criticism. No one seemed to respect that the others might have different goals in mind, or be struggling beginners, or be unsure of themselves and in need of building up and support. I never wanted that to happen to our writing groups, and I think I can say with confidence that it hasn't.

As the adult leader, I also try to point out unique things about each child's writing that I notice. Usually these are positive things, such as seeing that a child has been brave enough to try a very new approach, but sometimes I point to common problems that all writers need to grapple with. For instance, once a girl read her very well developed fiction story, and I heard that she had suddenly switched from the third person to the first—"she did this" had become "I did this." This opened a quick discussion about how writers had to be consistent and choose one way or the other, and that she had the option now of going back and rewriting it all in first person, or keeping it in third. Others shared how they had dealt with this issue in their pieces too. I think the student gained from this without feeling she was "picked" on.

One thing we don't discuss is mechanics—things like handwriting, spelling, or punctuation. Although at some point a "spelling club" might come in handy, we have enough to talk about right now just with the composing process! We accept and are all pretty good at deciphering inventive spellings, and no one is made to feel they can't fully participate because of their lack of finesse in these areas. We are interested here in people's ideas, and we never have felt the need to introduce red pencils to mark up technical mistakes. (I remember one homeschooling mother being seriously asked by her school superintendent if she *had* a red pencil. Did she need one? They'd be more than happy to give her one if she didn't have one!)

Sometimes of course our response to pieces read at the meetings is quick and direct—we all find ourselves laughing aloud over a particularly funny piece, or the kids call out "READ MORE!" when I say it's time to stop my reading of Jacob's pages long *Math Land* escapade. The writers know they've been appreciated and heard, and often that's all that's needed, or all we have time for.

If time allows we all write together after sharing our writing from home. With an earlier group it worked very well just to have the kids free write on any topic they chose. The kids expected this and often used ideas they'd gotten from the earlier part of the meeting. After just a few sessions almost everyone was able to get writing quickly. These would then be shared and after that the kids would zip outside to play.

We began introducing other types of writing "games" with the new larger group, and this has worked even better than free writing. One thing that has always been a hit is for the kids all to write on a similar topic—maybe a shared experience, maybe a common theme such as "My Bedroom" or "My Road," and then we guess who wrote each one. Often the children themselves think up these topics during the meeting, other times I've planned one in advance. Once decided upon, the kids scatter about the downstairs of our house with paper and pencil and write furiously for about ten minutes. I then collect the pieces, being sure not to let anyone see anyone else's writing (a little fanfare and drama never hurts here...). Then the fun begins. The kids have "ballots" and number their paper from one to however many people took part (mothers are encouraged to write if they are not busy chasing toddlers!). As I read the stories aloud, the children all try to guess the authors. Often there is lots of head scratching and cries of "Read number five again!" but it is amazing how often almost everyone guesses correctly—they can recognize each writer's voice and style and typical approach to a task. They listen attentively and critically and with purpose.

What follows are some of the writings generated at our writing club meetings during these games. Again, these were dashed off, top of the head writings, not pondered over and polished, and I think they are often charming and delightful. Enjoy! Our topics have included *Dogs, My Road,* and *My Bedroom.*

It's a Dog's Life
by Ian Latinette (age 14)

Arf! It is I, Spot McFido, here to remind all dogs of the saying, "A dog's best friend is his human." Keep this in mind, for there have been disturbing stories about mistreatment of humans. The Society for the Prevention of Cruelty to Humans

is determined to prevent these happenings. Support your local
S.F.T.P.H.! "Have you licked a human today?"

Dogs
by Anna Latinette (age 6)
Dogs are nice. Dogs have wagging tails that are soft. Dogs
are good for watching for robbers. They are good for friends.

My Dog
by Andrew Glendening (age 9)
My dog is a funny one. He will do just about anything to
get food. He will also jump around like a rabbit. He has a
bed, but it's a wreck because he chews on it. When he plays
ball with us he likes to think it's a rat and shakes it around.
And the strangest thing he does is watch TV. His favorite
show is "Nature" and when he sees a dog he barks.

Our Sneaky, Impatient and Guilty House Dog
by Jesse Richman (age 12)
At first she was very guilty about being in the house and
would not come in. Then she begged to sneak in. We made
vain attempts to keep her out, but for all but a few purposes
now her guilt levels and our resistance levels are lowered, and
this house dog has no other house than our own.

My Road
by Autumn Speck (age 10)
Our road is like a rollercoaster when you go fast on it.
There is a big, big hill that my sister and I ride our bikes on. I
said, "I will ride down with no brakes." That I know was
dumb, but I did it anyway. I flipped over the handle bars on
my bike and got hurt, but, luckily, I didn't break any bones!

My Road
by Ian Latinette (age 14)

Our road is long and winding, in the country. We have a couple of neighbors within sight and steep hills in two directions. The only problem is that our road is connected to the highway, causing noise pollution and killing our pets. I have ridden my bike the length of our road, and, boy, was it difficult! I think we are located in one of the best places we could be.

Parents at the writing club try to write in these games every time we can.

My Road
by Susan Richman (age 38)

When I cross my road to go to our mailbox, the road is a quiet crisscross of tar drips plugging up cracks. But quick. Watch out—dart across fast before that lumbering thunder off in the distance becomes a banging, barging fierce coal truck pounding by, squeezing the oozy tar flat. Squeezing the quiet into a roar.

My Road
by Jacob Richman (age 9)

A monster, killing animals,
Our road.
Running at 45 miles an hour,
Our road.

My Road
by Jesse Richman (age 12)

As if being in need of paving is not enough, PENNDOT [Pennsylvania Department of Transportation] seems to have decided that quantity is better than quality. Accordingly they expand my sides almost every year without properly preparing the surface. This means that my shoulders are nonexistent and badly worn.

My Road
by Molly Richman (age 6)

Rushing, seizing,
One car, two cars,
Then a line, then two again,
Then one.
A rushing road.

My Road
by Andrew Glendening (age 9)

My road is dangerous. The speed limit is 55 and it is narrow, but so far no one has been hurt. And to make it worse it is curvy and there are lots of cars on it.

My Bedroom
by Micah Latinette (age 8)

It's a little bit cold at first, but as I lay I roll around and find a place that is warm. I try to go to sleep but it takes a long time. I finally drift off to sleep about a half hour later. I hardly ever wake up. My mom usually wakes me up by calling me to come to eat breakfast.

My Bedroom
told from the point of view of mice
by Jesse Richman (age 12)

Hello! It's just one more day at the bedroom tour agency. Here come some prospective viewers. "Hello, who are you? Do you feel brave enough to take the tour?" Most of them do, so here we go!

Our first stop is the floor hideaway. A floor board fell out of here a few years ago and things began to accumulate. First there were a few candy canes and halloween candies, then those disappeared and were followed by all sorts of other junk. It's so bad these days that we cannot take you through it. Now here we are coming to a dresser. Come on up to the top, there's another way down. There's a lot of junk up here, so watch your step. There are three old watches up here, some model swords, speakers, penknives, scraps of paper, pens, alarm clocks, and many other things. What? Do you have to go so soon? Well, good–bye! Come farther some time!

My Bedroom
by Ian Latinette (age 14)

My room has two super single beds, two dusty dressers (one covered with combs, cassettes, stones and explosives), a permanent layer of dirty clothes on the floor, and a passage to the attic. Generally, if you excavate through the clothes at the foot of my bed, you will find about a dozen–odd books. My room is shared with one other member of my family at all times. The closets I am not going to mention, because it seems that I would need TNT to blast the contents apart for sorting. My room—a jungle to you is home for me!

My Bedroom
by Laura Speck (age 11)

You walk in and stumble over boxes of dressups and odds and ends. You never know what will be there, it's always different.

My Bedroom
by Molly Richman (age 6)

"Children, clean up your bedroom. You ought to have done it yesterday."

"Well, Mom, it's clean already."

"Well, I will come up and see for myself."

"Oh, no, no—not yet."

"Why?"

"Because."

"Because what?"

"Because because!"

We hope we've given you a taste of what fun a writing club can be, and that you'll try it out in your own area, finding a format that's right for you.

9. Creating Poetry

I'm holding in my hands two poetry books, both handmade by my sons when they were seven years old. These books sit on our shelf of "Written by Children Books," and I've just picked them up now after not looking at them for maybe a year or more. The memories come back as I flip through the pages. I remember Jesse dictating his poem about the wind, called "Still Silence," with it's opening line, "I wonder what would happen if wind was tied up in a sack?" and ending with, "Still air is when all the balls of wind are away from a place." He'd been thoughtful and wondering and imagining as he'd told me those words, almost dreamy and yet intensely concentrating. And then I come to Jacob's poem about seasonal change, and I marvel at his seemingly inate ability to create a metaphor, or comparison, that I never would have thought of.

> Snow is wool of the earth.
>   It gets cut in the spring.
> The shears that snow is cut with—is warmth!

They were both using poetry as a way of wondering, of seeing, of tieing loose ends of experience together in new ways so that a new sense of reality was created. I think they understand poetry, and I'm glad I have these early poems of theirs.

But what is a poem? I sometimes wince when I see poems by children that are just exercises in reeling out strings of nonsensical rhymes. I don't deny children enjoy doing this sort of thing at times, and that the results can sometimes be quite humorous. Creating rhyming patterns can even be a help in beginning to learn to read. But are these jingles poems? I'm not so sure. In choosing the poems for this anthology I have tried to look for those poems that give us strong images, succinct and telling and personally meaningful. These might or might not incorporate rhyme. I feel that often, for grownups but even more for young writers, rhyme can get in the way, making writers put down any number of artificial thoughts that mean nothing to them. The only saving grace is that the result has an obvious rhyme scheme—therefore the writer declares it a poem, beautiful or not.

I remember once reviewing a thick rhyming dictionary, one of those reference books for serious poets which lists all the possible rhymes you might not have thought of on your own. I cringed to think of students using a book like this as a way to create yet more doggerel rhymes that had no other thing in their favor but their rhymes, but when I read the foreword to the book, I was relieved. The author actually agreed with me! He felt that poets should *never* use a forced rhyme, or even distort word order just for the sake of meter or rhyme. He also cautioned against using old flowery language full of *thee* and *thou* or, worse, *'twas*. He felt rhyme had to be used very carefully and skillfully, or it just got in the way of things and cluttered up a poem with gilt edges of distracting frivolousness.

I have included a short listing of books of poetry in the "Resources" section that have been especially helpful in our family. Several are collections of poems written by children, and many of these are strong on image, rather than being overly dependent on rhyme. We have also always enjoyed Japanese poetry, which does not have any rhyme structure. Flora Arnstein's book *Children Write Poetry* is especially helpful and inspiring, as it takes a group a children through several years of weekly poetry workshops, showing how their poetic vision grew gradually over time. When the children first began, most wrote complete doggerel—rhyming stuff with no sense. By the end of the book you will be astonished at the children's sensitive and personal work.

Here is a poem that does use rhyme carefully and skillfully. See if you can picture these two girls, working together, enjoying rearranging their words and their thoughts.

Poems
by Rachel Melis (age 10)
and Nica Christensen (age 9)

Sitting in the bedroom
Writing poems with a friend.
Thinking of the many ways
Different words could blend.
Many sheets of paper
Lying on the floor,
Many are done
But we can always write more.
Putting words together,
Taking them apart,
That's just what poems are,
Another form of art.

And here's a poem that doesn't use rhyme but captures the strength of feeling and vividness that is the hallmark of great poetry.

Roller Skating
by April Blair (age 10)

When you put your skates on
You can already feel
The freedom
Rising from your toes.
Then off you go
Feel the wind
Whipping your face
There you are
flying around the rink!
Slow down!

Dorien, our next author, sent me her "Writing Autobiography" to help others understand how she goes about writing.

Writing Autobiography
by Dorien Casses (age 9)

I am a nine year old girl and I love reading and writing. I like writing because it gives me a sense of freedom. One day I decided to write something. I didn't want to write a story (that would take too long) so I wrote my first poem. It's called "Impartable" and it's about two of our favorite toys, Moe the mole and Karen (Karen's a beaver). One day we sat down to homeschool. I was answering questions in my English workbook. There was a question with the word "impressionism." Mom told me what it meant. Later on that day I sat down to write. I wanted to write something really

pretty. Soon "Impressionism" was done. A week later I had
an idea. I thought about how silly and clumpy grasshoppers
seem, so I wrote "Grasshoppers."

Impressionism
by Dorien Casses (age 9)

It's not the music,
       but the sound of the music.
It's not the sun,
       but the feeling of the sun.
It's not the leaves,
       but the color of the leaves.
It's not the rose,
       but the smell of the rose.
It's not the fruit,
       but the taste of the fruit.
All of these five senses,
       Why do we have a limit?

Dorien wrote that she got the idea for the shape of this next poem
after reading *Joyful Noise: Poems for two Voices*, by Paul
Fleischman (1988 Newberry Honor Book). The poems are meant to
be read by two people reading simultaneously, as in a duet,
sometimes sharing words, sometimes saying different words,
sometimes syncopating back and forth between the two voices. It is
a wonderful idea for others to try, and I hope that Dorien inspires
you to try out this innovative poetry form. It reminds us again that
poetry is meant at its best to be read or recited aloud. Read this
poem with someone else. The words opposite should be read

together. Take turns reading the other lines.

Grasshopper
by Dorien Casses (age 9)

hop	hop
grasshopper	
hop	hop
	playing
hop	hop
singing	
hop	hop
do you	do you
know where	
you came from?	
hop	hop
	from my egg
hop	hop
but where else?	
hop	hop
	from my long
	dead mother
hop	hop

I was delighted to receive another poem for two voices, this time from Nica Christensen in Wisconsin. Nica says she loves to write, and I think it certainly shows in her wonderful, aware, and thoughtful poems that follow.

Chickadees
A Poem for two voices
by Nica Christensen (age 10)

In the air

Two chickadees

Jumping higher and higher
Together as one   Together as one
Skipping a stone

Whirring wings
Their little hearts beating   Their little hearts beating
Away.

Nica's mother wrote to let me know something of Nica's writing background, and I think you'll find it helpful. Note too that Nica would never have developed her writing abilities to this extent in the school she used to attend:

One of the reasons we chose to homeschool Nica was because she did so *little* writing in public school. In all of third grade she wrote only one "creative" paper and it was about Mars, which she wasn't even interested in. The rest was all fill in the blanks. No exaggeration!

At home Nica writes daily. She seems to have a list of topics in her mind and each day she just gets out pencil and paper and writes. Sometimes it's letters or book reviews (usually of a book that really moved her) or an article for a newspaper published by a nearby homeschool family. Last year she wrote lots of poetry—usually about things she'd seen or experiences she'd had. She corresponds with friends, relatives, and penpals around the world, and always writes an interesting and very readable letter. She has submitted work to *Cricket*, *Skipping Stones,* and *Stone Soup.*

There are many reasons why Nica likes to write, but I think the main thing is that she is a "word person." We read to her a lot, she reads to herself a lot, and she always writes about topics that are interesting to her. She loves music and poetry. She has a small flock of ducks and geese and is often inspired to write poems about them. She plays Suzuki violin and the banjo and loves to sing. I think writing is just an extension of this gathering of sounds and syllables and rhythm which she is in tune with in the world around her.

Nica looks on nature and life about her with a quiet concentration and perceptiveness. What a feast of poetic images!

Lines to a Crow and a Sumac Bush
by Nica Christensen (age 10)

Sitting on a sumac bush
An ebony black crow.
Black against red,
A checkerboard.
He sits and eats the luscious berries.

Fall
by Nica Christensen (age 10)

Fall is a leaf drifting slowly on the wind, slowly to the ground.
Fall is a golden sunflower.
Fall is the loud bird songs that echo and ring through the
    woods.
Fall is the rush before the frost and Fall is the harvest.
Fall is the crisp wind that rustles the leaves of the oaks now
    scarlet and golden.
Fall is working hard stacking firewood and coming in for hot
    spicy apple cider!
Fall is a leaf drifting slowly... slowly to the ground.

Fall in Wisconsin
by Nica Christensen (age 10)

The sound of fall birdsongs fills the air.
Bluejays land on sunflowers.
I love the rush before the frost as we harvest pumpkins.
Trees wave in the wind.
Brightly colored leaves fall to the ground.
We take beautiful walks in the woods through crunchy leaves.
Trees wave in the wind. We smell the wet ground and fresh
    air.
I remember crisp mornings,
Wood crackling in the stove,
Pots of brilliant gladiolus,
And tomatoes on the windowsills.

One Mother Spider
by Nica Christensen (age 10)

One mother spider
On the bottom of a chair.
One mother spider
Her egg sacks around her.
The young hatching.
Many spiders.

Spring
by Nica Christensen (age 10)

Crocuses opening up to show their blue and violet petals.
The nights are short and the days are longer.
The air is crisp and clear.
Running in the field, picking dandelions.
Spring has come.

The First Wind of Spring
by Nica Christensen (age 10)

Wind, wind laughing as it goes
        running, running across the fields.
The trees sway to and fro, just a breeze
        and it blows lightly across my face.
Leaves fly high looking like butterflies
        and the seagulls soar.

Where the Quiet Meets the Waves
Bark Bay September 1988
by Nica Christensen (age 10)

It started raining, just a sprinkle.
Bubbles in the rain, bubbles in the water.
Raindrops were bouncing off the water.
Three otter heads popped up.
The canoe drifted quietly through a small channel
With prickly bursting seed pods growing off the reeds.
When you touched them they fell to many pieces.
Huddled Hawk resting in a tree.
We canoed to a beach where the white sand met the great
      crashing waves.
Seagulls called and the wind roared.
There were beautiful silky rocks washed by the water.
White smooth driftwood for sword fighting.
Smooth glass for collecting.
Silky smooth feathers for your hair.
We threw off our clothes and jumped into the cold water.
We dove into the waves. Underwater it was white and
      smooth.
Back in the bay it was quiet. A blue kingfisher flew by.

Seasons and their changes are always something that makes us
thoughtful and wondering. Here is a poem by Jennifer Trynovich
showing the contrasts of winter, and a poem about going out into the
coldness and the night by Mika Perrine.

Winter
by Jennifer Trynovich (age 13)

Beyond frosty window panes,
Lies a barren land of a dozen plains.

Out where nothing wants to grow,
Where wintry winds just blow and blow.

But inside the fire and its glow,
Contentedly makes us forget the snow.

And we forget the dim, dull light,
Of this barren wintry night.

Shadows in the Moonlight
by Mika Perrine (age 11)

The Moon has a radiance
        that entrances me.
The steady crunch of our feet on
        the icy snow
        calms me.
And we stop to
        listen to the silence,
As if there's something
        to hear.
As we turn we marvel:
        Shadows in the moonlight,
Shadows in the moonlight.

Snow means something different to young Aram Melis. He has been able to capture many images of snow in this spare poem. The form of this poem, a cinquain, is a listing of metaphors ending with the actual name of the thing being described, is a very good one for anyone of any age to try. Kirsten Winston's poem was written just after a sledding time outside with her sister.

Snowflake
by Aram Melis (age 7)

Snowflake,
Sugar, white rabbit,
Skiing, skiing, sledding, dreaming;
Floating,
Falling
Snow.

Snow
by Kirsten Grace Williams Winston (age 4)

It's snowing!
It's snowing!
The girls are getting cold.
They said to their mother
"We are getting cold."
So they went inside
And they replied,
"We can't go out anymore."

April Blair watches snowflakes very carefully and thoughtfully and lovingly in order to write this next poem. She catches the intense concentration of observation that can mark a fine poem. Molly Richman, too, has grasped the important idea that poetry is about creating images and about seeing how one thing is like another thing.

Snowflakes
by April Blair (age 10)

Flutter down to the earth
crystal clear
so tiny
so fragile
As one floats gently
onto my hand
it melts almost immediately
Snowflakes are so beautiful
cold
yet so lovely

Snow
by Molly Richman age 6

Falling like a storm of feathers,
Making mounds.
As cold as goose bumps,
But as soft as a pillow—
            It's snow!

Here is yet another image of snow—this time it is cast as tiny troopers, signaling battle for some. But not for Holly Tobey!

Snowfall
by Holly Tobey (age 12)

Floating down in parachutes
Come the white and feathery troops.
Covering field, and fence, and wall;
Snow is not welcomed by us all.

Some do battle the snow packed road;
Such as truckers with heavy load,
But for some of us—who at home can stay
We bid the troopers tarry, and play.

Enjoy the strong rhythm and building repetition of this next poem.

Christmas Lights
by Sara Taylor (age 9)

Lights in the window,
Lights on the tree,
Lights in the twilight,
Lights by the sea.
Lights, lights, lights wherever I can see.
Lights, lights, lights, they're twinkling at me.

Kristi also saw lights at Christmas, and more, giving her poem an element of contrast.

Christmas
by Kristi Kashner (age 8)

Christmas has snowballs
Christmas has stars
Christmas has holly
Christmas has Christmas trees
Christmas has lights
And most of all
Christmas has Jesus
      And Jesus has me.

Molly wrote this next poem while we were out in our van on a super highway and she noticed that there were fewer cars on the road than in the day time. Fortunately she found a scrap of paper and pencil—good things to keep in a vehicle if you want to nurture writers along!

Highway
by Molly Richman age 6

Rushing,
Rushing like a river.
But at the night
It goes slower—
That's what a highway is like.

Jacob began this next poem at a writing club meeting, during one of our writing "games"—here all the children were to write about a house. He later reworked his idea into this poem, creating a reflective mood, helping us all see and feel in a new way.

House
by Jacob Richman (age 9)

A house, a towering giant,
Never growing,
Making small movements
Which it has no control of.
Little movements—
    A door shutting.
Little sounds—
    A door slamming,
    The tinkle of a faucet dripping.
Little sounds.
What a giant—
But how helpless,
    How quiet.

Family life can inspire a poem, such as this one from Tim Kirkland. He'd just had a run in with his little brother, and is learning patience and forbearance. Writing can help us gain perspective—and some of you may want to remember this little poem for times when things get rough! In the following poem, Greg Darling captured what it's like to have a dog as a playmate in this next poem. Sounds just like some dogs I've known!

Little Brothers
by Tim Kirkland (age 9)

Sometimes a pain,
Other times a gain,
But they are so small
And you are so tall—
         It's not fair
         To be a grouchy bear
         With your little brother.

Trapper, Our Dog
by Greg Darling (age 12)

He likes to play with his ball everyday,
He likes me to scratch his belly,
But when he jumps up on my back,
He turns me into jelly.

I let him go, he runs all around,
And then a few hours later
I look around, he's nowhere to be found,
He's such a tardy traitor.

But in the next hours
He runs through the flowers,
And then he's home again!

The Lerew girls all learned about Haiku poetry from a family friend who first wrote a Haiku about all of them. The friend then explained a simple structure of this old Japanese form: 5 syllables in the first line, 7 syllables in the second line, and 5 syllables in the third line. They all tried their hand at it, including their mother. A parent's active involvement in her own writing, and sharing this with the children, is so often a help and encouragement. Gets us feeling both the exhilaration—and the insecurity and tentativeness—of creating and sharing. We wonder, maybe even anxiously worry, how our little efforts will be accepted by our children, and find that maybe because of that we are more ready to hear their works with loving hearts and cherishing—and excitement. I wonder if the Lerew girls also had a chance to hear some translations of Japanese Haiku poems, as their voices seem to match very well to the Japanese essence of capturing a small moment, seeing meaning in a fragment of life that might have just slipped by unnoticed.

Grammy's Good Glasses
by Dory Lerew (age 9)

We look everyplace
They are almost always gone
How will we find them?

The Small Bird will Sing
by Dory Lerew (age 9)

The small bird will sing
Beautifully all day long
Will you come and hear?

Do Not Eat the Core
by Jennifer Lerew (age 11)

> Do not eat the core
> Throw it outside your back door
> You see, it's a tree

This next poem gives me the same feeling as a Japanese Haiku, but without the strict syllable counts. April felt free to develop her own unique structure, but the essence of a brief surprise, a small epiphany experience, is the same.

Woodland Creatures
by April Blair (age 10)

Look!
See it?
Scurrying across the forest floor?
It's a chipmunk!
Look there!
White–tail deer prancing across the stream!

And here is a poem from someone else who also was surprised by suddenly seeing wild deer up close. I think she'd take this experience over the usual cartoons any day.

A Call to the Window
by Rachel Melis (age 10)

One Saturday morning watching cartoons
A call to the window we answer.
For there in the yard stand seven tall deer,
Staring, looking straight at us.
They pause for a moment
Then reach for the ground,
Nibbling the sprouts of new grass.
Then all in one bound they leap for the woods,
Leaving their beauty behind.

Jake and his sister Elisabeth live right under a wild geese fly way, and were able to capture the image of it in poems.

A Winter Dream
by Jake LaForet (age 12)

When winter's frosty bite chills
The darkened streets at night,
And all the stars that shine above,
Burn so fiercely bright,
The wind blows cold and the ground does crunch,
As I walk along the stream,
And the geese fly over from the lake,
To complete a winter dream.

Where Geese Fly
by Elisabeth Holly LaForet (age 8)

When winter comes and winds are cold,
And all the rivers freeze,
The geese fly south above our house,
They sail above the trees.
They make such noises as they fly,
Honk–honk each bird will say,
They follow their leader in a game
I think they like to play.

In this next poem, I especially like the echoing of the last line in
each stanza, and the repetition of the word "rustling" to give a calm
soothing effect, just like a breeze.

The Breeze
by Shaw Lynds (age 8)

Ask me a question,
I'll answer with ease.
My voice is like murmuring
Through the trees.

Do not fear,
The breeze is here.
Rustling, rustling
Through the leaves.

I especially like the spare form and strong rhythm of this next poem, all achieved without resorting to any rhyme scheme that might have trivialized the strong meanings and message.

My Father's Hands
by Amanda Strunk (age 12)

My father's hands are worn,
        cut,
        bruised,
        hurt,
        for me.

My father's hands are rough,
        callused,
        blistered,
        scratched,
        for me.

My father's hands are blemished,
        wounded,
        painful,
        injured,
        for me.

My father's hands are scarred with love
        for me.

The next poem also has a strong structure and rhythm that gives meaning and delight. Again, no rhyme was needed to help us feel that this is indeed a poem. The poem was first published in the children's section of our *Pennsylvania Homeschoolers* newsletter, the "BackPack," edited by Madalene Murphy.

City Rain, Country Rain
by Tracy Elizabeth Kuehne (age 10)

Rain on the apartment roof
Thunder bolting down!
Rain splattering on the cars,
Flooding the streets,
Running down the umbrellas
And all man's creation.

In the country, rain fills my ears
With a soft rainy lullabye.
It collects on the flower petals,
Making little pools.
It waters the grass and trees
And all GOD'S creation.

Molly wrote half of *Mazes* on her own one Saturday, and left her paper lying about in our project room. I spotted it on Tuesday, told her how much I liked her beginning, and she grabbed it to finish it up. She told me afterwards that the two poems just printed above were her inspiration for the structure of listing and contrasting. It shows again how hearing good writing can be the best inspiration for your own creative work. Molly thought about the wind with her second poem.

Mazes
by Molly Richman (age 6)

Mazes,
I mean *natural* mazes,
Like on trees,
Or when "Jack Frost" comes on windows too.

Mazes,
I mean *not* natural mazes,
Like on roads,
Or when you sew and your thread gets tangled up.

Mazes,
I mean all kinds
        of mazes.

Wind
by Molly Richman (age 6)

Wind, singing in the air,
As I hear it, I say:
"Who is singing, tell me?"
And then it goes away.

Christian Murphy in the next poem contrasts the natural world with
the man-made, creating strong images with layers of meanings. I'll
always think of Nathan Mellis's poem whenever I am tempted to
kick a lumpy old stone as I walk along a quiet dirt road. Could it be
a toad?

Poem
by Christian Murphy (age 14)

A silent natural missile
Gliding through the water
Non−destructive
Yet caged
A great swimmer
But confined
Unable to catapult at full speed.
Could you
If you are confined in walls of glass?

The real missiles
Are they caged?
Can they not exert
Full destructive power?
Yet we destroy the whales
Not the bombs.

Summer
by Nathan Melis (age 9)

Lying in the grass looking up into the sky,
Watching the birds that fly;
Getting up, walking along singing an old song,
Kicking a pebble on the road,
        That hops along like a toad.

Emily Murphy has worked as a volunteer at the fascinating Mercer Museum of American Life in Doylestown. She has been able to see the back storage rooms, cluttered with implements of past years, and out of that experience she was able to create this poem, again a poem of contrasts.

The Museum Warehouse
by Emily Murphy (age 16)

Thick black dust covers everything.
No housekeeper
Worth her weight in lead
Could allow her habitation
To get this filthy
Downstairs
Shelves full of knives, ladles, bowls and spoons
That will never hold another piece of food
And fire engines
That will never again fly down a street
Metal gleaming and bells ringing
With three snow white horses pulling
The pride of the Doylestown Number One Fire Company
Upstairs
Chairs that no one will sit on again
And cradles that no baby will ever cry in again
There is a sense of abandonment here
A need to be loved.

The final poems in this section are all by Sandra Blair, a young girl with a poetic vision let loose. Enjoy her images of nature. Her mother, Ann, writes that Sandra first learned to feel spontaneous with her poems and enjoy the act of composing and revision when she first tape recorded herself saying them aloud. Later the tape could be listened to and the poem transcribed. She has now compiled a whole book of poems, illustrated them in color, and given them as gifts to grandparents. Sandra has the fresh eyes of a poet, savoring whatever her day brings her.

Butterfly in the Garden
by Sandra Blair (age 7)

As the wind blows
A butterfly flies
As the hiss of the wind
Goes across the sky
The butterfly starts to land
On a rose
Near the end of the valley
Of rose petals
As the sun shines
That butterfly stayed
In the same garden
Of Always.

The Tulip of the Valley
by Sandra Blair (age 7)

As the sun shines on the tulip
As the wind blows
Clouds move
As my hand touches a petal
Of the tulip
The breeze blows
As the tulip starts to fall.

The Red Rose
by Sandra Blair (age 7)

The grass is sweet as the roses blow.
It's very nice.
The roses are tipping their petals
There are lots of things, there is more to it all.
It is a poem that I am telling
Of the sweet roses
It is a little rose that never tipped over
The grasses tipped
The sun is shining
All you have to do is shine when you are a sun
        .... when you are a sun.

10. Imagining
—Close to Home

I remember a few months back as I was reading over the submissions for this anthology. I was spending an evening trying to sort the pieces into categories for the different sections I was planning for the book. Here was a large pile of stories full with family life—stories about mischievious baby brothers and loved pets and getting lost, all clearly true stories that really happened. Here was another pile bouncing with talking frogs and fairies and princesses—clearly fiction.

And then I held another story in my hand and I didn't know quite where to put it. There weren't the obvious trappings of folk tale type fiction, and yet somehow I wasn't quite sure the piece was intended to be a family memory. Something told me maybe it was imagined, but imagined in this real world we all see around us rather than in a world you only find when you go through a magic wardrobe or when you get sent through a "wrinkle in time." I even found myself making a few phone calls over some of these pieces to check on their proper category, and I finally decided these close to home fictional stories needed a category of their own.

I realized that fiction writing can have many guises. It can seem so down to earth and plausible that we wonder if the story really did happen to the writer—it seems so clear that the writer is telling in sharp detail what has actually been lived through. The characters are contemporary, they live in neighborhoods like you or I do, they do everyday things.

Some of the stories I was sorting gave themselves away as fiction only because they were set in different time periods. Other than that, they ring true to life, and leave us wondering if the writer perhaps was related to the character—maybe she's writing down a true story her greatgreatgrandmother told her... You'll meet some stories like that here. Others are neighborhood mysteries or imaginings about animal friendships.

I decided to leave for the next chapter the fables and folk tale types of stories, the ones with not only animals doing the talking and thinking, but also maybe beans and almonds, binoculars, trees, and even a volcano on Antarctica. Fancy and whimsy take big turns here, and you can just feel the writers enjoying these tastes of freedom from day to day normality. I think that maybe these writers all look at the "real" world a bit differently after writing these pieces, beginning to see story ideas all about them, as if all the world is talking to them. Day to day moments become jumping off points to imagined dialogues and intrigues and plots. Simple objects or creatures become characters and personalities yearning to tell their sides of things.

It's certainly interesting to watch how different children react to the idea of fiction writing. Some dive into the fun of it immediately, rarely coming up for a breath of the "real world," while others shy away from it. For a long time my son Jesse resolutely stayed away from fiction as being too frivolous and ungrounded. He instead stuck to narrations about things that had really happened to him, and kept journal entries and wrote down nature observations. One of his early forays into fiction was actually made by simply writing *as a crayfish*. It was summer, and I'd suggested he write something about the crayfish that he'd caught in our creek. I was imagining an informative, maybe slightly humorous, essay about how he'd captured the creatures, set up his aquarium, read about crayfish, and observed their actions and interactions. After a short time of writing, I saw him start to really become absorbed in the task, pencil flying. He looked up in a while to tell me excitedly that he'd decided that a straight "report" would be deadly boring, so he was instead going to write from the point of view of one of his crayfish. And so his self-published book, *A Crayfish Abroad*, was born. In the later sequel to this first book, Jesse let the floodgates loose even more, and imagined whole crayfish governments and empires and dainty crayfish princesses.

We hope this and the following section open all of you up to the delight that fiction and imagining can be. It is certainly not the only type of writing that people can do, and some feel downright uncomfortable with its loose ends while it's being spun out. But these writers have all taken the leap of fiction, and I think you will all agree these writers have learned and gained, and that we're all richer for their wonderings.

Julie Hoerr's mother writes to say that Julie has always been homeschooled, and taught herself to read before any formal instruction was begun. Now a fourth grader, she reads every chance she gets, and often writes "for the fun of it." She often likes to write directly onto the family's computer, although she mostly prefers the time honored pencil. Typing is still a bit slow going for her. I think you'll be able to see how Julie has been able to use realistic fiction writing as a way of sorting out her feelings about new situations, a way of extending her empathy in her imagination.

The Strange Surprise
by Julie Hoerr (age 8)

I stood there and stared dumbly at the moving van as it moved swiftly down the road to the house next door. "I wonder if they have any kids," I said softly to my friend who stood next to me.

The door popped open and out came my little brother

Jason. "C'mon, Lizzy. Mom said to bring these to our new neighbors." I didn't blame him for wanting to go. He's only four!

I took the bag of just baked chocolate chip cookies from him and started over and almost at the same time said, "Wanna come with me, Meg?" I call Megan, my friend, Meg for short.

She sighed, squinted at the sky, looked at me, and said, "I guess."

So the three of us walked, what seemed like a mile to me, a few steps across the lawn and up the steps. I wondered if I would have to use the big, shiny knocker. Finally I found the doorbell and rang it. A girl about our age answered it. "Mother, door," she said. Her mother came up, stepped in front of her, and opened the screen door. I studied her carefully. She wore a dress, nylons, high–heels, and the ugliest, but sort of fancy, earrings. She said, "Hello, kids. Come in."

Their house was empty except for the carpet on the floor.

"H–here," I stammered as I handed her the cookies.

"Why, thank you! Did you make these yourself?" she asked.

I shook my head. "No–o–o." That time it came out clearly.

I turned around to look at the girl. Then my heart leaped into my throat. She was in a wheelchair! She must have noticed my shock because she motioned for me to come over. So I went over.

"I had a problem when I was born," she whispered. Everyone was leaving so I said good–bye quickly.

"Come over when you can. I live next door," I said.

Her mother smiled. "I'm glad you two are becoming friends."

I left quickly. "Friends?" I thought.

Well, an hour later she came over, and in the midst of playing Old Maid, I whispered to Megan, "I didn't expect to be friends with someone who is handicapped!"

The next two stories are both from the Crouthamel girls. When I wrote to the family asking for some background about how the girls had written such good pieces, their mother, Gail Crouthamel had much to share:

Anne (age 8), Robbin (age 7) and their sister Holly (age 5) have many individual interests, but their two greatest shared interests are reading and music. All three girls play the violin and piano. Anne and Robbin enjoy reading mysteries most of all. Probably the favorite part of the girl's day is "Free Reading Time," when each girl is free to read what she likes. I read aloud to the girls each day too. We watch practically no TV. The girls also have ample play time. For children, I think that the combination of plenty of enjoyable reading and enough time to exercise their imaginations through play, is great preparation for writing.

Anne and Robbin usually spend about 30–40 minutes each day working on their writing. In addition, they each keep a journal that they write a page of "what's new" in each day. Anne and Robbin have both really enjoyed some of the *Writing Strands* writing course assignments. One assignment suggested writing a story about walking along and hearing a noise. That assignment resulted in Robbin's story, "Surprise in the Field." The girls' stories are all fiction.

The procedure the girls use for writing a story is as follows:

1. Discuss what type of writing you will do and why, with Mom.

2. Think about what you would like to write about.

3. Write a rough draft in pencil.

4. Read story to yourself, plan where paragraphs would start, look for misspelled words.

5. Read story aloud to someone, change anything that doesn't sound the way you want it to by crossing it out or adding new parts.

6. Have Mom go over the story with you.

7. Recopy the story in cursive in pencil. Read a sentence then copy it, then reread it, to avoid the frustration of missed words before going on.

8. Share the story with someone!

Of course their Daddy is always interested in hearing the girls' stories. Also we recently started a "writing club" with the girls' cousins who also homeschool. Once a week the club meets and each child brings something they have written to read to the others. Everyone really seems to appreciate the positive feedback.

Anne and her sister Robbin both enjoy writing about getting new pets. When I asked the girls' mother if they did actually own lots of pets, I found out that writing was a sort of wishful thinking for the girls. "We have one pet, a dog named Willy. We'd really have to live on a farm to have all the types of pets that the girls crave!" Fictional writing like this can help us imagine as vividly as we can what it would be like to have our hopes come true. And who knows—these all *could* happen!

Jenny's Surprise
by Anne Crouthamel (age 8)

One day in late October, about 5:00 p.m., a little girl's mother told her that she should go out and get the mail. The little girl's name was Jennifer, but everyone called her Jenny. As she walked out to their mailbox, she shivered. It was getting windier and colder every second. It was also getting darker and darker by the minute.

When Jenny reached the mailbox she looked inside and there was no mail! She wished she had not come out to get the mail. Suddenly, she heard a little rattle coming from a trash can near the mailbox. She decided that it was probably a skunk or a raccoon. But, she wanted to find out what it was, so she went very quietly over to the trash can and looked inside.

It wasn't a skunk or a raccoon. It was a tiny orange–marmalade kitten!! Jenny picked it up out of the trash can and put it inside her jacket. Now she was glad she had come out to get the mail! She ran back into the house and she and her mother gave the kitten some cream and a basket with a soft cushion in the corner of their family room.

That night, Jenny's mother and father let her sleep downstairs with the kitten. Her mother and father said that they would put an ad in the paper the next day. So they did, it said:

FOUND: A small orange–marmalade kitten with a white spot on her head. To identify, call 297–8372.

After two weeks, no one had claimed the kitten. Jenny's mother and father said that she could keep the kitten if she took care of it herself. Jenny promised that she would. "Oh, thank you! Thank you so much!" she cried. "I have always wanted a kitten!" She named the kitten Cuddly, tied a big blue ribbon around her neck, and they had a party to celebrate.

After the party a man knocked on the door. He asked them if they had found the kitten he had left for them in the trash can. "Yes," said Jenny.

"Do you want it back?" asked Jenny's mother.

"No, I just wanted to make sure you got it," said the man.

"Hurrah!" shouted Jenny, "Cuddly is *really* mine!!"

Siblings hear each other's stories. Maybe you can see the influence of Anne's story on this one by Robbin.

The Surprise in the Field
by Robbin Crouthamel (age 7)

I was walking along in a field when I heard a noise. It sounded sort of like a puppy barking, but not quite. It was different from the beagle barks that I knew. "Oh, dear," I thought, "It might be a bear!" But it wasn't. I hid behind some bushes as the sound came closer. I was scared! I shivered. The sound came even closer. "Help!" I thought, "I must escape!" I looked around wildly.

Suddenly, I burst out laughing! Coming toward me was a puppy that looked so small that I thought he was just a few weeks old! He was a Boston Terrier. He was so cute! I picked him up. He was so, so, so cuddly! I took him to my house and my mother said that I could keep him if nobody claimed him.

My mother started to call people on the telephone. Everybody said, "No." But the last person she called said, "Oh, he must be from my dog's litter!"

"Would you like him back?" asked my mother.

"No," he said. "Besides, my dog had eight puppies, not including the one I just gave you." (I got on the phone just in time to hear all this.)

"Yay!" I shouted over the telephone, "The puppy is mine! Thank you so much!" After I hung up, I turned around and scooped up the puppy. "You're mine!" I told him.

The puppy snuggled against me and licked my cheek. "You are the best puppy in the whole world!" I said.

Stephanie worked long and hard to finish this next story about an imagined camping trip. Sometimes it is tempting to give up on a task when the going gets tough and the ideas are not coming just as easily as in the beginning. I applaud Stephanie for working through to the end, as she has created a fine and very funny story. I just hope the next *real* camping trip her family goes on is not as filled with mishap as this fictional one!

The Best Summer Ever
by Stephanie Maier (age 10)

"Hey, Dad, are we almost there yet?" I asked. "It's getting hot in here."

"Yes, almost there. Do you want the air on?" asked Dad.

"Yes," everyone said.

Dad, Rebecca, David, and I were going on a camping trip.

Mom was in New York visiting her mother so she wasn't able to come with us.

As we were driving along we went over a bump and all of a sudden a big green thing slid in front of the windshield blocking our view. We ran into the curb and we heard a swishing sound like air coming out of a tire. It was!

"Okay, everyone, out of the car."

When we got out we found that the tent which had been on

the roof, had slid in front of the window.

While David and Dad fixed the tent, Rebecca and I unpacked the trunk. It took half an hour. We finally got everything unpacked. When we got to where the spare tire was kept, it wasn't there. We all looked at Dad.

"Well?" we asked.

"I forgot to pack the spare tire."

"Great!" I said.

"Well," said Dad, looking at a road sign. "There's a gas station about a mile from here. Who wants to walk with me?"

I said I would. Some camping trip this was turning out to be.

As we walked, I asked if we were almost there yet.

"Yes, there it is," said Dad.

"Look," I said, "it's closed."

"Well, let's keep walking."

"Holy smokes!" said Dad as we came to another gas station. "We walked four miles."

Meanwhile, back at the car, another car had stopped with a man, a woman, and a dog.

"Having trouble?" asked the lady.

"Do you need some help?" asked the man.

"Woof," barked the dog.

"Well," said Bec (we always called Rebecca *Bec*), "we have a flat tire. My dad and sister went to the gas station."

"I see. I might be able to help you. Do you drive?"

"Yes," said Bec. She is 17, David is 13, and I'm 10.

"Well," the man said, "here's a spare tire if you want it."

"Oh, thank you so much, but would you be able to put it on the car for us?" asked Bec.

"Sure," the man said.

Soon the tire was on the car.

"Thank you again," said Bec.

"Good–bye," she said as she and David drove off.

Back at the gas station we were just about to buy a tire when I thought I saw a car that looked just like ours.

"Hey, Dad," I said. "Look at that car over there. It's just like ours. Even the people look like Bec and David, don't they?"

"Yes they do," he said and he turned away."

"Dad, look! They are Bec and David," I said as Bec got out and waved to us. Dad quickly paid for the tire and we ran over. "What are you doing here?" asked Dad as he packed the tire under the tent.

"Get in the car. I'll tell you all about it." We got in the car. Dad got into the driver's seat. As Bec and David told us what had happened I must have fallen asleep because the next thing I knew we were at the camp site.

After we unpacked and pitched the tent we took our hiking gear and went on a hike. After a while I said, "Dad, I'm tired and hungry."

"Yes, me too. Let's head back to camp."

After about an hour, I asked, "Are you sure this is the right way?"

"Of course," said Dad. "We won't get lost!" But we did! It took us two hours to find our way back to camp. When we got back we were so hungry that we had third helpings of our lunch. It was stuffed cabbage. (You don't usually have stuffed cabbage on a camping trip.)

After lunch it began to rain. There were lots of groans as we got into the tent. We played Monopoly until bedtime.

The next day was beautiful. We went fishing and caught lots of fish.

We were going to be camping for two weeks. After about

three days we noticed food missing. The next morning we found out why. Around 3:00 in the morning, a raccoon visited our campsite, took a banana, and knocked over some pots, and woke us up. Dad said that from now on the food stays in the tent.

The next two weeks sped by quickly but we had a lot of fun. We went on hikes and took a boat ride and the boat turned over. We all swam back to shore. That is, all except Dad. The current took him the other way and he kind of floated down a waterfall. It wasn't a big one and we found him down the other end of the lake. All too soon we were packing to go home.

In the car I fell asleep. When I woke up we were almost home. "Gee," I said, "this has been the best summer ever!"

"Yes," they all agreed.

"Home sweet home," I said as the house came into view.

"Home sweet home," everyone said.

Many kids seem to really enjoy reading mysteries, and for those children an ideal way to begin writing longer pieces might be to imitate the style of the books they so enjoy reading.

This first mystery was actually *not* directly inspired by mystery reading, as I found out when I asked Mark Lama to tell me a bit about himself as a writer. He wrote back the following:

> Since I began writing in the past two years, much of my writing has been voluntary. Usually the rule is that as long as I write, it's fine. However, I do write reports and business letters.
>
> I don't get ideas from books (or read mysteries). My stories and poems are usually under my own inspiration. The story I am working on now I thought up in the shower! It takes about two weeks to write, correct (I get some help from my mom with that),

and type my story. Poems take one or two days.

When I first write a story, I write fast, not worrying about punctuation or spelling, so I don't lose my ideas. I like to work alone in a quiet place. Concentration is important to me because I can write better. Distraction makes me lose my ideas. I don't like to get other people's ideas when I'm writing. I only like help with rewording and grammar.

I write almost every day. I think that the most important factor in learning to be a good writer is practice.

Notice how Mark mentions getting ideas even when he's not actually sitting down with pencil in hand. Some writers call this "writing without writing." Several other parents have written to say the same thing—that when their children write frequently and regularly, they begin spontaneously coming up with topics at any odd moment. The blank piece of paper is not a problem because the children actually have been thinking all day about new possible writing ideas. If children know that they will soon be writing again, and that they have control over what they write, then they begin to realize that almost anything in their lives can be a beginning idea. They begin imagining just how they might put a thought; they begin thinking like writers, ready to seize upon their fleeting ideas and make them concrete.

Mark's mother added that she also thought that one other ingredient in Mark's learning to write has been that he's read and listened to hundreds of good books. He has developed an ear for a story and how it can be put together.

The Case of the Pantry Raider
by Mark Lama (age 9)

Ira came in the kitchen and opened the pantry door. The potato chips were gone! Someone had been getting into the pantry. Ira ran out the door determined to find out who it was.

The first place he stopped was his friend's house next door. He said to his friend, "There is somebody raiding my pantry. Come help me find who it is." So Ira and his friend set out to find who it was.

At first they could not find anything, but then they saw a potato chip on the sidewalk. "A clue!" Ira shouted. They walked on. When they came to a wastebasket, Ira peeked in, and there was a potato chip bag! "Another clue," Ira said. "We must be hot on his trail." As they walked on, they saw some potato chip crumbs leading behind a house. Ira went up to the door and knocked. Nobody answered. "Oh, well, there's nobody home," Ira sighed. "Let's go back to my house." As they left they saw a boy walking quickly away from the house and down the street. "Hmm. Looks suspicious," said Ira. "We will continue the search tomorrow."

The next morning Ira went to get some chocolate chip cookies before he left. They were gone! That made Ira even more determined to continue the search.

He called his friend and said, "The chocolate chip cookies are missing. Meet me outside."

After they met they walked on the same sidewalk they followed the day before. Suddenly they saw a chocolate chip on the sidewalk. "We're on his trail again," Ira said.

As they walked they followed a trail of cookie crumbs and a few scattered chocolate chips. Then the trail abruptly cut across the street and disappeared in the grass about a hundred yards from the house they had come to the day before. Ira said, "I am going to go and knock again."

He did, and this time a woman answered. "Hello, ma'am. We're detectives. Has anything strange happened here?" they asked her.

"Yes," she replied. "My son didn't come home for supper last night and was missing again at breakfast this morning."

"Thank you," they said. Then they left.

Ira said to his friend, "Her son must be the one who is raiding my pantry."

"Why didn't you tell her that?" asked his friend.

"I didn't want to embarrass her," Ira said.

Just as he spoke a boy threw a chocolate chip cookie bag into a trash can. He walked towards the two detectives.

"Quick! Jump behind that tree! He hasn't seen us yet," said Ira. So they jumped behind the tree. Just as the boy reached the tree, they jumped out and blocked the sidewalk.

"Stop!" they said.

"What?" The boy looked up startled.

"Get him!" Ira said, and before the boy could say anything more, they took his hands and marched off in the direction of his house. As they walked Ira said to the boy, "We've caught you now. You were the one that stole things from my pantry." Ira added, "Your mother's been worried about you."

When they reached the house, Ira knocked. The woman answered.

"You found my son, you gallant boys. Come in and have some doughnuts." They were friends ever after.

Here is another mystery story. Noah has actually written three long mysteries all with the same children as detectives. He's found a secret that many writers love—the sequel! When children start writing and when they have say over topic choice and when they feel in tune with what they are writing about, they begin seeing more possibilities. The completion of one story stops being an ending, and becomes instead a jumping off place for the next adventure. Writing builds on writing.

High St. Detectives—*Volume 2*
by Noah Snyder (age 7)

Dad (Chuck) woke up and ate breakfast. For breakfast he had Nutra–Grain flakes and bananas. He wanted an apple... but where were the apples? There was the bag, but where were the apples? "Oh well," Dad said, "I'll have some fruited yogurt... Hi, Noah. How are you?

"Fine," answered Noah.

"Bye," said Dad as he went out the door to go to work. A minute later Dad flew into the house and he said, "Where's the car? Noah, have you seen the car?"

"No, where is it?" Noah asked.

"I don't know," Dad said.

"Where is Mike?" asked Noah.

"I think he is upstairs," said Dad, and Noah whizzed up the stairs. After checking upstairs, Noah whizzed back down and said, "He's not there."

Looking confused, Dad said, "He was there when I woke up."

Noah got an idea and said, "Do you suppose Mike stole the ca—?"

Suddenly Jesse, Noah's eight year old brother, interrupted. "HEY, Noah, let's go. It's time to go to our Little League game!"

Riding along on his bike, Noah noticed something. "What are those tire marks and that odd scrap of metal?" he asked.

Instead of answering, Jesse yelled, "Come on!"

Noah continued talking anyhow, "Those tire marks are heading toward the baseball game and they start where Dad's car was parked last night. Okay," muttered Noah, "We'll tell Kurt about these mysterious things when we finish the game."

(Kurt is Noah and Jesse's friend who lives up the street.)

After the game, Noah and Jesse were talking and Noah said, "What a great game... 700 – 0! I had 75 home runs! And your superduper stops at the plate kept them from even getting close, Jess!"

"HEY, there goes our car that was stolen," yelled Noah. "Signal Kurt on the walkie talkie," Noah commanded. While Jesse gave Kurt the message over his walkie talkie, Noah rode after the car.

Kurt and Jesse also took up the chase from different directions. Kurt took the alley instead of the road, so the car got away. So the three boys rode to Noah and Jesse's house. The boys asked if Kurt could stay with them for lunch. His mother said no.

While Noah and Jesse pigged out on ravioli, Noah said, "Maybe Mike took the apples and drove to school."

"But what was that scrap of metal?" asked Jesse.

"Maybe it was part of an experiment," suggested Noah. "You know how Mike is always doing experiments."

Noah and Jesse finished lunch and sat down on their front porch. Then Kurt came down to see them. "HEY, Kurt," said Noah, "Have you seen Alfie, the kid you said stole things from you?"

Kurt said, "Oh yeah, you're working on THAT again."

"Right," answered Noah. "Let's go."

"HEY, wait for me," said Jesse, as Noah and Kurt jumped on their bikes.

"Wow, you're fast!" Kurt told Jesse. "Jess is gonna be the first to the corner!"

"No, we'll tie——me and Jess," said Noah as he caught up to his brother.

Just in time Kurt caught up to the others and shouted,

"Three way tie!"

As a car drove by, Noah told Kurt to get the license number in case it would be a good clue. Kurt said, "I don't have our detective's notebook."

Noah handed the notebook to Kurt. Kurt wrote, "*596–HOME*, Minnesota plate."

"I think I know that plate," said Kurt.

"No wonder," said Noah, "It's a bicycle plate!"

"That's Alfie's bike plate," Kurt yelled.

"Dunt da dunt dunt, Dunt da dunt dunt da," Noah and Jesse sang the music used when clues are found.

"Fast," Noah told Kurt, "turn to page 3. Hand it to me. Let's get Dad."

Noah talked about the mystery with his dad, then came back out to Kurt and Jesse. Noah told Kurt, "Don't forget your—"

"What?" Kurt interrupted.

"—sister," Noah finished his sentence.

"Yeah," Kurt said, remembering that his sister, Angie, had stolen the ball in the last mystery case. "That's it!" cried Kurt.

"What is it?" asked Noah.

"That's why she was gone last night, and she brought home a car just like yours!"

"Or, maybe two blue VW vanagons were stolen yesterday," said Noah.

Joel, Noah and Jesse's six year old brother who was out playing with his friends said, "I think I have a clue!"

"What is it?" asked Noah.

"Yeah..." said Kurt.

"Come on, tell us," said Jess.

"Well, I saw somebody and he showed me something that he found on the street next to his neighbor's house. It said,

'XXY hidden at 35.' What does XXY mean? My friend thinks it means blue van because he's intercepted their codes a couple other times."

"You mean he's been in on other cases?" asked Noah.

"Yep, and found criminals," said Joel.

"Does he know the rest of the gang members?" said Kurt.

"You took the words right out of my mouth," said Noah.

"I guess you could go over to his club tomorrow night," suggested Joel.

"Come on, let's just go over to his house. Where does he live?" Jesse asked Joel.

"297 Queen Street," said Joel.

All the boys went to Joel's friend's house. Joel's friend, Mark, would only tell Joel the names of the thieves in the gang. He did not trust the other boys since he did not know them.

When the boys arrived home, Joel told the names of the gang members. Their names were Kristen, Luke, Matthew and Stephen. Mark also told Joel where this gang met. Since they met in Mark's neighbor's back yard, Noah, Jesse and Kurt, went to Mark's house again the night of the meeting. From Mark's bedroom they watched the meeting with special binoculars. These binoculars also had special auditory microphones that could pick up sounds from far away. So the spies could both see and hear the gang's meeting.

"I think it's Stephen," Joel says. "He's doing most of the talking.

Mark said, "Plus, he's the leader of the gang, I think. If they haven't changed it."

At the same time, Noah and Kurt both said, "Let's go get them before they leave the meeting."

"There's our stolen car!" said Noah.

"Let's see who gets in it!" said Jesse.

"Matthew did!" said Mark.

"We'll signal the police," said Kurt. "Then, during their next meeting, we'll work with the cops to corner the gang members."

After a few days, Joel burst out the door to tell Jesse, Noah and Kurt, "The meeting (panting to catch his breath) is this... afternoon!"

"Did you tell the police?" asked Noah.

"Yes, said Joel, "I just did."

"Let's go to the meeting."

As their meeting was ending, the boys ran down from Mark's room, burst into the meeting and caught Matthew, the car thief. Just then, the police came. "Hey, you got 'em! Good work!" said the police officer.

"I was just thinking of something," said the other officer while blocking the doorway so none of the gang could escape.

"You thought maybe you got the wrong gang," said Luke.

"Don't you think there must be more than one guy in on this crime ring?" continued the policeman.

"Yes... the whole gang should get it for organized crime," answered the cop.

"Oh no," groaned the gang members, "They got us. We've never been caught before."

"Now Stephen, since you are the leader, you'll come to my office and tell me all about this," said the officer.

When they arrived at the police station, the policeman took Stephen to his office. Detectives Noah, Jesse, Kurt, Joel and Mark overheard Stephen yelling, "That little boy, Mark! He intercepted our code that Matthew dropped out of a hole in his pocket. How does he always intercept our codes?"

"I don't know," said the police officer, "but our town is very lucky to have detectives like Noah, Jesse, Kurt, Joel and Mark.

That closed the second mystery solved by the High Street Detectives.

Mary Tisdale has tackled a very hard topic—writing about a little girl's experience with loneliness and abandonment in the year 1884. I think you'll agree that she does a remarkable job of creating unique characters and gives us the rich details to help us feel empathically into the situation. Contrast this Christmas with the Tisdale family Christmas traditions described by Mary's brother in the family newsletter section. I think writing this piece, and so vividly imagining another person's life in such stark contrast to her own, probably helped Mary really appreciate the many important gifts she has in her family and home.

A Very Sad Christmas
by Mary Tisdale (age 10)

Riding in a carriage was a beautiful, petite girl with green eyes, coal black hair and very dark skin. As the little Black girl arrived at the white house in which she was to stay, she set her eyes hard on the woman near the doorway. All the girl's belongings were taken in by the driver and set on a thickly padded red chair nearby, and the girl was left standing alone by the door.

The woman shoved the girl inside the doorway and said, "What is your name?"

The four–year–old girl looked frightened but answered slowly, "My name is Rebekah Love."

"Well," the lady commanded, "Go put your clothes in the first room you see."

"Yes, Ma'am," Rebekah said meekly. She pulled her bags up the stairs and found her room was on the left. The bed was in the corner of the room, and running to it, she sobbed, "Oh, Mommy, why did you send me here? Why did you have to die?"

She sat up and looked about her. The room was very dirty and had junk on the floor. Not wanting to put her clean clothes in the filthy drawers, she went down and said, "My room is dirty."

"I know," snapped the woman. "Go and get on an old outfit."

The girl looked frightened by the woman's voice and quickly ran up the stairs. The woman followed with the bucket and box. When Rebekah had finished putting on her oldest clothes, which were a red shirt and blue slacks, she put on a spotted blue bonnet and a pair of socks and shoes. She looked far different from the lady who was standing behind her with the bucket and box. That woman was wearing a flowered pink dress, a small pink cap on her head, and high black shoes.

Now, since Rebekah was dressed, she took the bucket and asked, "What am I to do with the bucket?"

"Clean the drawers, of course," the lady answered.

"Oh," said Rebekah sarcastically.

"Well, get going," said the lady descending the stairs.

Rebekah did not know how to scrub very well, so you can guess how well she did the drawers. She managed to do as well as she could and put her clothes in them. Then, she walked around picking up all the junk.

It was soon supper time and the bell rang. After supper the young lady said, "Go outside if you have finished your room."

"All right," replied Rebekah. As Rebekah got on her coat she thought about how cold it was. It was a very cold December day. Since it was December 23, 1884, Rebekah knew it was almost Christmas. But she also noticed that there were not any Christmas decorations anywhere. At her home they had had lots of decorations.

Before long it was bedtime, and Rebekah went in to warm up before she got on her blue nightgown. That night she cried herself to sleep.

In the morning she was in a happy mood and got dressed while humming a tune she had heard in her church. It was Christmas Eve, so she outfitted herself in a blue dress, because at her home she had always had to dress in blue. She found her good high black shoes. Then she ran downstairs for breakfast. The lady was wearing a white and blue striped dress.

"There's your breakfast," the woman said, not even looking up from the cereal she was eating.

Rebekah looked at the cereal before her, wondering what it was. She looked at the lady ahead of her and saw that she was heartily eating her breakfast. Then Rebekah sat down and ate her breakfast quickly. She was looking forward to evening and was excited about it.

After breakfast Rebekah hurried outside, so she could get away from the grumpy lady. But she had not been out there very long when the lady called her in. Wondering what she wanted, Rebekah followed her up the stairs. The lady had just walked into the room when she started talking.

"I want you to put on a red dress because red is brighter. We are going over to a friend's house until tonight," she said, walking out of Rebekah's room.

Rebekah soon had on the red dress. In a few minutes the lady came from her room and, calling Rebekah, went outside.

The lady's friend's house was very boring to Rebekah. There was absolutely nothing to do but sit. At lunch she had plenty to eat, but the food was insipid to Rebekah. Soon it would be time to sit again, Rebekah thought, but surprisingly the friend said, "Go outside for a while and play."

Rebekah agreed readily and slipping on her coat ran eagerly outside. Play did not last long, for soon she was called inside because it was time to go home. At home she and the lady made ready to go to church. Rebekah was so tired she did not want to go. She did not enjoy church as much as she thought she would. On the way home she fell asleep, but was jerked awake when the horses stopped. The minute she got in the door she slipped on her nightgown and went to bed.

Christmas Day always brings thoughts of family, and that was why the lady did not see Rebekah until the latter part of the morning. Rebekah had busied herself in her bedroom as much as she could, and then when she had nothing more to do, she went downstairs where her very cold breakfast was waiting. Not knowing what to do after breakfast, Rebekah wondered if the lady was in a good mood and would give her presents. However, when Rebekah asked the lady, she replied, "What presents are you talking about, Rebekah?"

"Why, of course the presents we always get on Christmas," answered Rebekah.

"Well, you're certainly not getting any this Christmas," replied the lady. Loneliness and sadness were the only gifts that little girl had on her fourth Christmas.

And here is a story of someone overcoming loneliness through a surprising companion—a bear. Micah Latinette had the chance to work on this story over quite a long period of time, and get feedback from other homeschoolers at our regular writing club meetings. He has just begun to type directly into the family's computer word processing program, and finds that is *much* easier than writing things out long hand. I am sure that all the wonderful read aloud books Micah and his family have shared over the years have helped Micah grow as a writer; he has those books rambling around in his mind as he works on his own stories. I think you'll agree that Micah's story is a very tender evocation of friendship between people and wild creatures. Many of the children in our writing club appreciated that the ending was happy, but not *overly* happy. And in case you're wondering, Micah does live out in the country and does love horses and riding, but he does not have a bear—yet!

Bear Story
by Micah Latinette (age 8)

Early one morning I was riding through the woods. I heard something far away. It sounded like thunder. I looked at the sky but it was not lightning because the sun was shining brightly. Then I turned around and saw something that was unusual. It was a herd of wild horses! They were thundering across the meadow and coming right towards me!! Quickly I grabbed my lasso and hid behind the clump of blackberry bushes. Just as I got behind the blackberry bushes do you know what I saw? A grizzly bear devouring the ripe berries! I quickly lassoed the bear. It tried to get away but I had tied the end of the lasso to a tree. It was running around the tree and got caught in the rope.

I walked out of the bushes. Where was my horse? He must have run away with the wild horses. How am I going to get the lasso off the bear? The bear was not struggling anymore. It started to unwind so the rope was long enough that the bear could reach me where I was standing next to the berry bushes.

I got ready to run, but I knew that the bear would chase me so I decided I would play dead. The bear rolled me around. It tickled a little bit. It seemed like the bear was tame. I knew that the bear could not be tame, but he did not hurt me. I wondered why the bear was walking around me.

I got up very carefully—the bear licked me! I untied the rope from the tree. I was hoping that the bear would run away through the woods. I wondered what it was going to do so I watched him. He was watching me. We watched each other for awhile. He walked towards me sniffing my boots. I saw that he was friendly, so I began to walk home. The bear started to follow me home to my house! I had to walk backwards so I did not have to turn around to look at the bear to see if it was still there.

I have a little house with five windows and three rooms. But I did not want to put the bear in the house because it was too big and would get into everything, especially food. I thought that he could stay in the corral. I led the bear to the fence; he didn't even pull on the rope. On the walk home the bear had been quite happy. He seemed anxious to get some food.

The next day I was making his food. It was dry bread and honey with milk. I was wondering if he was still there. I looked out the window—sure enough, he was laying down on the grass. When I got to the bear, it stood up and let me pet him.

After he ate I took him for a walk. I did not bother to close the gate of the corral since my horse had run away with the wild horses. When we started it was fun. The bear would run around me, tangling me up. So I named him Twister. Twister seemed to be having a good time.

We came to a huge meadow. We saw something moving around in the meadow. It looked like the horses that my horse had run away with!! I left Twister in the woods. I got on the ground so they could not see me. Since I did not know what I was going to do I lay on the ground. I thought that I could scare the horses to my house and have Twister keep the horses by the corral. They would be afraid of him and they would run in and I could close the gate.

My rope was on Twister. I had to get my rope so I crawled quietly to Twister. He was sniffing at the horses. Quickly I untied the rope. I got back on the ground and started to go back to the place that I had been hiding.

I was looking at the horses but I felt something on my back. It felt like something sniffing my back. I turned around and Twister was there. I took him to the woods and left him there and I crawled back. The horses were eating the grass. I started to crawl around the clearing.

I was about to the horses when I looked back at the woods and I saw Twister in the woods making noises. He was walking over the leaves. If he scared the horses they would run away in the wrong direction. Maybe I could take Twister to the other side of the clearing. If I tried to get to Twister the horses would see me.

I had to do it. It would be hard. I tried to think of a way to get Twister back to the other side of the clearing without the horses seeing us. I tried to think of an idea, but I had to do it quickly because the horses might run. So I crawled back to the woods.

But where was Twister? I looked everywhere but he was not there. I was so sad I couldn't do anything. So I went home.

I did not want to make any lunch, so I just sat there. But later I did take a walk. It was not the same without Twister. So I did not do anything.

In the evening when it was a little bit dark I heard something. It sounded like someone walking through the woods. I knew nobody would be outside. I went outside just to make sure but there was no one there but me, so I went back in the house.

The next morning it was a nice sunny day. So I took a walk—then I heard the sound again. I snuck to the woods and there was Twister! I ran over to him. "Twister, you came back! Where were you?" He just looked at the house. "So, you want something to eat. All right, you can have some." We walked off to the house happily together.

Matthew Formica is an aquarium buff, and has learned a lot about the ins and outs of keeping fish. How to communicate that in writing? Instead of just sharing his knowledge in a factual essay, he decided to create a fictional story using all that he knew about fish. What a good idea!

Once Upon a Fish
by Matthew Formica (age 11)

As the intoxicating sounds and smells filled John's heart and brain, he knew that he could easily spend hours at the pet store.

His dad had promised him a fish tank with some beautiful tropical fish for his birthday, and today, March 5, 1989, was it! He knew that he would enjoy his fish. He also knew that everyone always teased him about how he always started projects and never finished them.

He had a brother and two sisters, all of them younger than himself.

John hoped that he could get set up and settle down with his fish within two months. You see, there was a contest for kids that were beginner fish keepers. The prize was five hundred dollars! He would buy himself a new bike with it if he won.

His father had said that he could go to the pet store by himself.

"Hi, young man, and what may you want?" said one of the workers in a great booming voice. "No, no, don't tell me. Let me try and guess. Do you want... a Sting Ray? No, no, too dangerous. Do you want... a job? No, no, you're too young. Then what do you want?

"Um... er, sir..." stammered John.

"Well, come on, boy! Speak up, speak up!" the worker boomed.

"Well, sir, you see, it's like this. I would really like to start a freshwater aquarium."

"I can get you started! By the way, what is your name?"

"My name is John, sir. What is yours?"

"Oh, you can just call me Mike."

Mike got John supplied with all that he would need to get his tank running. John got such things as an under gravel filter, a Whisper brand air pump, and some brown and blue gravel. As his father later said, "With all the gadgets you can buy, you barely have enough money left to buy any fish!"

Oh, the days passed quickly for John. Between going back and forth to the pet store for supplies, going to school and doing his homework, he worked feverishly on his fish tank. His dad helped him some, too. It takes a few days to about a week after setting up the tank for the good bacteria to start growing and the tank to start becoming stabilized.

A few days after setting up the tank, something strange happened! John was looking at the empty water in his tank and was hoping that he could get some fish soon. Then he noticed that the water was all milky! He rubbed his eyes, hoping against hope that they were just playing tricks on him.

When he looked again, the water was still slightly milky-white! He ran to his dad. His father had told him never to interrupt him when he was working except if it was an emergency. Boy, was this one!

"Dad, Dad, come here!" John yelled to his father who was writing a report.

"How many times have I told you to never come and interrupt me?" said John's father.

"Many times, Dad, but this is really important. The water in the fish tank is sort of whitish!"

"What!!! What did you say? How in the world did your breakfast milk get in the fish tank is what I would like to know!" said John's father.

"I didn't stick my breakfast milk in my fish tank!"

"Oh, well I am sorry. Let's go look in your book about fish and see if it can tell us what this is all about," his dad said. They realized that it was fine that the water was milky, since it was only a few days after they had set up the tank and the bacteria had not settled yet.

A few happy days later, John's mom took him to the pet store. Mike, who was now John's good friend helped him pick out four Zebra Danios (small fish with stripes). Sadly, though, one of them died. When he checked the PH (how acid or alkaline the water is) it was seven point four! That is way too alkaline for Zebra Danios! After lowering the PH, be bought more fish.

As the weeks flew by, John started teaching his fish some tricks. He would need to if he was going to get anywhere in the contest that was coming up.

Before he knew it, it was the day of the contest! The morning dawned bright and cheery. By the time his mother had driven him to the school where the contest was, he was in fine spirits.

The contest required every contestant to have his fish do tricks for five minutes with special lighting of their choice. Then, the five judges give the contestant a rating between 1.0 and 10.0, with ten as the best.

The contest was to take place in the school auditorium. There were two contestants before John, and when his turn came, surprisingly, he was not very nervous.

He had his three fish jump from one tank into another. The judges were not very impressed. Then, John tapped on the glass three times. The fish started doing flips in midair while jumping from tank to tank! The judges started whispering and pointing together. Then John tapped the first tank once. The fish used their bodies to bring a piece of coral up to the surface where they flipped it up out of the water to him!

After John's turn, there was about fifteen other contestants, and it was difficult for John to wait. Finally, the winner was announced! John's heart fell to his feet when he heard that he was *not* the winner. He started to walk away, when he heard the loudspeaker boom, "and in second place is a fine young man named John. Thank you, John, for a great performance."

John's heart jumped back up into place. He had won second prize! That was two hundred and fifty dollars! John was so happy that he felt like flying.

When one of the judges handed him a trophy, John was so happy that he dropped it twice.

On the way home,][ZYCQRSUWV6?2m3A@;wld do with the money. He would not buy a new bike. John decided that he liked fish keeping so much that he was going to use the money to buy more fish and equipment.

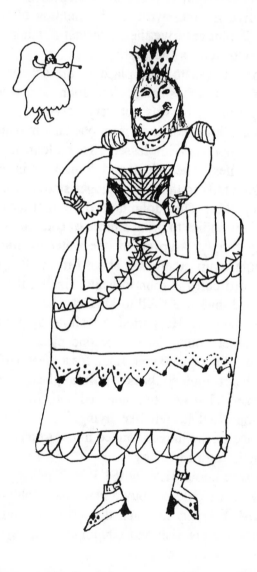

11. Imagining
—Whimsy and Wonder

In thinking about the type of imagination needed for the more whimsical fictional stories included in this chapter, I found myself thinking again and again of the charming story Christine Wilkie, a homeschooling mother of four children, once shared in our newsletter. Her 8 year old son had just taken an achievement test and had apparently missed all of the questions dealing with "ability to differentiate fact from fiction." Christine wrote:

> This last spring, what I believe to be an important insight was gained during our annual standardized testing at home. I review my children's tests before sending them back to be evaluated, and in the reading comprehension section of Aaron's test (Aaron is my second child, who was eight years old when he took this test) was the following:
>
> > In each group of sentences below, put a mark by the sentence which tells about something that could happen.

Then came the sentences:

> a) A bus enjoyed its lunch.
> b) The letter arrived yesterday.
> c) The tree decided to take a bath.

Aaron's response to this first group was, "a) A bus enjoyed its lunch." I was a little concerned that such an easy exercise should have been answered "wrong." Had Aaron misunderstood? The next group read as follows:

a) The soup was greedy.
b) The jewels dug a hole.
c) The rooster crowed at dawn.

Aaron's answer: "b) The jewels dug a hole." I was beginning to get worried now. What had happened? Why these "wrong" answers? The next sentences were:

a) The people sold food.
b) The fence went fishing.
c) The bird caught the bridge.

This time, Aaron's answer was "c) The bird caught the bridge." Oh, no! I was really in a fright by then. What was wrong? Was my son learning disabled all this time and I never knew it? Was he "acting out" his underlying disgust at taking these tests (even though he was telling me he didn't MIND taking them!)? Was he suffering from delusions—some deep seated problem with perceiving reality? What was happening?

As calmly as possible, even managing a tremulous smile, I called Aaron and showed him the part of the test I was reviewing. "Aaron, these answers are very, uh, interesting— could you explain them to me?" I asked nonchalantly. "How can a bus enjoy its lunch?"

Aaron looked at me very matter-of-factly and said, "Its gas! A bus would enjoy its GAS for lunch." Then it hit me. Aaron had focused on the word "could" in the directions, and in the world of a voracious reader who is as imaginative as children come, a world that still has fairy tales, monsters and a little bit of magic, all kinds of things *could* happen. And for all that his answers weren't what could *really* happen, they made perfect sense in his child's way. What eight-year-old isn't still hearing and seeing stories with horses that talk, machines with big eyes and smiles, and lamps that grant three wishes? I was relieved, and happy. I liked Aaron's answers.

I asked him about the others. "Well, if jewels are sharp, they can be used to dig a hole in the ground, can't they?" was his explanation for the second "wrong" answer. I was still puzzled about this bird catching a bridge business. Aaron explained, using his fingers as a bird's talons to illustrate, "If the bird was flying, and landed on a part of the bridge like this," and he made a grabbing motion with his hand, "You could say it caught the bridge!"

By now I was smiling. How many times had I read literary metaphors that would describe a certain action or scene in just this manner? I told Aaron that his answers were very creative. I was more than satisfied with his answers now that I understood them, because I felt they evidenced an imagination and perception beyond the superficial viewing of things. However, I knew that when I returned the test, those answers would be marked "wrong" by a computer, somewhat lowering his over-all reading score, and no one evaluating such a test without knowing Aaron would ever see what I would say were thoughtfully creative perceptions overriding a fill-in-the-blank-space world.

How wonderful that our children do *not* have to spend their lives in "fill-in-the-blank-space worlds." Our children have the chance at home to let their minds make unusual connections, open ended connections, and fit puzzle pieces together in new ways that don't match a preset frame of reference. They don't have to be always mechanically sorting out fact from fancy in separate, never to overlap categories. Instead they can imagine and invent and melt together what they know with what they wonder about.

Writers seem to always love the fun of imagining they are something else, seeing the world through new eyes, even through things that we don't normally think of as having eyes. This has a long tradition in literature written for children, also. Hans Christian Anderson loved to use this device to the fullest, becoming fir trees, tin soldiers, spoons, and more, and children seem to love the chance to try this out for themselves.

I know that, in our homeschooled children's writing club, this sort of writing is often very "contagious"—a child usually catches onto the fun of this approach from hearing another child's experiment. Hope you catch the idea from Sunshine. And watch out—you may not be able to look a bite of chili in the eye again after reading this story!

Teeney's Journey Through Life
by Sunshine Civitarese (age 9)

I am a kidney bean. My name is Teeney.

I have five brothers and sisters, and I would be lonely without them. My favorite brother's name is Beaney. We are identical, and we are kidney beans too! I could not get along without Beaney. So, where you see Beaney, you see me.

I am getting bigger, and there is a rumor that we will be picked soon. (What does *picked* mean?)

Now I am two weeks old and it is 3 o'clock, then—my house is shaking, moving, HELP!!!

Beaney says, "I think we are being picked and I do not like it!"

I said, "I don't like it either, and to think I've been looking forward to it!"

And then a bright flash of light and I'm being taken out.

"Good–bye Beaney!" I cry.

"Wow, this world is big," says someone beside me. I turn and look.

"Beaney! I thought I'd never see you again!" I cried.

Now I am in a very small container in a very cold thing. (I think it is a refrigerator, but I'm not sure.)

I start whining.

"Oh, hush," says Beaney. Because he is older than me. Iguess he knows better, so I hush.

We are all put in a pot, some white stuff and some gooey stuff added, and then cooked. I hated it all. It really hurt to be cooked.

Hey! Now we are all mixed up into chili!

Then I find myself looking into a little girl's face. "Yum! this is great chili!" she says.

It hurts to be eaten, but I am glad the girl won't starve.

Sunshine wrote back to me when I asked her to tell about herself as a writer. Her letter follows, and gives further insight into how she goes about the work of writing. You'll notice, too, how her fictional story grew from an actual experience.

How I wrote Teeney's Journey
by Sunshine Civitarese (age 9)

One, day, when I was in the garden weeding, I started thinking about how a bean would feel as it got picked, shelled, and finally eaten. Maybe I could make a story out of that, good enough to be published! I thought about my idea a few days, then one evening sat down and wrote, "Teeny's Journey Through Life." My mom helped with grammar, spelling, etc.

I like writing, but like it best when I do it of my own choice, not when Mom tells me to. I write about my family sometimes, but most of the time I make things up. My favorite things to write are poems, limericks, and even some knock–knock jokes.

I have been homeschooling since I was five. One of the reasons I like homeschooling is because I don't have to follow the textbooks all the time. If I am interested in the human body, I don't have to wait until I get there in the science book, Mom just takes me to the library and we look it up together. I think homeschooling is fun, and I hope more people will be doing it soon.

And here is another story of the journey food goes through to get to our table—but this little almond doesn't exactly want to get eaten! I can imagine Emilie asking her mother where almonds come from after a shopping trip to their food co–op, and her mother's response touching off this delightful story.

Jack Almond
by Emilie Smith (age 8)

Once there was an almond growing on a tree. His name was Jack. All of a sudden a boy climbed up the tree and shook the branch where Jack was hanging. The boy climbed down the tree and picked up the almonds that had fallen off. He took them to a truck and put them in. The truck drove to a food co–op. There someone ordered the bag of almonds that Jack was in. The bag was taken to a truck. The truck drove to the house that the bag was supposed to go to.

The next day the almonds were put in a pan, and the pan was put on the stove. The almonds started to fry. But Jack managed to jump out of the pan. He jumped off the stove and into the garbage. It started to stink.

One day the garbage was picked up and put in a big truck. The truck drove to a dumpster. While the men were taking the bags out of the truck to the dumpster, Jack jumped out of the bag and ran back to where the tree was that he grew on. And there he settled down in the grass—and sprouted!

Sometimes these types of "first person" stories can take the form of a riddle, often a good beginning place for younger writers, but great fun for all ages. Here is one by Jeremy Fisher.

What Am I?
by Jeremy Fisher (age 7)

I have four eyes like lenses. I help people see things that are far away. Sometimes people hang me on something they call their necks. When they need to see things that are far away they look straight into my eyes and turn something like a dial.

I have many brothers. I am camouflage color, but some of my brothers are black, blue, or brown. People use me when they go hunting, at baseball games, and for bird-watching.

What am I?

(Answer: binoculars)

Jeremy's older brother, Joshua, also enjoys writing in the first person from a "thing's" point of view. Here's one everyone at our writing club enjoyed. My favorite part is the one thousand fingers!

The Tree
by Joshua Fisher (age 8)

Hello! I am a tree. My name is Bark. I have 50 arms and 6 toes and 1,000 fingers.

Here come some people with boards, nails, hammers, a screw driver and other tools. They are putting something on me. I wonder what they are going to do? I hope they won't hurt me.

Ouch! Eech! Yow! Help! These people are giving me splinters. The thing they are building is starting to look like a little house. The building is done.

Here come some children. They are going in the little house. They put a sign on it and it says:

C–L–U–B H–O–U–S–E

H–m–m, I wonder what that means?

Our writing club once challenged everyone to write about Antarctica, a topic we were all studying in our homes during the Trek Across Antarctica Exploration. I asked the kids to write from the point of view of something or someone from the continent, animal, human, or inanimate object. When we read them aloud, everyone had to guess who or what was doing the telling. Here are some samples of those pieces, written very quickly under a 15 minute time limit.

What am I?
by Ian Latinette (age 14)

Brr! It's freezing here in Antarctica. I really don't like it here, but since I can't fly or swim, I can't ever leave. I am unusual in being the only member of the Drosphilae family to live in this cold wilderness. Excuse me, my teeth are chattering so much I can hardly talk—this weather is enough to freeze your wings off! But enough talking, get inside before you solidify. Nice talking, bye!

(Answer: the wingless fly of Antarctica)

What am I?
by Jacob Richman (age 9)

I had lived a quiet peaceful life until now, when a small hairy thing fell into me and gave me a large scratch, as well as pouring a lot of cold snow into me. It feels like when you put a pipe cleaner in your mouth and turn it around five times! So over all I think this Trans–Antarctica Expedition has caused me too much hassle to be worth anything at all.

(Answer: a crevasse——which one of the sled dogs has just fallen into!)

What am I?
by Jesse Richman (age 12)

A little bit ago (a few million years) I was in a forest. That was when I was in my prime and I hardly noticed the telltale signs that it was getting colder. Years came and went and it got still colder. Animals started to go to the sea. I just sat and smoked. Ice came and covered everything except for me. I just sat and smoked. The ice is still here, and I still smoke. What am I?

(Answer: Mt. Erebus, the only active volcano in Antarctica)

What am I?
by Molly Richman (age 6)

I was just sitting happily beside my mom when I ("Help!") started to ("Mommy!") sail away. Then I came into a little nursery which was being invaded! And then the murderer came, for guess who? Me!!! Then with the most vicious manner crunched me up!! And all I could remember from then on was being EVERYWHERE.

(Answer: a piece of the huge ice shelf breaking off, crumbling, and finally melting, and so being "everywhere")

What am I?
by Laura Speck (age 12)

I was just sitting there nice and peacefully with people passing by not often, maybe once or twice a week since it was so cold. When out of nowhere there came a group of men with dogs and they came right up to me, touched my head with a hard, cold hand (not saying that I was hot or anything—it was just quite a surprise to me). It did not seem much of a surprise to all of the men or to any of the cameras or tape recorders. But I was glad, do not ask me why, because I don't know.

(Answer: the actual south "pole" when the explorers reached it——there really is a funny barber shop style pole with a big mirror ball on top to mark the spot!)

What am I?
by Autumn Speck (age 10)

One cold summer day I was lying quite still when all of a sudden something stepped on me and then a whole bunch of things stepped on me and then something else slid on me and then it was over. And as I layed there, I thought that maybe someday it would happen again.

(Answer: snow, with the expedition moving over it and passing on)

Next is a very well developed and delightful piece by Will Moffat, showing how this "first person" idea can continue with older writers. Will is part of a weekly group for junior and senior high school students in home education programs, and they often work on writing as part of their activities together. Will's mother, Judy, writes to tell how this story came about:

> This was an exercise in descriptive writing inspired by *Free to Write* by Roy Peter Clark. After reading several examples to Will and the kids in our group, they wrote paragraphs about themselves as inanimate objects which they shared the following week. Prior to beginning the first draft he jotted down any inspirations he had about the object he would be. Will and I worked on the revisions together. I would read his rough draft back slowly to him and he'd interject where he'd want a change. He also worked on revisions himself. I'd also give my thoughts about the changes he'd made.

My Life as a Goodyear
by William Moffat (age 14)

Hi, I'm a Goodyear tire and I would like to tell you my devastating life story. But let me get one thing straight: the only "good year" of my life was when I was fluid inside that beautiful Central American rubber tree. After I was sucked out of it and frozen into a ball, my happiness ended.

At some Goodyear tire factory, I was boiled at such scorching temperatures that I thought I would evaporate. Unfortunately for me, I didn't. I was then mixed with other chemicals and poured into a donut shaped mold. When I had dried, my new form was unconcernedly popped out and thrown to the floor. That didn't tickle, as I was stiff enough as it was.

Anyway, I was sent to the inspector. First the heartless guy tossed me into a sunlamp chamber where I felt like I was going to crack or peel apart. After I was taken out of there, that lead–hearted inspector put me into a deep freeze. I wasn't ready for that since I was from Central America.

I survived though, and was stamped and sent to the shipping department, and from there to a Goodyear tire mart. There I was tossed onto some cold, rusted, steel hooks to await my fate.

After about a week of hanging mercilessly, I, along with three others of my size, were sold to some teen–age boy with a bright yellow convertible. The man who ran the tire mart put me on a funny looking machine. The next thing I knew I was being stretched to amazing lengths. A rim was placed in my middle making me solid. A hose was then fastened to a little projection on my body. I then began expanding until I was so full of air that I could have blown out the Great Fire of San Francisco! A cylindrical metal object was then attached to the little projection which I have learned is a valve. Involuntarily I blew into it. Part of it slid outward. The tire man unattached it, studied it, and grunted in satisfaction. A little plastic cap was screwed onto the valve. The other three tires received the same treatment.

That done, we tires were placed onto the yellow car's axles. The teen paid the man (I still don't believe I was only worth sixty dollars!), and with we four tires part of his dream machine, screeched onto Route 30.

Well, that kid drove too fast. Once he came suddenly to a *Stop* sign. He stopped so fast that we four tires slid and received the biggest brush burns of our lives. He "peeled out" when he started up again and that didn't help those brush burns at all. At his house his family all complained that we smelled like burnt rubber.

After two years of sliding and peeling out, we tires were thrown away. While we were awaiting the trash man, a blue van with a family inside stopped by us. A tall man who I heard the family call "Rich," came over to look at us. He picked my up and hoisted me into his van. If he was rich like the family said he was, I wondered why he didn't just buy a new tire. In the family's basement, I was cut in half with two thin rings attached to me on either side. Then I was roughly turned inside out, bolts were pounded into me, chains were fastened to those, and bright yellow nylon ropes tied to the chains. I was being made into a tire swing, to my dismay. I was taken far into the family's backyard and hung on a thick, black walnut tree branch. I was pretty popular those first few days, but am now hardly used at all. Now I am just mercilessly hanging there by those chains and bright yellow ropes, which remind me of that horrid Corvette and reckless kid. And if the word "reckless" meant "having no car accidents," it was the wrong description for that teen-ager.

Now we move on to fable and folk tale type stories. I enjoy the happy ending of this next story, and the simple kindness shown by the old man and the grateful heart of the crow. It has the flavor of an old fable to me—with the modern addition of a veterinarian!

The Poor Crow
by Hope Tobey (age 10)

Once upon a time there lived a crow, and an old man. One day the crow fell from his perch in a tree. The old man, named Harvey, found the poor crow, and took him to a veterinarian.

The vet said that the crow had laryngitis, and that there was really nothing he could do for the crow. So Harvey took the crow home.

When they reached home, Harvey asked the crow, "Would you like to live in this tree above my pond?"

The crow nodded his head, yes.

Charley the crow lived in that tree for many years.

One day Charley ate something that he had never seen before. Something growing by the edge of the forest, which was at the edge of a dandelion patch, which was at the edge of the pond.

All of a sudden Charley could speak again. So Charley went to search for the old man, Harvey. When he found Harvey he said, "Thank you for letting me stay here, and get well. Now that I can talk again though, I had better be on my way. I will never forget your kindness."

Elisabeth LaForet writes regularly, and added in a letter "I love to read books and I cuddle down on my bed when I read. My favorite books are *The Bobbsey Twins*, the hardback old ones. I read every one I find. I also read Robert Frost and Robert Louis Stevenson. I memorize poems, too." Here is one of Elisabeth's ventures into composing a simple animal folk tale. Writers often have fun with the idea of creatures, or people, doing just the opposite of what they should be doing.

The Cow that said Quack
by Elisabeth LaForet (age 8)

Once upon a time Daisy the cow stretched. She usually said a MOO when she stretched. But, oh no! This time she said a quack.

"Quack!!"

She said, "Quack" to Farmer Ziggy.

She said, "Quack" to Big Piggy.

She said, "Quack" to Big Borsey Horsey.

Now those mischievous animals changed sounds! The red rooster said, "Baa," and the lamb said, "Cockledoodle doo," and the duck said, "Moo." The hen said, "Ne-e-e-e-ey", and the horse said, "Pluck Pluck." All of the farm animals said strange sounds!

Suddenly the animals saw the lamb on the barn roof and he was crowing! He scared the wits out of Framer Ziggy! The rooster said that he wanted his old job back and his mates agreed.

So, they exchanged sounds and got their old sounds back. And all of the farm yard was jolly ever after.

This next animal story was printed up and bound into a little book with a construction paper cover, the whole thing tied together with yarn. This simple bookbinding method helps makes the story feel like a finished product, ready to give as a gift to friends and family.

Peter Babysits
by Alicia Mae Kuehne (age 8)

Once upon a time there were five little rabbits. They lived in a burrow. Their names were Mama, Papa, Peter and Jane. Peter was seven, Alice was four and Jane was one month old.

One day Mama said, "I am going to market."

"What will you buy?" asked Alice jumping up and down.

"I'm going to buy vegetables and clothes. Peter, please watch Jane and Alice. Good–bye."

Alice ran over to the fence. She climbed up on the fence and began to walk across. She didn't know that she wasn't supposed to.

Meanwhile, Peter was counting how many minutes had gone by. He didn't want to watch his sisters because Jane was always crying and Alice was always getting into things.

After Alice had gotten steady she began to run across the fence. Suddenly she tripped and fell off!

When Mama came home Peter told her what had happened. Mama told Peter that he should watch his sisters more carefully.

Mama licked Alice all over. Then she washed some of the carrots, parsley, apples and lettuce that she had gotten at the market and they chomped on these for supper.

I hope you thoroughly enjoy this next little story, which takes us into the imagined worlds of the young, showing how a child can transform the most mundane event into a feast of imagination.

Mid–Morning Attack
by Taryn Lynds (age 11)

Princess Allison ducked as they came at her again and again. She tried to run, but tripped on some old corn cobs and fell down to the hard, cold, dirty ground. Then, looking up she was just in time to see another feathered creature come rushing towards her. They were fearsome beasts with red, fiery eyes, with claws and beaks as sharp as swords.

"If I could only escape into a cave or a brave prince could come to the rescue like in all the stories, then I'd be safe!" she thought as she threw her hat at them to give her time to run into a nearby shed, only to find three more screeching and flapping their wings with fury. Startled, she jumped back and escaped behind a heap of grain. Then catching her breath, she heard her mother calling.

"Allison, time for lunch."

"Coming," Allison called back, dusting the feathers off her jeans and brushing the dirt off her straw hat which she had thrown at them. Then, picking up her egg basket, she walked to the house.

"What in the world have you been doing, Alli?" asked her mother, as she walked into the kitchen. "You're a mess. Just look at yourself."

"Sorry, but I had a little trouble with the chickens. I don't think they want their cage cleaned," said Allison, as she hung her hat on the hook.

Here Taryn has her cat tell the story. All cats indeed seem to feel they are regal beasts deserving royal treatment, and this cat takes that to the hilt. Enjoy how Taryn is able to sustain the tone of writing that we associate with medieval times. You can tell she must have read a number of novels or histories of this time period to be able to imagine it all so well, and through a cat's eyes at that!

Edwina, A Medieval Cat
by Taryn Lynds (age 10)

Good morrow! My name is Edwina the IV. I am of a very royal breed of cats. In fact, I belong to Queen Arabella of Donnybrook. Once every 12 new moons we have a fair here at Donnybrook. It is such a merry time of year with the smell of hams and spices in the air, with dancing and singing and music everywhere.

And sausage... AAAH that sausage. It wasn't my fault. It was just something inside of me that made me do it. It was like what I have seen little brachets doing when they know they should not steal but when they are so very hungry, they do. It was like that, but only I was not hungry. Alas, I must go on.

It was the second day of the fair and the smell of hams was in the air as I have said before. I was in the royal carriage with the Queen Arabella when I decided to go take a look around. I hopped out of the carriage when the queen was waving at some nobleman. So, down to the far corner of the fair I trotted, where I knew the meat was kept.

When I got there I saw pork chops, chicken breasts, and hams, but my eye was caught by the sausage, the beautiful long strings of sausage. I looked around to make sure no one was looking. I leaped for the sausage and caught it in my jaws. Then I ran. I ran for my life all the way back to the carriage to eat my prize in peace.

However, when I got there, Arabella took the sausage away from me and threw it out the window. Then, she told me I was very naughty to do such a thing. I was so disturbed, I just sat there the whole day, listening to the singing outside and asking myself why I ever did such a thing.

Rachel Wilson has already published two delightful picture books on her own. This was her longest story ever, a remarkable accomplishment for someone her age. Rachel is an excellent and avid reader, and has also always enjoyed hearing stories read aloud—this has all helped develop her sense of story and character and plot. To give you a feel for how Rachel went about writing this story, we've included first her brainstorming "Idea Sheet" that she used to help her think of the next possibilities when she was part way through with her story. She was fully aware that she, as the author, could choose between any number of endings. If you ever feel stuck when writing a story, you might want to try an "Idea Sheet" also to get new ideas going. Also see if you can see which ideas Rachel decided to use and which she laid aside—for this story at least!

"My Idea Sheet"
by Rachel Wilson (age 7)

Rosebud returned to the garden (describe the morning).

Fairies have meeting.

Fairies tell Rosebud that don't like to talk much, can fairies call Rosebud "Rose", yes.

Rose tries to warn fairies Ma is watering the garden.

Rose gets lost, fairies come and help find way back.

Rose gets stung while parents at meeting, fairies take care of Rose.

Maybe Ma finds fairies, keeps secret from Pa.

And now on to the story of Rosebud. And watch out—it looks like Rachel is planning on doing what so many good writers love to do. She's already tossing around ideas in her head for a sequel!

Rosebud
by Rachel Wilson (age 7)

Chapter One

Once there was a little girl named Rosebud who was playing in her mother's garden all by herself. The flowers were in full bloom.

Suddenly, she noticed a beautiful flower she hadn't noticed before. She walked over to it. When she got near it, Rosebud heard little voices. She looked in the middle of the flower and there were lots of little people dancing and singing in a circle. As Rosebud looked closer, she saw that they were fairies.

It seemed to Rosebud that the fairies didn't notice her. They didn't look up at her and just kept on dancing and singing until one little girl fairy saw Rosebud and screamed, "Mommy, Mommy!! There's a *big* thing watching us!"

Chapter 2

At that point all the fairies disappeared and Rosebud sadly went back into her house to think about what she'd seen.

Later that night when Rosebud was looking into the darkness of her room, she saw a little light. The twinkling light came closer and closer until it landed on Rosebud's nose! To her surprise, it was the tiny fairy she'd seen that afternoon.

The fairy whispered to Rosebud, "Come back to the garden tomorrow." The light then faded from Rosebud's room and the fairy was gone. The little girl, Rosebud, wondered if she had only been dreaming, but as she fell asleep she determined that she would visit the garden anyway.

Chapter 3

When Rosebud woke up she remembered what the fairy had told her to do. Maybe she had been dreaming, but she would go to the garden anyway to find out. Rosebud hadn't noticed that it was raining until she looked out the window. Now she'd have to wear her raincoat and boots... phooey!

After Rosebud dressed, ate her breakfast and put on her raincoat she went outside to see if she could find the fairies. When she reached the garden, she looked for the fairies in the flower where she had seen them yesterday. Rosebud found the fairies were busy having a meeting.

Rosebud said, "Hello," and all the fairies were so startled that they fell right off their tiny chairs! Once they saw it was Rosebud, they all settled down. Rosebud asked them what they were having a meeting about and they said, "You!" Then what seemed to be the leader stood up and introduced herself. In a very tiny voice the fairy said, "My name is Columbine and I am Queen of the fairies. This is my daughter, Princess Hollyhock, but most of us just call her Holly. We fairies don't like to use long words. We've heard your mother calling you Rosebud and we wondered whether you would mind if we called you 'Rose' instead?" Rosebud answered, "Why, Yes! I've always wanted a nickname and Rose would be just perfect."

Chapter 4

One sunny day Rose's parents were at a meeting. Rose was all alone and she was bored. Suddenly she had an idea! She could go visit the fairies.

Because it was summertime, Rose was allowed to go barefoot and Rose loved being barefoot. While she was running, Rose stepped on some clover. Rose yelled, "Ouch!" and stumbled to the ground. She had not noticed the bee on the clover, but when she looked at her foot she found out that she had been stung. Rose got up and limped the rest of the way to the garden. When Rose got there, she found all the fairies were having a good time. She watched them for a few moments and then one of the fairies noticed her and shouted, "Look!"

All the fairies turned to look where the fairy was pointing. A fairy by the name of Lily could tell that Rose was in pain and said, "What's the matter?" Rose told them she'd been stung by a bee.

At that point all the fairies started flying around and filling big pails, small pails and tiny cups with pollen from different flowers and then dumping them into one big pot. When the pot was almost up to the brim, they all stopped and Columbine, the queen, told Rose, "Pour this pollen where you were stung and you will feel better instantly."

Rose gratefully took the pollen and poured it on her foot and it did feel better! So Rose thanked the fairies and went back into her house. This happened none too soon, because about ten minutes later her parents came home. She was very lucky because Rose did not want her parents to find out about the fairies...

Chapter 5

One day Rose was just so busy with classes that she had no time to go and visit the fairies. Late that morning when all the fairies were just minding their own business, Rose's cat took a walk through the garden. The cat brushed up against the fairies' flower house and all the fairies jumped from their seats in horror! Being fairies, they knew what a cat meant— trouble! So they all started throwing things at the cat. Now this only made the cat angry and it scratched the flower right down to the ground. And all the fairies fell scattered around the place where the flower was laying. Just as all the fairies thought they were about to be devoured by a cat, a bird came fluttering by. And if you were a cat, you'd be a lot more interested in chasing a bird than a bunch of fairies... which is what the cat did.

When the fairies recovered, they realized they didn't have a home anymore. Their flower home had been completely torn apart. And so they began to look for another suitable place to live...

Chapter 6

It was decided that they would break up into groups to search for a new home. The leaders of the three groups were Columbine, Hollyhock and Tulip. But there was one problem. Who would stay behind to take care of the fairy children? Just then, out of the crowd, came PawPaw and he volunteered to babysit. All the children cheered because they loved PawPaw's funny stories and the popsicles this favorite fairy shared with them.

Then all the search parties went different ways. Columbine's group went to the right, Hollyhock's to the left and Tulip led her group straight ahead. A few hours later, when all the fairies came together again, they told each other what they had found. Columbine had found some lovely sweet woodruff, but everybody thought they would get lost in it. Hollyhock's group had found a sunflower, but her mother, the queen, reminded Holly that the people shook the flower to get the seeds and they would lose their home too soon. So finally, it was Tulip's turn to speak. She had discovered mushrooms near Rosebud's house and all the fairies thought that was a wonderful idea. And so it was decided that they would live under the mushrooms.

When the fairies had all flown to the mushroom grove, they all started setting up their new homes. Each family had their own mushroom, with Queen Columbine's being the largest. While the fairies were still getting settled, a strange fairy that no one had ever seen before came up to Columbine and said, "Hello." The first thing Columbine said was, "Where did you come from?" The stranger pointed right next door. Columbine then asked, "Are there any more of your kind where you live?" The fairy said, "Yes, there are a lot more!"

Meanwhile, while Rose was at her ballet class she found

out that her next door neighbor, Rachel, had fairies living in her *house*! Rosebud and Rachel decided that they would try to have the fairies meet each other. They did not realize this had already happened that very afternoon. The girls promised to keep the fairies a secret between themselves. One can only imagine the adventures they must have had all together!

This next story shows a fine dramatic sense of story, and from a very young writer. Carina Strappello takes us on quite an adventure with her fictional character Lilly. Carina was already a very fluent reader when she wrote this story. She also is another one who writes very regularly. I remember her mother telling me that often at this time Carina would write a one page story every night just before going to bed. You can see that she feels fluent with her writing in a way that you probably can't match unless you write often. It is also interesting to watch the movement in this story. From the way the day opens the reader might think that certainly nothing good at all will be happening to poor Lilly, but just wait!

Lilly's Trip
by Carina Strappello (age 8)

"Wake up, sleepyhead," called Lilly's brother.

"I don't have to get up if I don't want to," Lilly said. She crawled out of bed and looked out the window. The sky was blue and the sun was shining. Lilly went across the room and shut her door. Yesterday was the last day of school, she thought as she put her clothes on.

Lilly was 9 years old. Her brother's name was Scott. He was 12 years old. Her sister's name was Mary. Mary was 14 years old. She was bossy. Lilly's family lived in the country on a farm. They lived in a huge house. Each person had her or his own room and bathroom in their rooms. The rooms were big. Every person had their own room except the mom and dad. They slept together. Lilly had her own horse named Starbelle. She had her own kitten, too. Her kitten's name was Muffin.

Lilly went outside to the big red barn to feed Starbelle. Starbelle neighed happily when she saw Lilly come in. Lilly gave Starbelle hay, oats, water, and a few carrots. She petted Starbelle's glossy black mane. She started grooming Starbelle, and then went back into the house to feed Muffin. Muffin hurried to Lilly as Lilly poured out some cat food into Muffin's pink bowl.

Next Lilly went into the big dining room to eat her breakfast. Lilly groaned, "Pancakes. I hate pancakes."

"You're so picky," Mary said.

"No, I'm not," yelled Lilly. "You're the one that's picky."

"What do you mean, I'm the one that's picky?" said Mary.

"Oh, be quiet," said Lilly.

"Girl's always fight with each other," declared Scott.

"No they don't," said Lilly. She ate her pancakes even though she didn't like them. "Mom," whined Lilly, "get me a drink."

"I just sat down, go get a drink yourself," said Lilly's mom.

Lilly got down from her chair, went to the kitchen, and got a drink. "I know what I'll do today. I will take Starbelle and go on a trip. I won't come back till tomorrow," thought Lilly.

Lilly ran upstairs to pack. Then she ran downstairs and told her mom.

Her dad came in when she was talking, "Let her go, it will be an experience," he said.

Lilly jumped up and down in excitement. "I can go! I can go!" she said. "I need a little tent for tonight. I need food too."

"Slow down," laughed Lilly's father. "We will get everything together soon enough."

When everything was ready, Lilly's father helped her put her stuff on Starbelle's back. Lilly climbed up on a space on Starbelle's saddle and she waved good-bye to her family.

"Be careful," yelled Mother.

Before Lilly went down the path. She heard Scott say, "That's no fair. Why don't I get to go?"

Lilly started down a path that led into the woods. Starbelle stepped carefully through the rocky path.

Lilly thought, "What if I get lost?" She ignored the thought and concentrated on the path. After what seemed like an hour, she came to a forked path. Lilly took out the map her dad had made for her and looked at it. She had traveled 10 miles. She decided to rest. She tied Starbelle to a tree and let her graze on the green grass.

Lilly studied her map. She had 12 miles to go to where she wanted to set up her tent. Lilly looked closer at the map. "I have to take the trail to the right," thought Lilly. Just then, Lilly heard voices coming down the path.   Lilly went back to get Starbelle. She had decided to follow them. Lilly got on Starbelle and quietly followed the men and the girl. After a while Lilly heard one of the men saying, "Let's stop here."

Lilly hid in the woods till it got dark and she could hear the snores of the men. Then she crept quietly to a tent. She looked in. The men were asleep. Lilly walked up to another tent beside the men's tent. She looked in. The girl was in it. Her hands and feet were tied together.

Lilly went up to her and touched the girl.

She woke with a start. "Who are you?" she whispered.

Lilly answered her reluctantly, "I'm Lilly. Who are you?"

"I'm Princess Angora."

"You mean you're a princess?" asked Lilly.

"Yes, I'm a princess," replied Angora. "And anyway, how did you get here?"

Lilly told her. "I am following you and I'll keep following you. How did you get caught?" asked Lilly.

"I was in the Palace gardens too long, and those ugly men came along out of nowhere and caught me," said Angora.

"There are rips in your dress," said Lilly.

"I know. They had to rip some cloth out of my dress to get the rubies and diamonds."

"I have to go," Lilly said to Angora. Lilly slipped away towards her horse. She lay beside Starbelle on the ground and went to sleep.

The next morning, she awoke to hear voices. She remembered yesterday what had happened. Lilly jumped up. She felt very hungry. She ate some food her Mom had packed for her. Then she got on Starbelle towards the men and Angora.

They started traveling again. Lilly followed, not too close behind. After a little while, the men and Angora turned up a rocky path on the mountain. Lilly and Starbelle followed. It was steep. Half way up the men stopped and put Angora down and propped her up against a rock and the men went to eat not beside Angora.

Lilly got off Starbelle and crept to Angora. Lilly whispered to Angora, "Come with me."

"I can't come. My feet and hands are tied up," said Angora.

Lilly got her pocket knife out and cut the ropes on Angora. They both crawled into the forest. "Hurry," said Lilly, "before the men come to get you."

They crawled to Starbelle. "Get on Starbelle. I'll get up behind you."

"I want to get home," moaned Angora.

"Do you know your way?" asked Lilly.

"No," replied Angora.

"I guess we can try to find our way. Let's go down the path to where I first heard the men," said Lilly.

Starbelle trotted down the path. They rode till they came to the forked path. "If we go the way to the right, we will come to my home," said Lilly. They turned to the left and started going again.

After a little while they came to another forked path. "If I remember correctly, we go that way," said Angora. She pointed to the left.

"I hope you're right," said Lilly.

"Things are beginning to look familiar," said Angora.

"When did the men kidnap you?" asked Lilly.

"Yesterday," replied Angora.

"Those men were walking and we are riding so we should be almost there," said Lilly.

A few minutes Angora said excitedly, "I see the palace!"

Starbelle galloped to the palace the rest of the way. Angora got off Starbelle and said to Lilly, "Can you come and meet my family?"

"I guess I can but I should be going home." Lilly got off Starbelle and went with Angora inside the palace. "It's beautiful," said Lilly when they got inside."

"Let's go up to my room," said Angora! They went up some winding stairs and through a hall. Angora opened a door and said, "This is my room." Her room had all the fashionable stuff.

"I like your room," Lilly said.

"Thanks," said Angora, "I think I should tell my mom and dad where I am."

When they reached the throne room, Lilly said, "You go in first and tell them how you got home."

"Okay," said Angora.

Lilly waited patiently while Angora went to her mom and dad. Finally Angora came and said, "You can come in now."

Lilly went in. After they came out, Angora said, "You can stay here as long as you want."

"Well," said Lilly, "I should be going home."

"Okay, do you want to go right now?" asked Angora.

"Yes, I would, I guess," answered Lilly. She said good bye to Angora and her mom and dad.

"Come and visit us someday," said Angora.

"I will," promised Lilly.

When Lilly turned into her yard with Starbelle, her mom and dad ran out and said, "Tell us about your trip."

"Well," said Lilly, "It's a long story..."

Stephanie Schultz says that she was mainly inspired to write this next story by her older brother Matthew's fictional story *The Time That Couldn't Fly,* and came up with this whimsical story of her own. So often homeschooled children do get very good ideas from other children—either siblings or others in writing groups or clubs. Stephanie and her brother attend a "Literary Club" every month with several other homeschooling families, where all of the children share stories they have written. Stephanie is also required to write daily at home during the school year—something that their mother tells me was initially greeted by groans and moans, but gradually gave way to the delightful writing that follows.

The Amethyst that Could Not Shine
by Stephanie Schultz (age 10)

Once there was an Amethyst that could not shine. Everyone laughed at him because he looked so ugly. He asked Mr. Emerald, "How do you shine?"

"I smile my best smile," said Mr. Emerald.

Amethyst asked Mrs. Ruby, "How do you shine?"

"I make sure my lipstick is on right," she said.

Amethyst asked, "Sister Diamond, how do you shine?"

"I just smile so my teeth show," said Sister Diamond.

He asked Brother Sapphire, "How do you shine?"

"I just make sure my hair is right," said Brother Sapphire.

Amethyst tried all these things but none of them worked. One day a girl came by and liked the amethyst. She decided to take it home. This made him so happy that he started to shine. He lived happily ever after.

And now for Matthew's story, which he says just popped into his head one day. Matthew reads widely in mysteries, comedies, and adventure stories. I think you'll be able to tell that Matthew has developed a fine ear for language through all his reading.

The Time That Couldn't Fly
by Matthew Schultz (age 12)

Once upon a grandfather clock, there were 12 little hours: 1 O'clock, 2 O'clock, 3 O'clock and so on, and there was Grandfather Pendulum, Pendulum for short. He was their teacher and advisor. All was well in that clock except for 12 O'clock. He couldn't make his hour fly like the rest of the hours. 10 O'clock and 11 O'clock were big and haughty because they had 2 digits, but 12 O'Clock was the biggest of all but he didn't boast. He may have been big but he wasn't strong. His hour was the slowest; he couldn't push the minute hand fast enough. All the hours teased him except for his one friend 7 O'Clock. 12 O'clock asked 7 O'clock for advice on how to make his hour fly, but 7 O'Clock couldn't give him any ideas except to go to Grandfather Pendulum. Grandfather Pendulum suggested lifting the *second* hand until he got really strong. So in his spare time he lifted the second hand and started getting strong. But 12 O'Clock was working so hard and fast that he was too tired to push the minute hand. Pendulum noticed how 12 O'Clock rushed and decided to tell all the hours a story.

"Let me tell you hours a funny story about a tortoise and a hare." Once Pendulum got to the part about the hare falling asleep, all the hours burst into laughter. "That's not the funny part," remarked Pendulum as he read on. "...'And when the hare woke and saw the tortoise about to win, he jumped to his feet and ran and tripped. Just then the tortoise crossed the finish line.' THAT'S the funny part," said Pendulum. So all the hours laughed.

"So you see, don't rush yourself: slow and steady wins the race, remember that," said Pendulum.

"Yea," 8 O'Clock teased.

So 12 O'Clock worked steadily and hard until HE could push the minute hand faster than any of the other hours.

To fully enjoy this next story, also by Matthew, it helps to know that the speeding roadsters you'll soon meet are really little children Matthew knows. The real Annie is four years old and Phillip is three, and they come along with their older siblings to monthly "Literary Club" meetings. Maybe they spend part of their time there zooming around on big wheels or toy pedal cars? Josiah and Erich are also members of the club. I can imagine the howls of laughter as

Matthew read his story aloud to all the club members—and how astonished Annie and Phillip must have been to find themselves in a REAL story! I can also tell Matthew has probably listened to many sports announcers giving blow by blow run–downs of fast paced events, as he mimics their style with such good humor and wit. I also like how Matthew lets the drivers in HIS race help one another out by sharing vehicles when necessary. Hearing this story may give your children the idea of using friends and family as the characters in fictional pieces. The writer will know he'll have at least some avid listeners!

The Grand Prix Race
by Matthew Schultz (age 12)

It was a hot day at the Grand Prix race track as four cars were getting ready for the race. One of the cars (driven by Erich) was new, sleek and shiny. His number was 88. He wore a chef's hat. Another one of the cars driven by Annie was a noisy, red hot rod with the number 12. Annie was wearing a football helmet.

The third car was driven by Josiah. he wore a regular racing helmet. His number was –1. The last car was driven by Phillip. he was wearing a sea captain's vest and cap. His car was a little beat up. His number 5,342,210,576,718.

The race was about to begin. Everyone got ready and gunned their engines, Annie the loudest. Suddenly the flag went down. Everyone put the pedal to the floor except Annie. She put it THROUGH the floor. Phillip offered Annie a ride in his car so they started down the track in Phillip's car.

When they rounded the corner, they did it too fast and did a spinout and hit the wall. A clanging noise followed so Annie asked what it was. "Just the bumper, it fell off," replied Phillip. Annie sat back in contentment. After about two minutes Annie complained they were going too slow. Phillip checked his digital speedometer and read 265 mph, so Phillip sped up to 290 mph. After a while Annie complained they were going the wrong way, so Phillip picked up a map of the track and started to study it.

"Keep your eyes on the road!" said Annie. Suddenly Josiah zoomed past followed closely by Erich. Phillip and Annie were only going 20 mph.

"We're out of gas," said Phillip, "Let me get some out of the trunk," and he started to open the door.

"Why don't you stop the car first," suggested Annie.

"No time," replied Phillip. So he took the gas can out of the trunk and ran beside the car while filling the tank.

When he was done, he was so exhausted from running beside the car that he took (or tried) to take a nap in the back seat while Annie drove. "The ride is so bumpy I can't rest," said Phillip grumpily.

"Just be quiet and let me drive!" retorted Annie.

"Be careful!" yelled Phillip, "You're going too fast!" They were going 394 mph.

"Nonsense!" Annie yelled back.

Suddenly they passed Erich. Josiah was in Erich's car! What had happened was Josiah hit a rock and flew out his window which was fortunately open and flew into Erich's passenger window which was also open and landed in the seat. Now those two were together.

The race was down to two cars.

Phillip and Annie had 20 miles to go but with Annie driving it was soon narrowed down to 15.

Meanwhile, Erich and Josiah were only going 250 mph. "We're never going to catch up!" Josiah remarked.

"Wrong!" replied Erich as he sped up to 350 mph. Soon

Josiah spotted Phillip and Annie ahead.

"Just a bit faster," said Josiah, so Erich floored it to 400 mph!

Soon there was only 7 miles to go and again the race was a tie.

The gap between the cars and the finish line was getting more narrow by the second. Six, five, four, three, two miles to go. All drivers and passengers were nervous. In 10 seconds there was only half a mile to go.

Suddenly Phillip exclaimed, "I see the finish line and they're ahead of us!" Annie went for a record breaking speed of 500 1/36 mph and caught up to Erich and Josiah. Again the race was neck to neck!

Erich was driving 500 mph and Annie was going 500 1/36 mph.

The race was a tie thanks to Erich's car being three inches longer.

"We were going 500 1/36 mph," Phillip bragged.

"Well, thanks to our longer car, we still tied you, so the extra 1/36 of a mile was no good!" Josiah retorted.

The mothers were the distinguished judges. "Who gets the trophy?" was everyone's question.

Suddenly Annie came up with an idea. "I vote we cut the trophy in half." Erich and Josiah did not like this idea, but if they weren't getting the trophy for themselves it was worth it.

"They were both going 500 mph," said Ann.

"Wrong!" yelled Annie, "We were going 500 1/36."

"Excuse me," replied Ann.

The trophy got split; Annie and Phillip got the top because they wanted the most gold but Erich and Josiah knew it to be more important to get the bottom because IT had the plaque.

12. Composing Longer Works

Some young writers have not only found their writer's voice, but are producing long, full length stories, and these are shared in this last section. Some of these writers worked on their stories over many months, slowly building up their characters and plots, working to rewrite and edit for continuity and clarity, and finally polishing up phrasing and delivery. These seem to me like piano students growing towards performing sonatinas with several complex movements. They've moved beyond the simpler folktunes or even minuets of their earlier recitals and are now tackling pieces that may take months of preparation, along with a much fuller musical understanding and interpretation. Just as often the most advanced piano students are asked to play the grand finale pieces that close a recital, so we have saved these stories for last here. I hope you'll agree these students deserve a standing ovation for their fine efforts.

You are in for a treat with this story. And besides just enjoying the well–structured plot and characters and the wholesomeness of the story, notice little things such as how new characters are introduced into the action. August doesn't explicitly tell who they are, but you know right away just what is happening, such as when the cat makes her first appearance. See how carefully August keeps the perspective of her characters in mind—not an easy thing when you are looking through the eyes of a mouse!

August is a very strong reader, who loves good literature, and her writing abilities clearly show this. She is thinking seriously about continuing work as a writer as she grows to adulthood, and already writes regularly and with great enjoyment. She finds that she has had much more time for writing during her two years of homeschooling than she ever had while in school. Turns out this is only a part of a longer sequence of mouse stories, which she originally began to share with her younger brother. I for one would jump at the chance to read anything else she comes up with!

Ruford

by August Beddingfield (age 14)

Waking up from a bad dream, Ruford found it very hard to go back to sleep. He was afraid from the tip of his tiny mouse nose to the end of his wiry mouse tail. Ruford kept himself awake for a long time. Finally his eyes heavily closed and he slept through the night.

The next morning Ruford decided that he did not need to tell anyone about his dream and after eating went out to play. It was a bright sunny day and he decided that the back of the house would be the best place to roll in the grass. "The pasture back there gets a lot of sun," he explained to himself, on his way to it. When he got there, he couldn't believe his eyes. He fell in the grass and looked about him. He was sitting in a tall green pasture with dots of white daisies, yellow buttercups, and blue violets. "Just like my dream!" he thought. Then as he recovered from slight shock, he shrugged the horrible thought off and began to roll and giggle. He soon forgot all about his dream. But if he would have remembered a little farther in his dream he would have turned around to see the large quiet feet coming closer. Feet belonging to the orange tabby body crouching lower. All of a sudden he was hurled into the air and he gave a little shriek as he hit the ground and was knocked unconscious.

When he came to, he didn't know where he was. He felt the predator's hot breath as he looked up. It was Marmalade! The cat who lived five miles down the road. Ruford put all of his attention into getting away. As Marmalade carefully cleaned her paws, keeping an eye on Ruford, Ruford thought, "I've got to escape fast!" Ruford's small black eyes scanned the forest quickly. He saw a little opening in a bush five feet away. He looked down at his feet and said, "Feet, you can't get weak now!" Marmalade finished washing and as Ruford looked up all he could see was the underside of her paw coming closer. As the five sharp nails came crashing down, Ruford dashed to the other side of the tree. He frantically searched for the bush. Marmalade wasn't going to lose him now! She raced around the tree. The bush was spotted and Ruford ran towards it. He made a running leap! *Crack! Crinkle!* He landed in the middle of a heap of twigs and dried leaves. He sat so still that he thought he was going to burst. Within a few seconds Ruford distinctively heard a sniffing noise. Marmalade's nose was hard at work. His hiding place would soon be found. "I don't have much time. I'd better find somewhere else to hide!"

Again he searched for somewhere to go. He turned and listened. He'd better do it quickly. He could already see the giant pink nose. Ruford saw a small passageway under the bush and out. He scrambled in the semidarkness of the leaves and tumbled out into the sunshine. "Good!" Ruford thought. Marmalade was on the other side of the bush. "Oh, no! If I run she's bound to see me, and if I don't she's bound to smell me out!" As the sharp nose came closer Ruford ran, looking backwards. "Argh!" He smacked into a log. "That's it!," he smiled. Ruford climbed into the hollow log and waited. Soon he heard noises. Marmalade jumped over the log. She saw him but she couldn't get at him. Defeated, she headed home with her tail in the air. You will never know how relieved that tiny mouse was, sitting inside that hollow log.

He scrambled out of a hole in the log. "Now I've got to go home," he said as he picked bits of dirt from his fur with his tiny paws. He looked around the forest with moss covered trees and a patch of clover. Slowly, a look of bewilderment crept over his face as he realized he was lost. Just how far had Marmalade carried him? His stomach growled with hunger. Ruford's little pointy nose began gliding over the ground. He found a few breadcrumbs and a few edible leaves. A shadow fell over him growing increasingly larger. He looked up in time to see two crinkly claws baring dark nails. The hawk came closer and closer. Ruford darted back into the log just as the claws nipped the end of his tail. The sound of the giant wings flapping together was so loud it hurt his ears. The wind that came from the beating of the wings caused the log to roll into a nearby tree. "Awk! Awk!" the bird screeched wildly. Ruford took it as a warning that he should not come out of the log. Maybe not until next week!   Ruford stayed put for a while. When he finally *did* pop his little nose out of that log, it started to bob up and down sniffing for danger. As far as he could see and smell, it was safe.

He scampered out, cautiously. "I still have to find my way home," he thought. He didn't know where to begin. He couldn't send for help, there was no one to send. He prayed, "Lord, I'm lost and I don't know what to do! Please give me an idea so that I can go home. Show me the way."

Meanwhile, back at Ruford's house... "He has been missing since early afternoon and now it's almost dark!" sobbed Ruford's mother. "It's not like Ruford to miss a meal. Not like him at all." She had been praying for his safe return. Mr. Mouse tried to calm his wife and sent her off to wipe her whiskers and relax in a cool bath while he went off to look for Ruford. Once out of Mrs. Mouse's sight a worried look came over his face. It wasn't like his son to miss *any* meal. Through a hole in the screen and down three steps, Mr. Mouse proceeded down the walkway and into the grass. He did not know where to start, but he was determined to find his son.

"The sun is going down," Ruford thought," and they are probably looking for me. I do wish I had some sense of direction or a sign that I could fol—, *Hey!* If I quiet down and listen, perhaps I will hear the bubbly brook." He quieted down and listened very hard. He heard the tweet, tweedle-leedle–leedle, tweet of the birds and the soft rustling of the leaves on the trees. He heard the chattering of chipmunks and squirrels, but no bubbly brook. An owl's hoot and the dark sky told him that he'd better find a place to sleep. Besides, the owl didn't seem very friendly. Ruford tried not to think about it, but he couldn't help thinking about whether he would ever get home again. He poked and twitched for somewhere to sleep. He found a hole in the trunk of a tree that looked uninhabited. He rolled, picked and pried until finally, he had the perfect sleeping quarters. Ruford looked about his tiny bedroom. He laid his head on a moss clump pillow, prayed and finally went to sleep.

Ruford's mother was very worried by this time. Not being able to sleep, she scampered about the house all night.

The next day a little girl named Janet and her little sister, Cindy were out gathering flowers. Now Janet was well acquainted with the Mouse family. She often brought little tidbits and morsels to them that were leftover from breakfast or lunch. On this morning Janet and Cindy decided to gather flowers in the forest. Cindy raced through the trees picking buttercups and dandelions. Ruford, who had been awake for just a short time, heard the familiar voices. He squeaked with excitement! Cindy heard the squeaking and followed it to a large oak tree.

Ruford stepped out of the hole in the trunk of the tree. His tail wiggled with joy. Janet and Cindy found some berries for Ruford to eat and then took him home. They met Mr. Mouse on the way and as he was weary from searching all the night, they gave him a ride home in their flower basket with Ruford.

As they approached the door of Ruford's house, Mrs. Mouse came running out. Ruford jumped from the basket and hugged his mother tightly. Janet sat Mr. Mouse down beside his family and she and Cindy skipped away. The three Mouses cried and laughed for it was indeed a joyous occasion. Mrs. Mouse made peanut butter and jelly sandwiches for lunch. Afterward, they all snuggled together and Ruford recounted his adventure. They thanked God for answering their prayers.

Over the years Ruford told his story to his family and then to his children and then to their children. And he never forgot to let them know that it had been answered prayer that rescued him.

Jessica Strappello is a voracious reader—*and* writer. She writes daily for a wide variety of purposes—international penpal correspondence, book reviews submitted to local library contests (she's won), descriptions of places visited on homeschooling fieldtrips, and even an article on homeschooling that has been accepted for publication in *Clubhouse*, a magazine for children put out by Dobson's *Focus on the Family*. I think part of the reason Jessica feels so fluent with writing is indeed simply that she writes so often, and her parents have encouraged her to use her own ideas and go with them. They do not respond with a heavy red pencil or diatribes about grammar or spelling. And because she reads so much, and from high quality literature with an emphasis on the classics, she has absorbed the sound of fine language, absorbed the conventions writers use to bring wit and humor and telling detail to a piece. She also has gained a fine sense of story structure, ably developing settings, characters, and conflict—and a happy resolution in the best fairy tale tradition.

The next story about Meagan the mouse is followed by its sequel. This idea of sequels is certainly one that adult writers for children use continually, and one that we might point out more openly to our children as a path for them to explore. Just think of the *Little House in the Big Woods* series—it was originally to be just the one book, but the one book grew. Our children can often grow as writers by seeing how their first ideas can grow into others, too.

Meagan's New Home
A Meagan Mouse Tale (Tail)

by Jessica Strappello (age 11)

Meagan Mouse lived in a castle. She wasn't a princess or a queen, but the humans that lived in the castle were. King Hubert, Queen Isabella, Prince Lewis and Princess Roseamund lived in the castle with Meagan. They didn't know she was there. Meagan lived in Princess Roseamund's room, in a little hole beside the big bed.

Rosa's bedroom had thick pink carpet, flowered wallpaper, and a big canopy bed. Meagan's house only had ten rooms, but the castle had 245 rooms. There were bedrooms, kitchens, music rooms, art studios, dining rooms, etc.. Meagan sometimes used Rosa's lavishly furnished dollhouse as her house—that is, only when Princess Rosa was out. It had 20 rooms and was a mini–castle. Meagan thought it was beautiful. Her house only had wooden furniture and match box beds. But the mini–castle had gold, glass and brass furniture, canopy beds and crystal chandeliers, just like the real castle.

Meagan got her food from Becky, the royal family's cook, in the kitchen. Becky didn't know about it. Meagan feasted on cheese, pie, lamb, turkey, beef, roast duck, cakes, cookies, pasta, apples, cherries, etc.

She got her clothes from Mary, the royal seamstress's sewing room. She got scraps of velvet, silk, satin, taffeta and rich furs. She was handy with a needle and her clothes were very pretty. Meagan bathed in Rosa's china washbowl which

Rosa didn't use (she used the marble sink).

Meagan often visited Maggie, another mouse, who lived in the greenhouse by the pools in the courtyard. Meagan rode in Lewis's mini–coach which was electric and could be steered. Meagan usually went at night since she wasn't sure of the royals' reaction to a mouse. The queen was very strict, the king quite stupid, and Lewis was even better than the court jester. Rosa was Meagan's favorite. She was quiet, timid and little. Queen Isabella thought her very silly.

Meagan thought life was quite perfect until a sunny Saturday when the unexpected happened. Meagan got up from bed at precisely 7:00. She got a bath and decided to wear her lacy pink satin dress. She went out of her hole and crept under Rosa's door. She walked to the kitchen, which was only a door away. She walked in and got up a breakfast of egg, bacon and jelly toast. Meagan sensed that something was different. The cook was busy making a huge cake with candles. Rosa was in the parlor with a blue satin, frilly dress. Big wrapped boxes sat on a table.

Meagan finally figured out what was going on. It was Rosa's tenth birthday! Meagan looked at all the elegant people streaming through the door—Dukes, Duchesses, earls and counts. Meagan got very excited! "Wow!" she thought, "Maybe I could stay and watch!"

She crept into a corner and bumped into something! "Hi! Meagan, isn't this grand!? I caught a ride over on the gardener's shoes! He was delivering roses!" said the voice.

"Maggie!" cried Meagan, "I haven't seen you in awhile. How are you?"

"Fine," said Maggie. "Look, they're sitting down to eat. And it's only 10:30! They usually have parties at 12:45!"

Meagan looked at all the people in velvet cushioned chairs

around the great table. "Look at that cake!" squeaked Maggie, "It's HUGE!" Indeed the cake was big. It had pink frosting and was 6 stories high!

After the food was gone everybody went into the Party Room. Rosa sat on a sofa. Meagan and Maggie watched from the piano bench. Rosa opened a violin, pens, jewelry, boxes, books, purses, mirrors, chocolates, dolls, portraits, diamonds, stuffed toys, and a tea set from China, parasols, doll clothes, dollhouses and lots of other things.

When everything had been unwrapped, the guests slowly started to leave. When all the guests had gone, the King said to Rosa, "Now, my dear Roseamund, your Mother and I have yet another small gift for you." He handed her a finely wrapped box.

"Do hold it carefully, dear," cautioned the Queen. Rosa slowly opened it. A small white head poked out among the wrapping.

"A white kitty!" cooed Rosa.

"Oh, a cat! Run, Meg, RUN!" screamed Maggie. Meagan did. She ran as fast as she could go, with Maggie close behind. When they reached Rosa's room, they scampered into Meagan's house.

"Ouch!" yelled Maggie.

"Whatever i–is th–the mat–matter?" panted Meagan.

"Ooh, that was close!" sighed Maggie. "My side is killing me!"

"What are we going to do, with that cat in the castle?" moaned Meagan.

"Well, I'm glad I live in the greenhouse! That cat better not come there," said Maggie.

"But what about me?" cried Meagan.

"I don't know, Meg. You could always come live with me

in the greenhouse. There's plenty of water because the hose drips and the gardener eats lunch there sometimes so there's food. I live in an empty pot. There's one right beside me and it's pretty big," invited Maggie.

Meagan thought a minute, then said, "Thanks, Maggie. But I've always lived in this castle. And, there's lots of food. And it's so perfect—or at least it was. Maybe Rosa won't bring the cat in here, or maybe it's friendly."

"I doubt it! But maybe you are right, maybe since the Queen's so fussy she won't allow it in here," Maggie suggested.

"Maybe. She will never let it in the kitchen. Anyway, I'll just wait and see. I'll move out with you if it gets too bad, okay?" asked Meagan.

"Fine with me!"

After Maggie had gone (on a maid's shoe while the cat wasn't looking), Meagan wondered what to do. Should she move with Maggie? Should she face the cat, or should she live all her life in fear of it? She finally decided to do just what she had told Maggie, wait and see. Right now she needed food. Her pantry was empty. But what about the cat?

"I'll go at night when the cat's sleeping," she said to herself. Late that night at 12:00 p.m., she crept out of her house. The door accidentally slammed behind her. "Oh, well, it's only a little noise," she thought.

But when she ran into a jack-in-the-box and it opened with a loud POP, Meagan gasped. But it was too late—the lights flipped on. "Who's th-there?" asked Rosa's trembling voice. Then she spotted Meagan. Unlike her Mother who would have screamed, Rosa bent down and picked Meagan up. "Oh, what a cute little mouse! Even with clothes! I'll have to keep Snowball out of here!"

Meagan started, then without thinking she blurted out, "W– will you really, honest?"

"A talking mouse!" cried Rosa. "Why, of course! What is your name?"

"Meagan Lucinda Castlemouse," answered Meagan.

"Oh, what a sweet name! Where do you live, Meagan?"

Meagan hesitated. Should she tell Rosa? She looked at Rosa's honest face and decided to show her. "I live in a hole behind your bed. It has ten rooms, but it isn't much of a house," replied Meagan.

"Oh, I just thought of something," Rosa cried, "You could live in my dollhouse. It's just your size, and I could bring you food. It has twenty rooms. I could keep Snowball out and you could invite a friend, too. I could borrow Lewis's electric train and you could ride it. I have two other dollhouses that could be a church and school!"

Meagan happily agreed and Maggie came to live in a dollhouse, too. And Snowball stayed OUT!

The End of a Tail

Meagan and the Joke

by Jessica Strappello (age 12)

Meagan Mouse sat in a cushioned wicker chair watching Princess Rosa brush her long hair. Meagan Lucinda lived in a castle. King Hubert, Queen Isabella, Prince Lewis, and Rosa lived there too. They didn't know that she shared their castle—well, Rosa did, but Rosa was different. The king was foolish, the queen was proud, and Lewis was a great friend of the court jester.

But Rosa... Rosa was different, Meagan thought reflectively. Rosa was kind, gentle, quiet, and very polite. When Rosa had found Meagan out, instead of raising a fuss, she had kindly offered Meagan her grand dollhouse to live in. It was a smaller version of the big castle, and had twenty rooms in it.

Rosa had a beautiful white kitten, but after she had found out Meagan, she had kept her door shut, and the kitten was not allowed in. Meagan thought of the small hole she had lived in before. Boy, was this better! Meagan still used the hole as a storeroom, but she didn't live in it.

Meagan suddenly started, remembering her expected company, Maggie Greenhouse. Maggie lived in the castle greenhouse. Rosa had said that Meagan could invite a friend to live with her, and of course Meagan had thought of her best friend, Maggie. Meagan had written Maggie (by way of one of Lewis's friendly carrier pigeons) to tell her. Maggie was coming tonight to view what was going to be her new home.

Meagan quickly jumped out of her seat on the dollhouse porch and ran into the kitchen. She wanted to have supper all ready for her friend. (Meagan got her food from the castle kitchen crumbs.) Meagan quickly got out some cheese, and cold tongue crumbs. Maggie was going to come over on the gardener's shoe, as the gardener had to come around 5:00 for his weekly pay. Meagan set the table, and was just placing the last dish on the table when Maggie burst in.

"Oh, Meagan! It's just beautiful!" Maggie cried. Meagan gave Maggie a quick tour, during which Maggie "ohhed" and "ahhed" enthusiastically. At last they sat down to eat.

"Meg, you wouldn't believe what I saw on the way over," Maggie said, "It's Halloween tomorrow night, and Lewis is getting up the most frightful costume. He's going to be one of those horrid black knights, like the ones across the sea! Becky, the cook is baking delightful orange sprinkled cupcakes. And the jester has made a silly list of mean jokes to play on people. The kitten, lucky for me, was snoozing. Oh, Meg, I just love this house. I can't believe I'm actually going to live in it!" Maggie said out of breath from her long outburst.

"Well, Halloween does sound nice, I wish we could do something fun," Meagan said dolefully.

"Yeah, I know what you mean," replied Maggie, then suddenly she brightened, "Hey, I know. You could get some scraps from Mary, the castle seamstress, and we could make costumes, and we could scavenge up some cupcake crumbs from the kitchen!"

Meagan's face glowed, "Of course, we'd have to be careful of the cat, but I'm sure we could manage. Why, we'll have our own private party!"

Suddenly Maggie's face got a wicked gleam. "Hey, I know, we could even play a trick (you know, 'trick or treat'). We could go to the royal dining hall, while the royals are dining, and clatter something over, then run away. They'll think the ghost of old Sir Humphrey's come back!"

Meagan looked doubtful. "Why would we want to do something like that?" she asked.

"Well, because everybody does it. I mean we could really get a good laugh!" Maggie said.

"Oh, all right, if you say so. Why don't you sleep here tonight?" said Meagan.

"Good, Meg, that sounds great!"

The two mice spent all evening and part of the next day getting their costumes and plans together. Maggie decided to be a witch, and Meagan thought a ghost would be easy. Maggie managed also to get most of her clothes and household goods over to the little castle. She had borrowed Lewis's small electric carriage and hauled it all over. It was decided that Maggie would have the room next to Meagan's for her bedroom. She had also snuck a few flowers from the green house and decorated the dining room beautifully.

Meagan had told Rosa that Maggie was moving in. "Oh, good!" Rosa had exclaimed happily, "I'll love having two mice as playmates!" Meagan had said nothing to her about the party. She just hadn't felt like it.

Maggie got Meagan's small, straw broom from her old hole and had fashioned a little gray flannel cape and hat. Meagan had simply cut out two eyeholes in an old white scrap.

Meagan felt badly about scaring Rosa so. (Although she didn't care in the least about the rest of the family, they weren't polite at all.) But Maggie skillfully calmed Meagan's fear, with the assurance that Rosa wasn't superstitious and didn't believe in ghosts.

Finally, after supper, the fun began. The two mice dressed

up in their costumes and ate their cupcake crumbs. Maggie said thoughtfully, "When I was small my brothers and I would dress up like ghosts and carry acorn wands and walk around the human family's jack-o-lantern and play all sorts of games."

Meagan looked surprised to see the rare serious look on her friend's face. But just as suddenly as the look had come, it was gone. "Come on, Meagan, let's go play our little trick," Maggie said quickly.

Meagan and Maggie cautiously made their way to the dining room. It was quite a way and by the time they'd reached it they were both out of breath. They quickly scurried up on the great shelves.

The family was enjoying their after-supper dessert. Lewis was full of tales about the boys' costume party he had been to. "And Father," he was saying, "Douglas dressed up like an imaginary creature, he was great! Two skinny antennas, a shiny suit, horns, and even a robotic horse that he designed."

Rosa shivered, "Oh, that's terrible, Lew. Douglas ought not to do that sort of thing."

"Young man, I daresay you shall not be allowed to associate with that great fool! I should have known it, his mother's simply dreadful!" the Queen indignantly sniffed.

Meanwhile Meagan and Maggie crept behind a large crystal goblet, and started whispering.

"Come on, let's push it over now," urged Maggie.

Meagan hesitated. "But Maggie——"

Suddenly she stopped mid-sentence, her whiskers twitched and her body froze.

"What on earth are you doing?" Maggie inquired suspiciously.

Meagan stammered, "I-I th-think I-I mean I just saw the-

the cat!"

Maggie gave a shrill scream and turned around. But, unfortunately a silver fork lay there and she tripped over it and fell head over heels! Meagan sprang into action. She ran over to Maggie.

"Maggie, Maggie, answer me! Are you hurt?"

A low groan came from the fallen mouse. "Oh, Meg, I think I broke my foot. Go, save yourself. Let the cat eat me!" she moaned heroically.

Meagan glanced around. "The cat left," she said. "But are you sure your foot's broken?"

Maggie nodded feebly. "I'm not positive, but even if it isn't broken, it's at least badly sprained."

Meagan looked desperate. "What should I do? Hey, I could use the electric coach of Lewis's."

Maggie replied, "Yes, but one of them would see it, and we can't have that, you know!"

"Maggie, they're finished with supper now, I'll go get the coach. You stay here. I'll bring it to the floor below the shelf, then we'll somehow manage to get you in it!" Meagan suggested excitedly.

"OK, but don't be long. The cat could come back," answered Maggie.

Meagan slowly crawled down the shelf. The family had gone to the parlor, and the servants hadn't come to clear the table off, yet. She hoped they'd be awhile. She ran across the corridor, raced through the Great Hall, and finally into Lewis's room. She hurried to the corner where the coach was kept. She spotted it and crept underneath and pushed the lever, then crawled back out and sat up in the seat. She put it on full power and sped to the dining hall. She drove underneath the shelf and parked it. Then she climbed back up the shelf.

Maggie squealed with relief. "I thought you'd never come!" she exclaimed. She painfully stood and clung to Meagan's shaking shoulder. They slowly and painfully got down from the shelf. Meagan helped Maggie into the coach and they drove home.

Meagan parked and dragged Maggie gently to the front door. She took her and tucked her in bed, after bandaging up the sprained foot. She brewed some hot tea on the real working dollhouse stove, and sat down in a chair beside Maggie's bed.

"Maggie, I don't think I like Halloween very much," Meagan began, but Maggie interrupted.

"I'm sorry I got you into this, Meagan. I really deserve this sprained ankle. You were right all along. It is mean and cruel to play tricks that can hurt someone. I never really did like the idea of witches and ghosts and goblins, anyway. Let's just forget about mean Halloween from now on, all right Meagan?"

Meagan nodded. "And we'll never play any mean tricks again."

And they never did!

This is Jake LaForet's first year of homeschooling and one of the very special things he is discovering is writing. As Jake writes:

> In my other school we did very little writing, but in homeschool I've found I have a talent for writing, and I enjoy it very much. My story was inspired by reading *Treasure Island*. My other favorite authors are Tolkien, C.S. Lewis, and Susan Cooper. I started to write this story in August. From then on I've written a part of it every Thursday.

It was just completed by winter, so Jake spent a long time on this story—it was no quicky, dash it off effort. I hear he's already begun another big story, ready to try his hand at contemporary fiction. Jake has learned how to take his time to work through a long piece.

Jake's mother wrote:

> I really believe that being able to communicate well through the written word is so important. It's important, no matter what vocation a person pursues. That's why we spend a lot of time on writing skills here in our home school—Forest Academy. We write stories every Thursday. It usually takes about an hour or so. Occasionally Jake has written half the morning....
>
> Homeschool has been such a blessing in so many ways. But one of those ways, and one which I did not anticipate, was in discovering that Jake loves to write, and that he's pretty good at it. I was in talking to his teacher last year, asking if Jake's class shouldn't be writing. (They did NONE all year.) So I determined to make up for lost time this year. It was just one of the things I wanted to cover. And in doing so, we made the discovery about Jake. He actually looks forward to Thursdays.

The Adventures of James Brustar

by Jake LaForet (age 12)

CHAPTER ONE

1763 Bristol was a busy seaport. Sailors were everywhere demonstrating their bad habits. Women stood in groups gossiping, boys chased each other, and girls played with rag dolls. Dogs nipped at the heels of the sailors, who yelled at the dogs and kicked them aside. Wandering chickens clucked noisily as they scuttled on the cobblestone street, sending feathers flying. Posters hung on the wall near the marketplace that listed mutineering sailors—one sailor in particular, whose name was Black Billy.

A lone boy stood by a dock. He watched as a seafaring vessel unloaded its cargo to be sold to the local traders. The boy was quite strong for his age, which appeared to be about twelve.

"Hey, there, you boy! What's your name?" called a tall sailor from the cargo ship.

"Who me, sir?" asked the surprised boy.

"Well, if it ain't you I ain't my uncle's nephew!" laughed the sailor.

The boy brushed the hair from his eyes and called back, "My name is James, sir."

"I'll give you two pence if you help me unload this cargo," said the husky sailor.

James' eyes widened. That was more money that he had

ever had in his life.

"Do you mean it, sir?" He ran over to the gangway. "Do you, really?"

"Course I mean it. Do you want the job or not?" repeated the sailor impatiently.

"I do! I do!"

"Then get yourself up here!"

For two hours James unloaded boxes and crates. There was tea from Morocco, muskets from Tunisia, tobacco from Virginia, rum from the West Indies, silk from China, and coffee from Brazil. He had never seen so much merchandise! Soon he began lagging behind the sailor. He was extremely tired from all the work. He picked up a box of silk and slowly walked down the gangway.

Suddenly, he tumbled down onto the dock. The unfortunate box fell into the bay.

"You dog!" shouted the sailor at James, as he charged down the gangplank.

James looked at the box bobbing in the water. It read, "Ten bolts of fine silk—price– 60 pounds—from China." James backed off against a wall. He was trapped!

"I bet you tripped on purpose because you thought I was paying you too little!" sneered the sailor.

"Oh no, sir," cried the boy in dismay.

"You will pay for it—100 pounds!"

"That's more than the silk's worth! You're gypping me!!" exclaimed James.

"You'll pay for it, as long as my name is Black Billy!!" roared the sailor.

Black Billy slowly walked toward James, his scarred hands threateningly out stretched!

CHAPTER TWO

James never was in a situation like this before. He had always been a quiet boy. But now James darted forward and rammed the enraged Black Billy in the stomach. With a roar of wrath, the sailor fell off the gangplank, nearly falling into the bay.

James charged up the gangway and onto the ship. He looked desperately for a good hiding place. He noticed that there were very few men around, and he saw no officers. They were probably in town. James heard Black Billy calling other sailors to help find him. He spotted some empty barrels lying on the deck. He glanced around to see if anyone was near. He saw no one. James squeezed into a small barrel which smelled strongly of rum. Minutes passed. It suddenly dawned on him that he was on the ship that had been mutineered. Then his blood ran cold! He heard, "Weigh anchor! The King's men are coming!"

James heard the sound of chains on wood. He had always liked the sound, but now it made his heart skip a beat! He peeked out on the deck through a crack in the wood. He saw Black Billy with an ugly knife in his hand. He was standing on the rough pine boards of the ship's upper deck, commanding harshly to nine, filthy men, "As soon as we're out of the port, start looking for that swine of a boy! And I want to see him dead or alive!!!"

"Sir, a clipper is trailing us!" shouted a man with a patch over his eye from the main mast. "Shall we turn to starboard and fire our guns?"

"Yes, and be quick about it!" yelled Black Billy, enraged.

The sailor scrambled down the mast, and ran past the barrels in which James was hiding fearfully.

With a sudden, unexpected jolt, the ship lurched to the right

at 90 degrees. As rapidly as it had started turning, it stopped.
James was beginning to feel seasick.

Suddenly, there was an ear shattering explosion. The ship
rocked as there was a splintering sound some distance away.

Two more shots, and then there was a sharp, distant,
crackling noise, and then a crash! All the mutineers were
running about, slapping each other on the back, shouting and
yelling and celebrating. Apparently the trailing clipper's mast
had fallen.

"They're turning back, sir!" cried a tall man.

Now there was no hope of rescue for James.

CHAPTER THREE

James was glad the ship wasn't hit, for then he would have
run the risk of being hurt.

"Come on! We all agreed that I'm the captain here! Get
searching for that boy! Now get movin'!" exclaimed Black
Billy.

Men began running below deck. Apparently no one gave a
thought that James was on deck in a barrel. He heard a man
yell, "He's not in the food hold!"

James grinned as he climbed quickly out of the barrel and
scooted after the man. He halted as another man wearing
ragged sea clothes emerged from a door. He was eating a
piece of salted meat. He walked down the hallway, his back
toward James, so he did not notice him. James gave a sigh of
relief, and slipped into the room which the sailor had just left.
Inside, there were shelves of water and rum and jugs of all
sizes. James stared at the meat. This would be a perfect place
to hide! But, he thought, some of those sea swabs would be
coming in all the time and getting food and drink. He looked
around the small room. He knew that ships had rock filled

bottoms for ballast, and this floor was very low in the ship. James attacked the floor boards with an iron bar lying nearby. In a moment he had enough boards ripped away so that he could squeeze in and be hidden from sight. The rocks that were used for ballast were only three feet below the floor. He would use this hiding place only when someone came in to get some food and drink. He could cover the opening with a crate of meat.

For five weeks, James hid in the hold, eating and drinking as little as possible. Black Billy thought that James had jumped off the ship, so he reluctantly gave up the chase.

CHAPTER FOUR

In June, an old man was leaning against the mooring in Norfolk, Virginia, a seaport in the New World. He looked up and saw a British ship coming in to dock. "More Redcoats, I suppose," muttered the old man, knocking his pipe angrily. "There's no stopping them! I'll wager ten shillings that there will be a war sometime," he said to himself, snorting indignantly. "Just give me a musket and I'll really show those Lobsterbacks!"

On board the British ship, James looked out the porthole at the oncoming dock. The ship glided up to the pier. One of the seamen tossed a heavy, thick rope down to the dock below. The longshoreman tied the rope to a mooring. They shoved a wide, dark wooden gangway to the ship. The mutineers went to make sure it was secure.

But before they were finished, James was on the upper deck. He ran down the gangplank, dislodging it from its setting.

"Get that brat! He knows we shot that clipper!" shouted Black Billy hotly.

"Aye–aye, sir!" yelled the mutineers.

James ran past the startled longshoremen. The longshoremen, who had never seen such a scene in their lives, did nothing but cheer James on. James darted down the cobblestone street.

Meanwhile, the sailors grabbed knives and pistols, and started to pursue James. James' heart was beating wildly in his chest. He looked desperately for a hiding place.

Wumpum!!!

James fell and landed hard on the cobblestone road. Then a tall man stood over him, glaring.

"Ah, sorry, sir," said James, getting red in the face.

"Wots the matter with you, boy?" asked the man.

"Some men are chasing me," cried James. He scrambled to his feet and tried running away again, but the man held his muscular arm out and stopped him.

"Let me go!" shouted James.

"Now, if I let you go, where will you run to, hey?"

"I'll go and hide!" James kicked out, but in vain.

"Sure, if I let you go, someone will think you're a runaway servant, and they'll be after you right away." The man looked sternly at James for a moment. "What is your name? Mine's Bartholomew."

"My name is James. James Brustar. Please let me go."

Bartholomew released his grip on James and looked kindly at him. "How about a hot meal at my home? You look like you could use one."

James glanced with relief at Bartholomew. "Thank you very much, sir."

CHAPTER FIVE

Bartholomew led James up a street past the marketplace. Suddenly a group a passers-by jostled James and he was separated from Bartholomew momentarily.

James felt scared. "Bartholomew! BARTHOLOMEW!" He began to panic when he got no answer.

Just then he saw three of the mutineers. They were running towards James, yelling. One had a naked sword, and another had a pistol, and the last didn't need anything because he had plenty of muscles.

The one with the pistol lowered it and fired at James, taking no notice of the crowd. He missed.

Another roar of a pistol came from the crowd, and the man with the sword dropped in his tracks. The two mutineers looked at their fallen companion and ran.

Bartholomew came forward holding a smoking gun. "Come, we must go," he said gravely, looking at the dead sailor, who lay face down on the cobblestones in a spreading pool of blood.

"Not yet! You are the cause of this!" said a little peddler who shook a cucumber which had a bullet hole in it. "You can have this for FREE!" He tossed the cucumber at Bartholomew. Bartholomew grabbed it in mid air and took a hearty bite.

"It's not every day I get free food from a peddler! Come on, now, James. We'll go to the constable and talk to him about this matter."

James suddenly realized how quiet the marketplace had become. He felt everyone staring at him. His face began to redden. He nudged Bartholomew to get him to start walking. The crowd watched the boy and the tall man disappear down the lane. It was only then that the people started talking about the shooting.

As they walked down the main street and a few narrow, twisting shortcuts, James told Bartholomew his whole story and how he had been kidnaped. Bartholomew laughed when James told him how he had hidden in the food hold. Soon they found themselves looking at a white washed house, with a sign hanging in front that said, "Constable." Bartholomew ushered James in.

A fat, bald man sat at a disorderly desk. When he looked up and saw them, his face lit up from a deep frown. He tossed a paper over his back. He smiled and said, "Why, hallo, there, Bart!"

At the name "Bart," James looked up at Bartholomew. Bartholomew smiled and said, "That's what Constable George calls me." And he winked.

James took a good look around the room as Bartholomew told George about the incident earlier in the afternoon. The room was furnished with two comfortable benches, a wooden chair in a dusty corner that looked like it would crumble if he sat in it, and a few old ships in dirty bottles on a shelf. The desk where George sat was cluttered with papers. The only place where there were no papers was where a chipped purple vase sat with some old withered flowers. It made a wide pink circle of dropped petals on the desk. The constable himself was a fat man with rosy cheeks and a short, red nose. His uniform was a little too small for his plump form. If he were a bit older, and had a white beard and white hair, he would have reminded James of St. Nicholas.

Vaguely, James heard "that young 'un" in the conversation between George and Bart. He focused his attention on them.

"I'll look into this," George was saying. The constable picked up his cap and slapped it on his bald head. He shouted to a skinny man in the back room, "Hey, you, John! Get two score of the King's men. Tell them to meet me down by the docks." With that he bustled out of his office. He called over his back, "Take that young 'un home with you." Before Bartholomew could say that he was planning to do that, the little man disappeared down the lane.

Bartholomew led James to a neat street which had beautiful landscaped gardens, both vegetable and flower. There were smooth green lawns and some houses even had some young fruit trees. Bartholomew and James walked up to one of the larger houses. Some would call it a mansion, but to James, it was a palace. His little house on the big, loud, dusty street back in Bristol was nothing compared to this. The house had three floors, plenty of emerald green lawn, many clean, clear windows, a few apple trees in the front yard, and flower beds all around it. Bartholomew turned the knob of the front door. James noticed that even the door was varnished to a sheen.

"Well, James, it looks like we're locked out. Just one moment while I fetch my keys."

"Sir, may I knock on the knocker?" James looked longingly at the shiny brass doorknocker that was shaped like a roaring lion's head.

Bartholomew cast a glance at James. He smiled, "All right, go ahead."

James grasped the knocker firmly and slammed it against its base. It made such a noise that it could have awakened the dead!

As they waited, Bartholomew spun his keys on his finger. James gazed in wonder up and down the street.

"Argh!!!" Bartholomew's keys flew off his finger and landed on the freshly cut grass beside the pathway. As he bent down to retrieve them, the door opened a crack and a tall, old

woman peered out. When she saw Bartholomew, she opened
the door wider and said in a scolding voice, "Mr. Cooper, how
dare you knock when you have your keys??"

Bartholomew opened his mouth to say something when
James spoke up in a meek voice, "Madam, it was I who
knocked on your door."

The woman put on her spectacles and stared coldly at him
for a moment. "Cooper, get rid of this filthy beggar at once!!"
she said, smoothing her skirts.

James' mouth dropped wide open.

"Mrs. Guigan, this boy is in my care." Bartholomew
shoved his keys into his pocket. "Follow me, James, I shall
take you to my master."

James followed Bartholomew into the house. Mrs. Guigan
closed the door, sniffed, and said, "Mercy on us!" and walked
away.

Bartholomew sighed as if a burden were lifted from his
shoulders. He rolled his eyes heavenward and beckoned
James to follow him.

Bartholomew led James through a hall. It was carpeted
with a thick, red carpet. The walls were covered with
portraits, probably family members. Then he led James up
some stairs, and to a closed door. Bartholomew tapped gently
on it.

"Come in," an authoritative voice said from inside.

Bartholomew opened the door and walked in. James
followed. Inside the room was a man in his early thirties. He
had brown hair in one of the new styles in town. His clothes
were in style, too.

"Welcome, Bartholomew Cooper. What is it?" The man
folded his hands in a businesslike manner.

"Well, Mr. Thorsen, I thought you might be able to provide

a trip to England for this boy." Bartholomew gestured to James.

"Why?" the man raised one eyebrow.

"You see, this boy lives in England. He was kidnapped by a group of mutineers and was brought here. Once they found out he escaped, they started a search for him. Three of them almost caught him. I chased them away, but had to shoot one of them. James' family must be so worried aobut him. Can you help him?"

"Yes, I think I can, Bartholomew. In four days, I will launch my *Lady of the Seas* for Southampton. Surely, once he is there, he could find somone to take him home."

James' heart leaped with excitement. He was going HOME!!!

CHAPTER SIX

At eight o'clock, Bartholomew and James stood at the docks with a small crowd around them, despite a light drizzle. The crowd was wishing James a good trip home on the *Lady of the Seas*. Some of them brought small presents for James, for over the time James had stayed at Norfolk, he had caught the sympathy of the townspeople. Rumors went around about him, too, saying that a score of men had been shooting at James, and that Bartholomew had shot them all. Or, others had said that Bartholomew had chased thriteen armed mutineers away from James with just his one gun. There were lots of wild stories that made people pity him.

As James and Bartholomew waited to get on board, James heard a familiar voice say, "Hey, you, Bart! How's it going, huh?"

Bartholomew turned around and looked down at George.

"Very fine, thank you," he said.

"Guess 'wot? I caught the mutineers! They're going to

London on a prison ship for trial. Hopefully, now they will be hanged!"

"Yes, hopefully!" chimed Mrs. Guigan, who suddenly appeared behind them. "Here, James, this is for you!" She held out a box to James. Her sudden change of attitude surprised both James and Bartholomew. Mrs. Guigan dabbed her eyes with a handkerchief.

"Um, Mrs. Guigan, don't you have anything else to do other than cry like a baby?" asked Bartholomew, hoping to make her leave so that James could have a nice, quiet departure.

"No, I do not have anything better to do and I am NOT crying like a baby. But don't you have somewhere else you could be—like playing cards with that fat constable friend of yours?" she snapped, highly insulted, and trying to insult him in return.

"Ahem, excuse me, lady!" The constable puffed out these words with some effort.

Mrs. Guigan put on her spectacles and took one look at George, then fled down the street, holding up her skirts.

"I wonder 'wot's got into her?" George said, after getting over the shock of being called "fat."

Just then, Mr. Thorsen came up to James and shook his hand, while he said, "Well, James, it's been nice meeting you. It's time to get on board, though." He smiled kindly.

James replied earnestly, "Thank you very much, Mr. Thorsen. I shall remember you all my life! And my parents would thank you, too, if they were here."

James picked up the boxes that he had been given, and as he walked up the gangway, he turned around and called, "Thank you, Bartholomew! Thank you all very, very much for all your hospitality and kindness. Good bye!"

He boarded the ship, and he sighed. He knew this would be a splendid voyage HOME!!

Samuel Ward has had a delightful time using a musical motif throughout this long adventure tale. He wrote his story while part of a homeschoolers study group that met weekly for special enrichment work with a resourceful, and dedicated, retired teacher. Samuel also has taken piano lessons and has learned about musical notation and vocabulary, which he put to good use here. He has a fine feel for the form of a fairy tale, built no doubt on all his wide reading. The following drawings by Samuel Ward illustrate some of the characters in his story:

The Tale of Trill

by Samuel Ward (age 13)

Hello my name is Sir Trill. I am a knight of the King of Keys and this is one of my adventures.

I rode along on my horse Value with my sword Cleaver at my side. I was trying to imagine why the King (His Majesty Measure, the Sixth King of Keys) had summoned me.

I rode along at a slow trot, taking in the sights and sounds. The trip to the city was *very* uneventful. As I entered the city gates and wandered around for a while, I saw two quarter men arguing with the owner of an inn. They were obviously becoming very angry. The quarter men advanced on the innkeeper who brandished his frying pan. I strode forward and asked what was the matter. One of them spoke up. "This innkeeper has cheated us by giving us mutton instead of roast beef."

I queried the innkeeper about the amount they had paid him.

He said, "Two pence, my Lord."

"That's ridiculous!" I exclaimed. "Two pence for roast beef. Two pence for mutton is totally unreasonable. So get along there," I said. They walked away.

The innkeeper thanked me. Adding that his name was Pinky, he asked me to stay. I refused and went on my way.

At the palace gate the captain did not believe me when I told him that I was Sir Trill, son of Sir Triad and Lady Legato. Just then a whole man walked up. It happened to be Rhythm, one of my childhood pals.

"Well, what do you know. It's Trill."

We walked off arm in arm, laughing and joking. I bet the guards were surprised. We went to his private quarters and talked until the church bell rang two times. Then I headed for the audience chamber.

In the audience chamber I awaited the King. Soon two whole men, the highest rank in the Keys Army, came in and announced, "His Majesty Measure, the Sixth King of Keys."

He entered and said, "Welcome, sit down." He explained that my mission was to find the *Lost Symphony*.

"If the symphony is not played at the crown Prince's coronation, he cannot become king. There will be discord in the kingdom without the symphony."

He also told me why the symphony was not in his possession. "The symphony was stolen by Chromatic Arpeggio, the former Duke of Thirds."

Just then, a half man ran in, saluted and gasped. "Your majesty, Chromatic Arpeggio's men have overpowered our outpost in the Sharp Mountains and have taken the garrison captive!"

"Impossible, inconceivable, he can't do that!" cried King Measure. Bringing himself under control he said, "You see, Trill, he is a *very* ambitious man."

He left me and strode away, calling for the latest reports on the situation.

I sought out the city's armorer and asked him for chain-mail, rope and a hatchet. Three days later, after searching all the new and old maps for the best route, I left the city.

The first day I rode hard, and by the end of the day started to leave civilization. On the second day I entered the flats and rode forty miles. On the third day before noon, I sighted a cloud of dust in the distance. It looked like a group of horsemen galloping in my direction.

I dug my heels into Value and we galloped off. My mount was going as fast as he could, but still the horsemen were gaining. Seeing that I couldn't outride them, I hid Value and myself behind a sand dune and waited.

The riders were wearing robes, and they had pointed beards. All of them bore scimitars and daggers at their belts. There were fifteen or twenty of them, carrying round shields, armed for a fight and undoubtedly looking for me!

I donned my chain mail and helmet, put my left arm through the straps in my shield, and mounted my horse. Drawing my sword, I charged, yelling at the top of my lungs.

They wheeled around and met my charge. They were superb horsemen and fought like tigers. Although I gave some hard knocks, I received even more.

After the surprise wore off, things did not go very well for me. First, I was unhorsed, whereupon Value ran off. Then I heard a shout, and a band of horseman galloped over the nearest dune. The nomads, seeing themselves outnumbered, fled.

When the horses came closer, I saw that they were led by Value and that there were no men on the horse's backs.

"How in a blue moon did you do it, you old stallion?" I asked.

"Actually, it was very easy," said my horse.

I almost choked; for horses, as a rule, do not talk in the country of Keys.

"Are you talking, or am I hearing things?" I asked.

"It's me," said Value.

"You talk!" I exclaimed.

"Of course I talk," said Value. "Bar the Great, the talking horse of the first King of Keys, was my great, great, great,

great grandfather."

"But where did you get all of these horses?" I asked.

"They were drinking at the water hole over there on the other side of those dunes," he said.

Value and I led the horses back and went on our way. The next day we met an old, old man. I asked him the way to Chromatic Arpeggio's castle.

He looked at me and said in a strange voice, "Ye shall goeth in an easterly direction."

Value disagreed. "We should go in a westerly direction."

I decided to take Value's advice and turned west. The path we were following took us toward a forest in the middle of which there was a clearing, and in that clearing was Chromatic Arpeggio's castle, Chord.

Determined to get the job done as quickly as possible, I planned to climb over the wall with my rope. Once inside, I would search for the symphony, and having obtained it, would depart by the rope, whistle for Value and ride away. By my calculations it would take no more than an hour.

Late that night, after blackening my hands and face with charcoal and wearing my darkest colored clothes, I attempted it! At twelve o'clock, exactly as the guards were changing, I crept near the wall. I then unslung the rope from my shoulder and threw it toward the top of the wall. In the end it took three tries before it caught and would hold my weight.

I climbed up the rope and looked around. As far as I could tell, the coast was clear. I climbed over the wall and crept toward the stairs. Seeing no one, I hurried to the bottom of the steps and could faintly make out the shape of the buildings, one of which I soon entered. It looked like a small palace.

Following dark passages, I found my way toward where I had guessed Chromatic Arpeggio's bedroom would be. I was hoping he had hidden the symphony there.

As I approached the door, I sensed danger! I ducked and a club came whistling over my head right where my head had been! Turning around, I saw three guards!

Once again I ducked the leader's club. Instead, I rammed head first into his stomach. He groaned and dropped to the ground. I charged the next man and got his fist on the side of my head. Ow that hurt! I swung my fist in his direction and missed, falling under my attackers. As I kicked and punched, trying to get up, one of them raised his club and hit me on my head! I then slipped into unconsciousness.

When I awoke with a headache, I was in a jail cell. I shakily stood up and looked around. The cell was small with one window. Sitting down again, I groaned. It was hopeless; there was no way to get out.

An hour passed, and then a guard came and escorted me to the throne room where Chromatic Arpeggio was sitting on the throne.

"Welcome to my palace," he said, speaking with a distinct accent. "I hope you are enjoying yourself." He laughed and went on. "I know why you are here." Seeing my surprise he added, "Etude, the royal spell caster, has used his magical powers to make you talk."

I looked where he was pointing and saw a short old man with a long nose. (The same man who had given me false directions earlier.)

"Now," Chromatic Arpeggio went on, "as many people here know, I love games. I am going to give you a chance. I will give you the magic phrase for the vault in which the symphony is hidden, but you will be in your cell all the time. So, unless you are a spell caster, you don't have a chance. What do you think, huh?"

"I think I've been in better situations," I replied.

He told me the magic phrase, but I will not reveal it in this story.

"Take him away." Chromatic Arpeggio said.

I was taken back to my cell.

For the next hour I paced the length of my cell, trying to think of how I could get out. Then I sat down against one of the large stone slabs that made up a large portion of the stone wall and thought.

Suddenly I heard a muffled blow and then another. Standing up, I saw that a stone slab had started to move! Soon it fell aside, and a dark haired girl crawled out.

When she saw where she was, she said, "Bother, these tunnels are worse than jumping in a hole and then realizing that you can't get out."

"What's the matter?" I asked.

"I'm lost, that's what's the matter," she said.

"Where does that tunnel go?" I inquired.

"Oh, the tunnels go all over the place. By the way," she said, "who are you?"

"My name is Trill, and you are my last hope. Do you think you can be back in an hour with weapons and get me out of here?"

"Well, I could, but Chromatic Arpeggio would be angry, and it's not good to make people angry. It would be fun though," she added.

"You haven't told me your name yet," I said.

"Well you never asked. My name is Melody. Don't worry, I'll be back in an hour." She left me alone and wondering whether I had made the right choice.

The hour passed slowly, but when I was certain that it had gone, I began to worry. What must have been at least another quarter of an hour went by, and then the stone moved, Melody pushed it aside. She stood up and handed me a sword, saying, "Don't complain. It was the best I could find."

I inspected it closely. It was a plain but sturdy weapon.

"It is just what I needed," I assured her.

"Now," said Melody, "before we go, I want to warn you. We are going to take a different route than I usually take."

"But why?" I asked.

"Because I think I was followed. And I also want to warn you of the Cat."

Before I could ask what the Cat was, she was crawling down the passageway. I stooped and crawled after her. The way was so low that I had to crawl on all fours, but it gradually got larger.

We came to a locked door. Melody took a key from around her neck and unlocked it. She turned around and said, "This is the lair of the Cat."

"But what is the Cat?" I asked.

"The Cat," she said, "is a large animal that guards these passages. What it guards, I don't know. But," she added, "it is important. No one is allowed down here except Chromatic Arpeggio and Etude."

My heart skipped a beat, for the only thing worth guarding this heavily would be the Symphony.

Do you think that there is a vault down here?" I asked her.

"Yes, of course there is, but why do you care about a vault?"

"Could you find it?" I asked, ignoring her question.

"Yes, I can find it, but I don't see why you want to go there." She led me through the maze of passages until we stood before the door of the vault. I said the magic phrase, and we entered.

There was nothing in the vault except a table in the middle of it. On the table was an oblong box. Upon opening the box, wonder of wonders, I beheld the Symphony. I picked up the box and closed the lid.

As Melody and I walked down the passage, I heard a sound of padded feet behind us. Melody glanced back and screamed. I turned just in time to see a large mountain cat flying toward me. Ducking, I tried to draw my sword, but The Cat jumped again and hit me in the chest. Melody picked up an old torch and struck The Cat over the head with it. The creature, leaving me alone, leaped toward her. Then I drew my sword and stabbed it in the heart. We hurried away, lest any other beasts were lurking nearby.

Five minutes later we were out of that hole. Melody and I left by the back door. When we reached camp, Value was not in sight. I called and whistled. "That dumb horse," I said.

We walked on in the direction of the Flats. The next day we ran into one of Chromatic Arpeggio's patrol parties. They took us to the outpost they had captured.

About two hours later we heard shouts and bugles. The door of our cell was opened, and there stood Rhythm! I was overjoyed.

Later I found out that Value had galloped to Rest and asked Rhythm for help. Rhythm requested aid from the King. It had been granted by the King. Accompanied by some of the bravest men, Rhythm had come after me.

Two days later we rode off. After three more days we entered the city of Rest. I was greeted quite royally, I must say.

Rhythm and I were promoted.

As for Melody, she rang true to my heart; but that is another story.

It is important to know before you read this next very long involved story by my son, Jacob, that Jacob has in the past probably been the most reluctant writer of all our children. If anyone says, "Well, my children just aren't writers and yours are, kids are just different," I tell them about Jacob. He was *not* always someone who enjoyed writing, quite the contrary. He wrote only when specifically directed to, wrote only briefly and with great difficulty, and tended to get stuck for very long periods of time on the same topic once he would get going. That is in his past though—people can change and Jacob has definitely changed his view about himself and writing.

Jacob was inspired to start such a long fictional piece after hearing the beginnings of Ian Latinette's king story and his brother Jesse's king story at our writing club meetings. He's had several opportunities to read parts of this story aloud to the writing group, and their good responses certainly helped keep him at it. He even has written enough further adventures for an equally long sequel. Another thing that has helped Jacob enjoy writing is learning how to touch type on our word processing program. Handwriting has always been at best a terrible chore for Jacob, and at worst an exercise in utter illegibility. But his fingers fly over the computer keyboard, and he can bang out a page in no time. Because he is still at an age where countless corrections in spelling and punctuation need to be made, the computer is again a treasure.

By the way, although Jacob's main character is a math hater, Jacob does not follow suit. Math is one of his very favorite and strongest subjects.

Math Land

or
The Trials of Governing Without Mathematics

by Jacob Richman (age 9)

Once upon a number there was a country called Math Land. The Prince of Math Land hated mathematics, so he thought of how he could escape from doing his page of problems in his *Miqoun* math book. He had an idea. Here's what it was: he would use the pair of binoculars and the mirrors he had got for his birthday. He put the mirror on the wall so that he would be able to see the answer booklet which was on the floor.

The only problem was his binoculars. He held them the wrong way. Instead of making the mirror look closer, it made it look farther away. The mirror broke off the wall, tearing off the wallpaper in a small region. And PLOP a math book which was called *One Billion Ways to Cheat in Your Math Book* fell down. He was extremely excited.

Then the King heard his mother coming in. When his mother came into the room, the King ran for his math book. Just as he started to pretend to study, his mother stepped into the room and said, "Oh, there you are, studying hard!" And then she left the room and the King went over to the book *One Billion Ways to Cheat in Your Math Book*. Then he started to read.

The first of the 1,000,000,000 ideas was "use a calculator." He thought to himself, "How would a calculator help me?"

Luckily he saw a sentence saying, "This calculator will add and subtract and find square roots and do your multiplication and division for you."

"Hmmmm," he thought, "What is this square root? And what is multiplication and division? I've only heard of addition with counting ice cream cones, and was rather horrible at that. I've never heard of division." He thought maybe it was a way of doing addition.

He decided to ask his father. His father said, "You ought to know it's not that! You are 14 years old!"

"I know." So he decided to go hunt for a calculator. After walking 10,000 millimeters, he came to a calculator store. Its advertisement was for "Calculators for Lazy Mathematicians." He thought this would be just what he wanted. Instead of getting a good calculator, he got one that was made for making errors! What they'd use it for was this: to see if you would be fooled by its faulty calculations. But he did not know that.

He was doing his lesson in the red book, when he remembered his calculator. He took it out of his pocket and began to type in his problems. He was done in 3600 seconds, a record time. His normal was around 9999 seconds. His father said to him after he had done his math, "You did that page as well as a two year old!" which meant he got it all wrong.

He decided to see what the next way to cheat was. It was "How to use a pair of binoculars to cheat." The next day he was taking his achievement test with about 50 of Math Land's brightest students. He took out his binoculars and started to look around. He scored at the 99th percentile. The reason was that everybody in Math Land, except for him, always scored at the 99th percentile on their achievement tests in math. He decided he would do that tomorrow, but he didn't have anybody to peek at so he decided he would do something else.

But right then the word came that his father was dead. At first the King was sad. But he quickly became happy because he wouldn't have to work in his red book which is the second math book in a series of math books for ages 6, 7, 8, and 9 and is normally used when you are 7. He would not have to do math (but this displeased his handkerchief carrier, whose job it was to smother his face with handkerchiefs when he cried).

He was asked questions like, "How many millimeters wide should the royal bridge be." He answered, "12 millimeters." The bridge was quickly done. He was the first person in Math Land to cross a bridge 12 millimeters wide. After that, Math Land called bridges of that widths tight ropes. (Note: he didn't know the difference between meters and millimeters—a meter is 1,000 times as big as a millimeter.)

The next thing the King was asked was how wide the royal chariot should be. He asked, "How wide is the bridge?" Twelve millimeters was the reply. "How about the chariot will be 9 millimeters?"

But when it was ready, he could not fit in. He could not figure out why. Do you know? So they put an ant in the minute chariot and a snail to drive it. After that the King ordered that the bridge be made 1,000 millimeters wide, or one meter. (Note: why he put the ant in the chariot and the snail pulling it, was to keep from being embarrassed, and a little bit of extra clowning, and it was a success.)

Now back to the one meter bridge. He ordered a 960 millimeter wide chariot. He had a goat drive it, and he set off on a parade. After about 1,000 millimeters they passed the snail on the other bridge. When the parade reached the other side they found that the snail was 1,200 millimeters from the start of the snail bridge.

When they were going back, they found that the goat had decided that the center of the bridge was a good place to stop. After 240 minutes they were on there way again, when the goat decided that he wanted to see the world. He turned around and the chariot flipped over and the King landed upside down—plop! The King landed on his back and found that he was being dragged in an upside–down chariot by a goat.

After about a miserable 5 minutes he reached the other side of the bridge. He wished he had made the road wide enough that the goat could turn around. After bouncing for about 2 hours, 32 minutes and 23 seconds under an upside–down chariot, he caught sight of Geography Land.

While he was there he found this out—that the world is round not flat. Here's how it happened. He stopped at the gates of a rather large castle. It was spherical and was on a turning base. It looked like a globe, but he did not realize it. He knocked on the door impolitely and said, "Let me in!"

A maid ran to the door in a frightened manner and asked "Who are you?"

He said, "I am the King of Math Land."

She said, "My name is Globea and you may come in."

He said, "What is this castle made to be?"

She said, "A globe, of course!"

"What's a globe?" he asked.

"It's a big map of the world."

He went in and immediately got dizzy because he was going around in circles. After about 30 seconds he fell to the floor. The maid picked him up and carried him to the hospital. They said that he was just suffering from dizziness. After about 10 dizzy minutes, he met the King of Geography Land, who was sitting down under, in a balcony off Australia. The

King of Math Land came dizzily in. He was asked to sit down and he did.

The King of Geography Land asked him "Who are you?"

He replied, "I am the King of Math Land."

"Oh." Then he said, "How do you find the area of a circle? I have been wondering."

The King of Math Land said, "I don't know!"

"You don't!"

The King of Math Land quickly left for a higher place. He found himself at the top of the globe. He took a rest in the Arctic Ocean. Unluckily he slid off, and when he woke up he was caught in between two of the Himalayan Mountains. Luckily there was a door, he went inside and said, "Can I please leave?"

"Okay." So he dizzily crashed to the door and left.

After traveling for about 2 hours, he came to Reading Land, which looked like a large floor covered with books. He knocked at the largest one and he saw a piece of the binding fly open and he stepped in. He foolishly asked, "Do you know how to read?"

"Of course! This *is* Reading Land!"

"Oh," the King said, "I come from Math Land."

"Come and sit down, and why don't you put your nose in your book."

So the King put his nose in a book, but after a bit the King got tired of just reading so he decided to take a walk. He crashed against everything, because he had his nose in a book. After about 15 dizzy minutes he could stand it no longer and he put down his book. He was asked in at a rather tremendous bookshelf. He quickly put his nose in a book and crashed around. After a bit he came to the King of Reading Land.

He asked "Can I please get my nose out of this book?"

The answer was "You may, but why would you want to?"

The King of Math Land quickly replied, "I want to!"

The King of Reading Land asked him, "Who are you?"

"I am the King of Math Land and I just came from Geography Land. It's a strange place."

The King of Reading Land said, "I just found a word problem in this book..."

When the King of Math Land heard that, he fled. The King got on his chariot and drove away.

After a while the King found Computer Land. Computer Land is shaped like a big computer, and people live in the keys. This looked like it would be a nice place to stop. The King and his goat and chariot got stuck between *M* and the space bar. Luckily the King remembered that the chariot only weighed 10 pounds. He picked it up and set off along the space bar. Unluckily, the goat decided that they should go to *C*, which was painted green and the goat thought it was a field. Luckily there was a door in the key and the King said, "Let me in!"

M ran to the door to see who it was. *M* asked him, "Who are you?"

He answered, "I am the King of Math Land and I just came from Reading Land. Oh, that's a horrible place and you always are supposed to keep your nose in a book."

"I agree," said mister *C*, "And these are my children *a, b,* and *c*."

Then the King asked, "Where is your King?"

"Oh, he's in the monitor right now."

So the King let his goat loose because he realized that the chariot would be no use in–between the keys. He was forced to stop at the disk drive where he took a nap. He saw a door in the disk drive. He went in and saw King Qwerty sitting on his throne. He was typing an invitation to the King of Math Land! The King realized that the letter Qwerty was writing was to him. He yelled, "I am here!"

King Qwerty turned around. He quickly deleted the letter and said, "I was wondering how to add."

Luckily, the King knew how to add so he explained how you do it. The King of Computer Land quickly said, "Now I will teach you how to touch type."

After two hours the King gave up touch typing and said, "I would rather go to the monitor." He went there by modem. When he got there he asked, "What is that?"

"Oh, that's the printer complex. Would you like to go there?" The King agreed. When he got there he found that the sounds were deafening. The King of Computer Land gave him a pair of hearing protectors. Foolishly, the King stepped on a conveyer belt which was feeding a printer. The King almost was covered with words, but luckily the printer stopped before he was at it. Then he ran back and ran off of the track full of paper.

When he caught up with the King of Computer Land, he found that his stomach was telling him to eat. He stopped at a restaurant and picked out a meal. He ordered a cheeseburger and French fries. After he ordered he found that he should have gotten *A*, *B*, or *C*. *A* was a hamburger and French fries, *B* was a cheeseburger and *C* was a cheeseburger and French fries. *Cheeseburger and French fries* just stood for extra printing paper. He put it in the trash can and walked away.

After a bit he saw a sign saying "Math Problem of the Week: 3+3." The King ran in and said "33!" When he found that his answer was wrong he recalculated and found it was "6." He gained a bit of math confidence from doing that problem.

Then he went back to *M* and took a nap—for 0 seconds because the noise of the computers was so loud. He got out of the bed and started for the space bar. When he got there he found that his goat had left that space. Luckily his goat had gotten stuck at *C* and after a bit of pulling the King was on his way.

He found that he was almost back at Math Land. His goat started to cross the 12 millimeter wide bridge. After about 1 foot they tipped over. The King did not know why. Do you? Then the King had an idea. Here's what it was. Since the bridge was at a dangerous slope going downhill, all he had to do was take a piece of bamboo, break it in half and hold on to it. He thought he would just slide across the bridge. But the problem was friction, and because of that his piece of bamboo lit when he was halfway across. The King fell into the water with a splash.

The goat just walked across the bridge they had left on and was home. The King's mother was worried because of just seeing the goat, so she decided to improve his Equation Playground. She ordered that the King should have a new calculus spiral to slide on.

The King emerged at the side of the river. He ran to the new slide and went down it. Then he went to his mother and said, "I went around the world, and I never found one of its sides."

His mother said, "Don't you know the world is round?"

Then he saw his friends, who were discussing the volume of the pi pool. Right as the King got there the problem had been solved.

The King said, "What is pi?"

"Oh it's a way of finding the areas of circles. You should have learned it in *Saxon 76*."

The King said, "I've not done *Saxon 76* yet, so why should I know?"

"If you forget, we'll teach you."

The King said, "Okay."

They started to explain what pi is. "Pi is a way of finding the areas of circles. All you need to know is the circumference or the diameter or the radius."

"What is the radius?"

"It's half the diameter."

"Anyway, what's the diameter?"

"It is the circumference divided by 3.14, don't you know? You have all those fancy Equation Slides."

"Yes, I do," the King said meekly. Then the King asked, "Why do you need to find the volume of the pool?"

"Don't you know that we are filling it up with water for you to dive in, and why we have to find its volume is so we don't waste a bit of water."

This was totally above the King's head, so the King of course was embarrassed and wanted to prove that he really deserved to be King of Math Land. But unluckily at that instant the King forgot how to even count ice cream cones. So he decided he would hold up his self esteem by showing off. Unluckily the King decided that he would do his clowning in-between a boat and the shore.

This would have been a good place for the King to show off, but unluckily the small stretch of water between the bank and the boat started to get wider and the King fell into the water.

Then the King got a great idea. Here's what it was: he

decided to start a program called "Math Haters Anonymous," which blossomed into a large organization. He advertised it in Reading Land and Geography Land and Computer Land. In the King's "Math Haters Anonymous" all the members wrote a book, with the help of the people from Computer Land. They wrote a book called *50,000 Reasons Why Math is Utterly Useless.* It contained many pages devoted to the subject of PI. On the King's brothers' request, this is a quote from one of these pages.

We believe that PIE is clearly more filling and much more tasty then PI, which is no good when you are hungry. You can eat PIE, but PI has no flavor and no cook can make her living selling PI. So why don't you stick with PIE, for it is more filling in every way!

The book the King's organization produced gained wide respect in Reading Land, Geography Land, and Computer Land, but there were also many sales in Math Land. The reason for *these* sales was that it became a tradition in Math Land that the teacher was supposed to read an excerpt from the organization's book before starting a lesson of school work. This was not as information, but to start the day off with a good laugh, like the laugh the excerpt you read gave you!

This next story was Jesse's first foray into fiction that was not somehow based on something in his immediate world. He was directly inspired by his good friend Ian Latinette's king story, *The Triumvirate*, which follows just after this story. The writing club heard all Jesse's drafts of this story, and I know that, like Ian, the club helped Jesse keep at his long task.

Jesse worked hard to pull his story elements into a tight whole. Often little funny details that he added in off the top of his head were later worked into the larger scheme of things, helping to round out the story. He was learning how an author works to craft a piece of writing, balancing story elements and themes. Often he would go back to rework a section, saying that he now realized that a certain character really should not have acted that way, based on what he now had decided about the character's personality. He definitely did not have an end directly in sight as he began the tale—there was no outline or roadmap made, or complete picture formed in his mind. It was much more like deciding which of many possible routes he could take at each point in the story, and imagining what the outcomes of each choice would be.

Maybe this is like the strategies used by good chess players—they can't actually have a complete picture of a game in their mind because all the info isn't there at any given point. But with each move there are decisions to make that affect the constellation of the game in significant ways, and the player tries to visualize as far ahead as possible. Gradually the appropriate strategy becomes clear, the game takes on a shape, and the end is in sight. Happily, writing allows you that wonderful option of going back and redoing moves you regretted you made earlier on, something chess won't tolerate!

The King's Closet

Or

The Laughable Tale of Evelitaurus Bombarous III

by Jesse Richman (age 12)

Once upon a time, a long time ago, on a distant island, there was a monarch whose name was Evelitaurus Bombarous the III. Although very few of his subjects knew his real name, Evelitaurus did not really mind since he much preferred being known as The King.

Although The King thought of himself in grand and powerful terms, most of his subjects felt obliged to think otherwise. One of The King's problems was that he was only 12, and The King was no bigger than other boys his age.

As in most monarchies, The King was the figurehead while someone else pulled the strings. In this case that somebody else was a page named Carl. Carl had set up a system of wires that were invisible to the human eye that fastened onto all of The King's clothes so that by running through secret passage ways he could run The King like a marionette.

Long ago The King had learned not to oppose these motions because when he did, Carl would yank up the robes so violently that they would fly into the air leaving his majesty standing in his underwear.

On the day of which we speak, Carl had the flu and was confined to his bed. The King woke early and began to fumble through his closet. The King's closet was bigger than most people's. The room was about 25 to 30 feet on a side. Drawers covered most of the walls. Chests and racks filled the floor. His Majesty wandered through his closet in a rather lost daze, trying hopelessly to find a suit of clothes that had never been yanked off him.

He was not having any luck, and was on the verge of despair. He began to lift up a robe made of purple satin planning to put it on. The robe was in one of the largest drawers. Excitement gripped The King as he saw light begin to come out of the drawer. He began to fling the robes, slippers, cloaks, crowns, stockings, and belts out at an alarming rate.

The light grew brighter. Finally The King got all the things out. If his hurried majesty had not been in such a hurry he might have noticed that the clothes he was removing were of an ancient style.

His majesty calmed his excitement for long enough to slip on a golden robe, and a leather jewel encrusted belt to which a sword and scabbard were fastened. He thrust his feet into a pair of embroidered slippers, and put on a cloak and a small crown. Then he jumped into the 4 foot high drawer and ran towards the light coming from the back of the drawer.

The light was coming around the edges of the small door. The King tried the lock with one after another of his keys. After trying the lock with most of the keys, none of which fit, it occurred to his majesty that a key might not be necessary, so he turned the knob and stepped inside.

At first the light almost blinded him, but as soon as his eyes had adjusted The King began to look around. There were doors all around him in the big circular room. There were labels above the doors the labels said things like "Fiction Hall," "History Hall," "Biography Branch," "Magic Corridor,"

"Complete Collection of Funnies"... I can't list all of the names because it would take too long. I will simply say that The King began to walk forward in a wandering line with his eyes shut. He came to a door and opened it. The door was labeled "Magic Spells and Wonders."

When he was inside The King saw that the hall branched, so he stopped and read the plaque above the branch. It said "Go Right for Old World Magic, Go Left For New World Wonders." The King suddenly forgot which way was right and which way was left. So he chose one pathway and walked down it. When he was at the bottom, he saw dusty shelves full of books. The lighting was an ominous blue. The King shivered as though it was cold, which was not the case.

Then The King chose one of the books titled *Beginning Magic for Young Sorcerers*. The book was very interesting and The King read in spellbound silence. As soon as he had put the book down, The King picked up another. It was not until the last book on the vast beginners' shelf had been hastily completed, and dropped on the floor, that his majesty realized that his stomach was strongly suggesting that he go to breakfast. So he hurried to the door and raced out through the drawer and into the closet.

The King was dismayed by the mess he had made and was about to put the first of the 999 pairs of slippers lack in the drawer when he remembered the "PickUp Spell." "The PickUp Spell" put all the many clothes back in the drawer. It also picked up The King and sat him down in his dining room where the cook was starting to clear away his untouched 30 course breakfast, and replace it with a "light" fifty sandwich lunch that would daunt the most gluttonous glutton.

However, The King was used to meals of such magnitude, and cut off one 25th of each sandwich and ate only the one

25th of each. Then, because he was still hungry, The King ate three more sets of 25ths and ran to find out how Carl was doing.

Carl had taken a turn for the worst and was delirious. The King tiptoed into the room. Carl mumbled to himself, "Gotta put new cables in, need to clear bats out of passage." Then Carl said quite clearly, "The ladder in my closet needs repairs."

The King went to Carl's closet in which hung Carl's only suit of clothes. The King pushed them aside and saw the ladder. The ladder was made out of rope and looked worn. The King, without a moment's hesitation, jumped onto the ladder and began to climb.

When he finally reached the top, The King used a spell to make two candles, both of which were not lit. The King tried to make a match without much luck. To make a very long story very short, The King finally got the spell right; the candles and his crown blazed brightly. He blew one (the crown) out and holding the others aloft, he began to look around. There was a pile of junk he, and his spells, had created at his feet, but his majesty paid no attention to that. Beyond the pile he could see what looked like pill boxes storage crates, tanks, and packages.

"I wonder where all of these things came from," thought The King, so he began to eagerly run and tumble around the room. All the pill boxes were empty, all the crates contained dust or mice, and most of the tanks were full of water, except for a few that were empty. The King opened all the packages without finding anything except for the sets of clips labeled *Robe Clips*.

Often he felt something like cables on the floor, but since he could not see them he decided that his imagination must be playing tricks on him, and he stumbled towards the ladder. He was about to go back to Carl's room when he noticed a corridor on the left of the room, behind a large crate. The King lost no time in getting over to it, mainly because the floor was clear. There was a slit in the floor through which light streamed in from the room below. Although he did not know it The King had found the beginning of the maze of passages with which Carl had caused him so much trouble and embarrassment.

Down under in his room, Carl suddenly began to feel much better. His fever was rapidly diminishing. Although neither of them knew it, The King had said a spell for curing Carl's flu when he was trying to light his candles. For a moment, all Carl could think of was how hungry he was, but then he remembered he had to clean out the bats from one of his string pulling passages.

Making his way to the clothes closet, Carl looked in. The ladder was swaying back and forth as if someone had just climbed up. Carl stopped and pondered this. Suddenly Carl began to vaguely recollect what he had told The King and his heart filled with dread. So his passages had been found, his stores plundered, his cables unwound and messed up!

Carl was so absorbed with these and other horrid thoughts that he almost forgot to get dressed. After he was dressed Carl grabbed a candle stub off his night table and raced off towards the kitchen to light it. He got distracted by The Kings lunch which was hardly touched and almost forgot about The King and his upcoming cleanup job.

When Carl finally arrived at the top of the ladder The King was already far off in a branch of the hall that led to above the armory. Holding his candle up high above his head, Carl looked about him with dismay. The room was a mess. Boxes, and crates were everywhere. At first Carl just stood and stared at the mess. Then he sadly got down on his hands and knees and began to neaten up the room.

After a while Carl began to see some queer bottles filled with green powder. Finally he could resist the temptation no longer. He read the label. It said, "Instant Princess. Add water until the consistency of soft mud is reached, then allow it to stand until a frog jumps out. Have a prince kiss your frog and you have a beautiful princess with golden hair, dressed up for a wedding."

Carl was about to drop the bottle, but his curiosity again got the better of him. He poured the powder into a pan nearby and began to add water. Soon a frog jumped out, leaving the pan empty. Carl was impressed by this display and began to manufacture frogs as fast as he could.

Meanwhile, The King had come to a door, unlocked it, and found himself surrounded by glittering swords, shields, armor, maces, lances, spears, and bats. Suddenly The King heard a pattering squashing sort of noise that if you used your imagination on could sound like an army on the march. Both of The King's candles suddenly went out, thanks to two adventurous and scorched bats. Then a harmonious chorus began to fill the room. The King had never heard a frog before, let alone twenty or thirty, and began to panic.

Down below, in the armory the guard was trying very hard not to hear the screams and croaks coming from above his head. He could stand it no longer when a princess covered with the remains of a bamboo bird cage landed softly beside him, and ran to alert the castle that he was either going mad or the world around him was.

Now back to The King. He had tripped over some armor in mid scream and his lips had smacked together on a frog. This was close enough to a kiss that a princess appeared, standing in a dress that was much to big for her.

The King first began to realize that he was not alone when he heard a high princess like voice rise above the din. It said "How silly of me to be afraid of these sweet little froggies. They are really nothing to be afraid of." the voice sounded as if its owner was trying to reassure herself that there was nothing to be afraid of.

Then The King suddenly, faintly, and vaguely remembering his manners and self control, summoned up all of the eloquence that he could manage with his thoroughly knotted throat, and croaked "Who are you, what are you, and how did you get here?"

The answer was a similar question it was. "Who are you and why do you want to know?" The question was much more audible but the speaker's voice trembled slightly.

Then The King said, the knots in his throat dispersing, "I am Evelitaurus Bombarous the Third, but I was not really seeking you at all, I was just a little lonely, and now who are you?"

"My name is Jane," said Jane.

"Let's get out of here fast" shouted The King, and without waiting for Jane's approval he began to mutter spells. Suddenly there was a crack of thunder and although the roof was still intact it began to rain. This was not what The King had intended, and it took him two wet minutes to stop the downpour.

Carl had heard the noise and was racing to investigate, the thunder and voices were coming from one of the passages he had not had access to. He did not put out his candle stub, although it was his standard practice to conserve. The reason for this was that he had a feeling that he would need a light

very soon. Carl was passed by many frogs all going the same
direction as he was.

As Carl approached the armory like loft it was still raining,
but when he arrived at the door the rain had subsided so that
by holding his candle high Carl could see the blurred forms of
The King and some one else, who he slowly comprehended to
be a princess.

The King stepped squeamishly forward trying not to tread
on a frog while the frogs attempted to trip him so that another
would get kissed. When The King reached Carl he groaned
and, said "What are these?" in a tone that was a combination
of exasperation and discouragement and the product of a small
knot that had returned to haunt him and make his speech sound
not very much different from the frogs' chorus that surrounded
them.

"Oh, these are instant princesses," said Carl brightly.

"How do you de-instantize them," said The King.

"You don't de-instantize them, you kiss them" said Carl
"You are so dumb sometimes that I fear for the kingdom.
Think of how *she* got here." Carl pointed at Jane "You kissed
her; that made her stop being a frog."

"A frog?" said The King blankly.

"A frog," affirmed Carl.

"Oh just like in the fairy tales!" said The King brightly and
kissed another frog.

Instantly the frog vanished and there stood a princess, who
said, "Thank you for rescuing me and thank you for making
me in the first place. Oh and in case your wondering, my
name is Jane."

Jane One made some whispered remark to Jane Two. I am
not sure what it was but I think it was something to the effect
of, "He is my prince, so you can't have him."

"How in the world could both of you be Jane!" exclaimed The King.

"If we were made the usual way," said Jane One, "We would not be the same but—"

Then Jane Two interrupted, "But that page over there left one grain of *her* powder in the pans. That grain which came from her bottle caused both of us to be Janes."

His majesty was paying only half of his attention to the Janes. With the other half he was finding out what happened when you put a frog in a cage and kissed it. The result was a broken bird cage, which Carl had planned to use for bats, and a princess who was covered with bamboo slivers from the cage.

"Who are you?" said The King.

"I don't have a name yet," said the princess. "You muffed up the spell so that I have to find it!"

"Oh!" said The King, "How horrid."

"And now," continued the princess, "I am kissed by a ragtag prince who has kissed two before me. Oh I can't stay here!" and with a loud scream off went the princess.

"What a melancholy person," said Carl, the Janes, and The King at once. The King decided to kiss more frogs, but all of the prissy princesses he produced ran away into the passage. When all the frogs had been replaced by princesses, The King, Carl, the Janes, and a procession of bats, walked or flew out of the loft–like room and into the passage. They had no sooner stepped into the secret hall, when a trap door opened under them, and all of those who had been walking, slowly (if falling head over heals can be called slowly) tumbled towards the ground.

They landed on top of four golden haired heads and promptly fell to the floor. The King got up and looked around.

The armory and hall were already full of princesses. Standing in the middle of the throng The King suddenly became aware of how wet he was, and he suggested to Carl that they both go to his room to change into clean and dry robes. Carl had no objection, so off they went.

The King only had royal raiment to lend Carl, so Carl wore The King's worst robes and his majesty wore his best.

As they walked off Carl drew his sword, and began to wave it around in a similar way to the way you or I would do if we suddenly found ourselves in possession of a sword.

"Put that back," said his more sword accustomed majesty.

"Why?" said Carl.

"Because otherwise I will be tempted into having a sword fight with you," said The King, as he reached for his sword.

Carl suddenly realized what a dangerous situation he was in. The King was an expert fencer and if he (Carl) did win, which he much doubted would be the case, he would be punished. Carl regretfully placed his sword back in his belt.

The castle was in turmoil. The cook was racing about with platters full of food. The 30 butlers were doing the same. Someone had lit a fire in the old banquet room, and most of the maids could be seen carrying armloads of quilts and sheets into the many guest bedrooms. After tripping 10 maids, 3 butlers, and the cook—who banged him on the head with a rolling pin—The King lost interest and wandered back to the armory.

His mother was there supervising the whole operation from her portable throne. When she saw The King enter, she called gaily to him, "Come on up and sit on Mommy's lap, Evie."

"No, thank you. I will make my own throne" said his very embarrassed Majesty. He lifted his hand, muttered something under his breath, clapped his hands twice, and there stood a throne carved out of a single lump of anthracite coal. "Not again!" said The King, as though this was not the first time he had attempted to make a throne out of a diamond.

Carl said "Turn it into a diamond." So The King hopped up and down three times and said some magic words. The coal began to glow. Then it began to shimmer. Then it turned into a pure diamond throne. Every one was amazed that it had worked, including The King, who climbed onto the lofty seat and began to try to scratch it with his pocket knife.

The pocket knife snapped in half without doing any damage to the diamond. The King looked up from trying to put his knife together to hear his mother say to him, "Carl will have to sleep in your room."

He was about to protest that his king size bed was for Kings only, but he thought better of it and decided that it might be fun to have someone to talk to. Since his mouth was open, he asked when they were going to have dinner.

"As soon as we have all the bedding in order," said his mother.

"Who needs a bed?" asked Carl, and since no one did, off they marched towards the banquet hall. The table was set, the candles were lit, and the old room—which had not been used for years—seemed to welcome them to sit down on its rotten benches and fall to the floor. Coats of arms and hero's swords hung on nails and rotted pegs and seemed ready to fall on the guests at any moment.

The King took his seat at the head of the table with a loud creak. The guests, namely the princesses and a few adventurous peasants, were told to stand until they were told to sit by his majesty. The King had scarcely finished saying those fateful words when the first bench spilled its inhabitants on the floor. It was followed in rapid succession by all of the other benches.

The King was about to disband the banquet when Jane One suggested that he make them all anthracite thrones. So The King stood up on his chair and began to teach everyone how to make anthracite thrones by making one for Carl. Soon everyone had caught on and was seated.

"Now if you want to make a diamond throne simply hop up and down twice like this" said The King, and he hopped up and down. He never did show the audience how to make a diamond throne, because his old wooden one fell apart with such a vibration that the tables collapsed, forcing everyone to move to The King's dining room, which should have been used in the first place.

After stuffing themselves, the guests retired to their quarters, leaving The King and Carl eating their fifteenth bowl of ice cream and arguing over whether the lowered calorie ice cream was better than the low calorie variety.

Suddenly they both realized that it was midnight and that they should be in bed. Off they went to bed, but although they got under the blankets they could not sleep. This was partly because of their satiated condition and partly because they were talking.

"You know," said The King, "I have for as long as I remember had my robes yanked off when I make certain remarks and you are not around. Do you know why?"

Carl paused uncomfortably. Was he going to give up his livelihood as a string puller or was he going to lie?

"Well?" said The King.

Carl looked and thought around desperately for some excuse to distract The King from his question. Finally he said "What should I call you? *Your Majesty* sounds too formal."

"Call me Evelitaurus," said The King, "and now, please

answer my question."

"So that's your name," mumbled Carl, and he began to desperately cast around for another distraction. "Where did you learn to do magic?" he asked.

"In a library inside my closet drawer," said The King. "Now WHEN will you answer my question?"

Carl began to hopelessly search for a new distraction. After a haste filled pause he said, "I will answer your question if right after that we go into your library to read magic books."

"GREAT!" said The King. "What is the answer?"

"I have been pulling your strings," said Carl.

"That sounds neat," said The King, "You will have to show me how you do it. Now let's go into my closet drawer library."

"Great," said Carl, "Let's go." So out of bed they bounded and back to bed they fled, because the castle was cold and a mouse who lived in The King's bed had eaten or chewed away most of the elastic on their pajamas. They soon found their robes and set out for the closet, holding two lighted candles above their heads. They emptied the drawer and entered the many doored room. The light and heat were in stark contrast with the cold and darkness of the room they had just left.

"This is it," said The King.

"This is what?" said Carl. "Where is the magic place?"

"Over there," said The King boldly, pointing at the wrong door.

"That can't be it!" said Carl, "it says 'Primers for starting readers.'"

"Well, it must be somewhere," said his majesty, in a most defeated tone.

"Then we will have to search for it. You start from that

side and I will start from this one" said Carl. The door turned
out to be at the center of the room, so that the two bumped
their heads together as they ran at it from different angles.
Carl got up off the floor and looked for The King but all he
could hear was the faraway mystical sound of a 30 layer
chocolate cake falling apart behind the door.

At first this puzzled him, but upon opening the door the
realization struck him like a disattached piece of chocolate
cake, which was the form the realization had taken. The
realization was that The King must have said some spell that
encased him in a chocolate cake.

So Carl, always thrifty, ran all the way to the kitchen where
he got two enormous trays, and a cake cutter, and staggered
with them through the castle to The King's Closet, and through
the drawer into the room, where he began to cut up the
wiggling cake.

Suddenly the top part fell off of the cake exposing The
King's icing-covered head to the light. His majesty's first
remark, after a lot of chewing and swallowing was, "Now I
know what it must feel like to be buried alive!"

"Neat," said Carl, without much interest. "Now stop
squirming so I can get this cake off. After half an hour of
scraping The King could move all of the chocolate covered
reaches of his body, and they set off through the door with the
now familiar title and chocolate icing on it.

They went to the Old World Magic Room. The room
looked strangely altered from The King's first arrival. The
books were thrown all over the place, and although it was
quickly fixed the situation gave a unkempt first impression to
Carl, and a small amount of chocolate cake to the books.

The mess prompted Carl to read the book titled "1110
Ways to Clean Your House and do other Tiresome Chores

With Magic, Also Stories of the Misuse of These Spells." The stories of misuse were frightening tales, like that of the *Sorcerer's Apprentice* who tried to get the brooms to carry water for him. Still, all in all Carl liked the book and so did The King—because of the cleaning effect it had on him.

After that both Carl and The King started to read at their own level, and besides for occasional mumblings, the silence was complete. Suddenly Carl shouted, "I have it! I have it!" and fell off of the pile of books he had bean using for a stool.

"What do you have to yell about now?" shouted The King.

"Very simply, I have a solution to the princess problem," said Carl. "Come here and I will show you." The solution turned out to be in the "Instant" section of the magic book Carl had been reading. "Now here you see," said Carl, "is the spell to make an instant prince."

"Just what we need," said Evelitaurus.

"And here," continued Carl, "is the spell to make an instant ship with crew. For an armada you just do *this spell* and a 40 foot high barrel appears. Dump the barrel into the ocean and there is the armada."

"Wonderful!" said The King.

But Carl was already making plans of what to do next. He said, "Come on, let's put a frog in every princess's bedroom and a diamond throne for two there, too."

Then The King, catching on, said excitedly, "And I just learned how to make a door in any wall, so we make a door lead out of their rooms to the sea, where a ship will ride at anchor for each pair, and we will have the whole court and the inhabitants of the village come to see them off. And we will serve chocolate cake from my unhappy enclosure."

"Great," said Carl "let's get to work!"

Off they went, or rather out they went, from the closet into

The King's mother's room. The Queen hadn't been able to sleep, so the door was opened quickly when they knocked. The Queen heard their plan and suggested a few changes. One change was that the whole procession leave the castle by the front gate instead of through the many back doors his majesty could hardly wait to make. Also she suggested, or rather commanded, that the diamond thrones be rigged up as sedan chairs manned by the men from the ships, who with the ships would soon be made into powder and de-instantized with a bottle of champagne.

Still, she did allow The King to make them all windows so that the harbor view could be seen by all in the morning. As for the chocolate cake, the cake that The King had occupied was deemed inappropriate and the cook and helpers were unwillingly roused and sent to the kitchen by Carl's "Sleepers Awake Spell." After all the details had been hashed out during the 60 minute talk, the busiest night that had ever taken place in the usually quiet old castle began in earnest.

Carl and The King seemed to be everywhere at once, which seeing as they were using magic, they almost were. One moment they were in the kitchen stealing pieces of cake, the next they were in the princesses' rooms distributing frogs, the next moment they would be back in the kitchen stealing cake, then when the cook saw them they would be outside christening ships with bottles of champagne. By five o'clock everything was ready, so Carl sent everyone to bed, including himself, with a little bit of magic. Silence fell over the castle, as every one fell asleep.

Jane One was the first to wake up and she roused the other Jane. They got up and began to look out the new window. Jane One was the first of them to notice the two frogs sleeping together in an oversize match box-turned-bed on the window sill. She did not faint, or even scream as some of the others might have. Instead she reached out her hand to touch the frog. The frog woke up, blinked its eyes, and hopped out of the box and down to the floor. It looked at Jane One, turned its head, and hopped off to investigate Jane Two, who was gaping at him from the safety of the bed. He apparently did not find her to his satisfaction either and hopped out of the slightly open door into the hall.

It was there that Carl and The King stumbled upon him as they emerged from their room rubbing their eyes and wondering if it was really morning. However, the sight of the frog and the bumps on their heads from falling onto the stone floor, jarred them awake. Because of the realization that something must have gone wrong and a frog was on the loose, they began the tiresome task of tracking down what room the frog had come from before the princess in that room woke up.

They arrived last at the Janes' room holding a bedraggled and bored frog. They had helped many princesses out of their fright and into the joy of having a prince (or as one put it "Now I have a prince of my very own at last"). They found both of the Janes to be up and marveling at a handsome prince that one of them, I think it was Jane Two, had created out of their one remaining frog with a mere smack of the lips. He, the prince, seemed to be almost literally singing the phrases of one, while telling the other how ugly she was. This was strange seeing as they looked exactly the same in their identical white nightgowns.

Carl, who had always thought of the Janes as a person and a half, was alarmed and surprised by the way they were being treated by this unknown prince, so with out thinking he raised his hand and "*ping*" there was the frog again.

Both Janes looked very relieved and one of them said,

"How crazy it was of this frog prince, wanting to take me away to his kingdom, which I got the feeling did not exist, and marry me there. Couldn't he see that although I *did* kiss him I am far too young?"

Then The King was overwhelmed by his own forgetfulness in putting a prince or two in the Janes' room, forgetting that they were younger than the other princesses by a few years, and were just different. He could testify to the fact that all of the other princesses were enthralled at having a real live, if instant, prince. He told the Janes the whole story of the idea of sending off all of the princesses with princes and diamond thrones to seek their fortunes and find themselves each a kingdom.

After His Majesty was done speaking. Jane One said "But weren't you going to keep a princess here to be your queen in a few years? Then you wouldn't have to do the sort of thing that King George the Third did of sending his pictures to all the princesses in Europe and hoping that a nice looking one would send back her portrait for him to hunger over."

"I never thought of that," The King mumbled. "But now it is too late. All of the princesses have kissed their frogs by now. Anyway I don't like any of them!"

The Janes, Jane Two in particular, were anxious not to be nuisances, and both were worried about staying around and getting in the way. They finally agreed to stick around, instead of departing for Europe, and see what would happen. That is not to discredit Jane One's hinting that although she did not want to be in the way, she was not against becoming Queen at some MUCH later date. With that, Carl and The King turned the frogs back into bottles of green powder and made the bottles disappear, leaving the Janes in a much happier state of mind.

In the other rooms the frog finding and kissing had gone well, greatly due to The King and Carl's help. The pairs of princes and princesses could be seen walking down the hallways to breakfast. The pancake breakfast was going well and the dining room was almost full. The cook was very busy and was throwing pancakes off of the griddles at the rate of about one pancake each tenth of a second, but even so there was always a line waiting for each one.

When the crowds of eaters had retired, the Cake Walk began. The Cake Walk facilitated the moving of the gigantic chocolate cake to the dock where it would be served. All 30 butlers were involved and it made a mouth watering spectacle.

After a much too long while the crews from the ships arrived, staggering under the weight of the diamond thrones. When the couples sat down in the thrones, they caused most of the bearers to drop them on the ground. This desperate situation was finally ended with the help of about 3000 helium balloons. The balloons were created by Carl, and fastened on the multitudes of poles, they made it so that the bearers had only to push the airborne chairs. The balloon filled procession got under way. The trip to the harbor was quite uneventful, at least for the first part.

Then the bearers started to complain that the much reduced load was still too heavy. They forced Carl to supply so many balloons that the thrones would have drifted into the air if it was not for the multitude of holders. This lack of weight caused a few of the bearers to break into a run. The others, who were not inclined to run, let go. That move was almost disastrous for the bearers and occupants of the weightless sedan chairs. As the remaining bearers ran they rose slowly upward, then as they came to a rise in the road they jumped it like a jump, and began to fly out of control and into the clear blue sky. If The King and Carl had not done some quick magic the whole airborne party would have most likely drowned when the balloons popped. As it was, they turned around and landed softly on top of the chocolate cake, and were eating before anyone else could reach the scene.

When The King arrived huffing and puffing, the first thing he did was get a large slice of cake and sit down in the shade to eat it.

The first thing Carl did when he arrived, was look for the diamond thrones. They were hovering about three feet above the chocolate cake, anchored there by magic anchors. When he saw them, Carl climbed up and began to push one balloon chair arrangement out over the ocean towards its ship, which was with the others drawn up along the pier in easy walking distance of its partying crew and guests. He let the chair down onto the deck, popped the balloons and went off for another magically anchored balloon and throne. The magic would hold the thrones down to a certain level but not prevent them from drifting, thus Carl could move them onto the ships without breaking the anchoring spell, and could wait to do that until the balloons had popped.

By the time Carl returned to the cake there were only a few not spoiled pieces left, but he managed to grab one and eat it as the couples and their sailors walked off to their ships. Those who remained, cheered.

EPILOGUE 9 Years later

Things have been quiet recently in the castle. Carl has given up string pulling and has become the Royal Adviser, which he describes as a more legal way of promoting his thoughts. The wedding announcements went out recently to all of the former instant princes and princesses. After the final ceremonies are over, they will be presented with their original frog powder bottles. To be wed are The King and Jane One, as well as Carl and Jane Two. And it looks like His Majesty Evelitaurus Bombarous III and his bride Jane the First will live, if not happily ever after, at least a long time in that position.

Ian Latinette shared this major story chapter by chapter all fall with our writing club. He always had a ready and willing audience, even when it took over 45 minutes to read the entire finished draft in January. He shared with us all how he got ideas, and admitted that he certainly didn't always know where the action would take him— he was in many ways riding along on the journey just like his characters. This made it especially exciting to see Ian pull the piece to a finish, as for a bit he felt he was wandering about the world with his characters forever, with no possible end in sight. He had the chance to realize that one of the strengths of writing is that you can always go back and change and fix-up as you need to, and make the beginnings consistent with what the ending turns out to be. Many people who have never attempted fiction feel, as I used to, that you somehow must have the entire plot figured out in detail in your head in advance, and the writing it down part is simply "dictation." Instead, it's often the act of writing that lets you know just what it is you might come up with.

As you'll soon probably figure out, Ian is a voracious reader, and has a unique sense of humor. What you wouldn't guess from this piece is that one year ago Ian hated to write, and wrote as little as possible and grudgingly at that. He felt his writing was boring, that his essays had the verve of a dull encyclopedia entry, and that he had nothing important to say anyway. His mother always felt he would enjoy writing fiction, since he enjoyed reading it so much, but any attempts ended up in frustrated crumples in the wastebasket. Ian felt his own writing just couldn't match what he was reading. I think you'll be just as glad as me that Ian has now changed his mind about his writing abilities. In fact, he recently told his mother that when he grows up he intends to be a writer. I think you'll agree that he already is.

The Triumvirate

by Ian Latinette (age 14)

Once upon a rather boring four o'clock in the afternoon, His Most Regal and Royal Highness, otherwise known as the King, had a Brilliant Idea. He forgot it almost immediately, but since he was not as Intelligent and Brainy as his advisor, Professor Compendium, and rarely had Brilliant Ideas on his own, it was time for a Grand Royal Celebration. So he made a speech that was to commemorate this occasion and delivered it to the professor, his servant Lackey, and his reflection in a full–length wall mirror.

His speech was long and tedious to listen to, and Lackey, moved by long acquaintance with the king's speeches, discreetly went to sleep. The professor listened with half an ear while brainstorming for his newest book.

Fortunately at that moment there came a loud knocking on the door. *Boom, Boom, Boom.* The king threw his notes at Lackey, who woke up and went to answer the door, rubbing a lump on the back of his head.

"Mr. Joe Bloe, from the patent office," he announced.

The patent office worker came in and greeted the king. "Your Highness," he said, then stopped, thinking of the best way to put it. He decided to put the matter plainly. "Sir, ah, I, I mean we, um,–"

"Well?" said the professor.

"Sir," said the patent office worker apologetically,"your subjects accuse you of making extra taxes, heavy fines, and long work days at a minimum wage of three cents per hour. They are tired of your 'oppressive rule', and so it is time for you to abdicate."

"Abdicate?" said the king.

"It is time for you to retire," said Joe Bloe, the speaker for the People. "Your Vice Minister is the one who raised the charges (and caused the problems, I might add), and he is the one that the people have chosen to lead them."

"I was almost positive that I didn't do those things" said the king triumphantly.

"You" continued Joe Bloe, "are to be taken to Dreadnought maximum security retirement home by the army of the Vice Minister very soon, so I do not have much time." He handed each of them a small packet filled with something. "Those are the donation from the retired king's fund. Use them wisely." and he was off, this strange ally, leaving three speechless people behind.

They were in prison. The Vice Minister had come with his army and taken them off to Dreadnought castle. The next day, after a light lunch of mule meat and black bread, for which they had to compete with hordes of rats, they were talking about the Good Old Days and the treachery of the Vice Minister.

As they talked, a strange packet fell out of the king's pocket. A rat ran out of a pile of straw bedding and started nibbling at it. It ate some of the powder inside and started to fly around the room! Soon the room was filled with flying rats, which began to fly out the windows. The king noticed this and mentioned it to the professor, who said that it was not a "Normal Natural Phenomenon."

The king and professor began speculating on the causes of "this levitation of the rodent population," but Lackey tried something a little more direct. He took a pinch of the powder and began to fly around the room.

"Come down here at once," said the king.

The next time the jailer opened the door to bring the next meal, he was mobbed by hundreds of rats who ambushed him from the ceiling, eating the food out of the dishes he carried and chewing on his leather tunic.

There were hundreds of rats, but there was no sign of the prisoners. They had Flown the Coop. They flew west, over the ocean to a small island where they congratulated themselves for their clever escape and then stuffed themselves with coconuts and mangoes.

They spent the night and part of the next day there, then flew farther west. In the evening they came on a large island, on which there was a large city, with a large castle in the middle. There was a martial parade in the main street, and heading it there was a large, nasty–looking man, obviously a military dictator.

The three decided that they would have to stop in the city for the night, because it was fast getting dark. So they landed in a park, hid their packets in a hollow log and walked forth into the dictator's city.

As the three walked into the city, they saw many subdued looking people and sometimes a large armed guard. As they looked for a hotel, night came. All of the people left the streets. Many more guards appeared, carrying lanterns.

"Excuse me," said the king to a guard, "but could you tell us the way to a hotel?"

When the guards heard someone ask them the way to a hotel, they quickly grabbed at them bellowing, "What's your serial numbers, ranks and names!?"

"Fly for it" said Lackey. "Huh?" said the others. So they

were captured and escorted towards the large and nasty castle of the large and nasty ruler.

"We captured the three UFOs," said the Captain of the Guard.

"Excellent" growled the dictator. "Put them in the 'softening up cell' while I think of what to do with them."

The three friends sat together in their cell and thought. They thought about traitors and armies and flying and coconuts, but mostly they tried to think of a way to escape.

Then, feeling in his pocket, the king found some flying powder dust. They divided it up and ate it, even though it was full of royal pocket fluff. Then they flew up to the windows, but surprise surprise! Their cell was deep underground and the windows were small slits leading up many feet. They couldn't get out. They sank back to the floor , feeling gloomy. "What do we do now?" asked Lackey to no one in particular.

"Come with me," said a guard who had just entered. He took them to the dictator, who said "You three are to be my new flying patrol for the downtown area. Anyone calling a meeting of more than three people, anyone not saluting the great flag of our country or doing anything listed in the Rule Book is to be reported to my Prime Coordinator. UNDERSTOOD? If you don't—I'll have you taken apart to see what makes you tick!!!"

"Gotcha!" said three voices at once. They flew to the park and picked up their packets, then began circling above the city.

"Do you know what I think?" said the king. "I think that we should fly away off of this island at once, leaving this nasty to take care of his subjects himself!"

"True," said the professor, but—" We shall never know what pearl of wisdom the professor was about to drop, for at that moment he spotted a group of four people.

On an impulse, Lackey flew down and told the people to go and hide in the park. The three continued to circle, spotting a group from time to time, and sending them off to the park to hide. So, by the end of the day, there were several thousand people in the park (which was large enough for them all).

While the king and professor made revolutionary speeches, Lackey had an idea. He flew to the dictator, and asked him for the key to the armory so that he could teach "those Rule-breaking civilians" a lesson. The dictator smiled a nasty smile, gave him the keys and told him "Don't overload the hospitals, boy, but give it to them!"

So Lackey went to the armory and loaded swords, armor, halberds and bows into a cart until the armory was empty. Then, he took it to the park and "gave it to them."

The people, who by this time were seething, were armed and ready. That night, near the entire population of the city started a march on the castle. "Call out the army, the guard and the special police!" yelled the dictator in a panic.

"But Sir," said the coordinator, "most of them have joined the opposing army. We have about fifteen people on our side, counting your cabinet ministers."

Just then an archer came to report the fall of the outer wall. On his heels was a man-at-arms, reporting that the inner wall and courtyard had fallen. "They were too much for us, Sir," said the archer.

"Are you forgetting rule #77841?" asked the dictator.

At that moment the windows had burst, and through the panes came a certain three people. The dictator threw his knife at them, but it broke, for they were wearing the best of his plate mail. Then he threw his scepter, crown and prime coordinator. All failed to stop their advance. In desperation, he lifted the great Rule Book and hurled it at them. They dodged, and the book tore out part of the wall.

After due consideration, the dictator, his eleven generals, coordinator and two soldiers were exiled to the small desert island, with a pocket knife, a fishing pole and a solar still apiece.

After the three friends left the island, they flew due west for the rest of the day. As night fell, they looked about for a place to land. Spotting no islands around, they began to argue about how they were to get any rest. As they argued, and as they flew, they failed to notice that as the moon came around a cloud, a large, faintly civilized island came into view on their right, where nothing had been a moment before.

It is important to note that this island appeared at almost the same moment the professor said "I do wish that SOME island would appear where we could take a nap!" Landing on the island, they found it as smooth as an egg and as empty as their stomachs. "What a barren place," they thought in chorus.

Only Lackey gave voice to their thoughts, saying, "What a cheerless dump. I wish there was a food shop nearby, or even a whole city of food shops!"

As soon as he stopped speaking they noticed a faint glow on the other side of the island, so they went to investigate. From far away, the glow seemed to come from thousands of food shops thrown together as if in a blender, thus making a large metropolis, smelling of rancid grease and stale bread.

When they entered the town, they found that the place where they had landed had disappeared, being replaced by a dead end alley. Even the professor found that something seemed slightly strange about all this, and remarked on it to his friends.

"Yes, it is rather different" remarked the king.

"Different?" shouted Lackey. "It's INSANE!!"

"Nice day for it" remarked a passing lunatic.

"We're going to get to the bottom of this!" said the king and the professor together. They instantly vanished, and Lackey wandered off to find some food.

Strangely enough, "the bottom of this" was the bottom of the ocean. The king and professor found this out, as they unvanished underwater near an ancient sunken ship. "Look!" said the king, "we're near an ancient sunken ship!"

"Let us go and examine this archaeological find," said the Professor.

So they went and examined it. It may seem strange, but the same powder that gave them their flying ability gave them the power to stay under water as long as they liked.

"Let's go inside and get all of the sunken treasure!" said the king. So they went inside. The inside of the ship was empty, except for a small bottle made out of a ruby. The king grabbed the bottle and said "That's all that is in here. Let's go."

As soon as the words left his mouth, they appeared next to Lackey, on the island, in the food shop city. He had a stomach-ache from too many greaseburgers.

"Something out of the ordinary is occurring here," said the Professor.

"Yes," agreed the king, "I wish I knew what is going on around here!" When he said this, the island began to shake and out of the small ruby bottle popped a small purple genie.

"Thank you, kind friends," it said. "I have been unemployed so long it feels good to be out and about. May I help you?"

The three were amazed at the sudden appearance of this strange creature, they couldn't speak.

"Well," said the genie, "are you taking your wishes or not?"

"Wishes?" the king managed to mumble dazedly.

"Yes, wishes. You get three wishes. Divided three ways that would be..."

"One apiece!" shouted the Professor brilliantly.

"Yes, one apiece." said the purple genie.

"Just a moment " said Lackey, "We have to talk about this."

They conferred for a moment and then the king stood up and said: "I wish that we all had three more wishes."

The genie frowned and pulled a scroll out of the bottle. He read it and said: "Look here in the contract: 'No person may wish for more wishes.' Next!"

The professor stood up and said: "How do I know that you really can do magic?" The Genie waved his hand and laughed as the professor turned into a frog, then a crab, then a worm, and finally back into himself.

"One left!" said the genie.

Lackey had been quietly thinking to himself and so he said: "I wish that we all three could fly without needing wings or pills."

"Wish granted," said the genie, "on one condition—that you take me with you on your travels. By the way, my name is Fred."

"Hi, Fred," said the three. "Of course you can come!"

That night there was laughter and feasting in the city of food shops.

The next morning, the four friends decided to rest and have a party on the island, celebrating the addition of Fred to their group. So, for the special festive day, Fred made another restaurant spring up instead of the first city of low-grade greasy fast food joints. This one was more high-class because the grease was several years younger, had also a wilted salad bar and (wonder of all) a real waiter who, it seems, had been in service almost as long as the grease and tablecloth.

After a festive dinner, Fred zapped into existence a triple pack of Rolaids(tm) which was welcomed by the feasters. As evening drew on, they all relaxed, floating in various positions.

"We thank you for the most enjoyable repast which you have made, and we are glad that you joined our party," said the Professor.

Spurred by this, the king was about to start a speech, when Fred gave a piercing whistle. "Ptwheet! Here boy, good boy!"

Almost immediately, out of the small red bottle came a small bluish bit of wispy fog. "Yirrruf!" it said.

"Fetch boy! Fetch the stick!" said Fred, and threw a bone which had just appeared at his feet. The wisp of fog ran after the bone, grabbed it and began to chew it happily.

"There," said Fred, "he seemed kind of restless in the house. You were saying?"

But the king was absorbed in watching the wisp of blue fog chew on the bone, and decided to forget his speech.

Lackey decided to liven up the conversation. "Mister Fred, I was wondering, why do you live in a bottle, and also, how did you get here, in an empty sunken ship under the ocean?"

"Well," said Fred, "As for living in a bottle, well, that's traditional. But, to explain the sunken ship, I must tell you the story of my life. You had better get comfortable."

"We are!" chorused the three at once. The Professor got out his notebook and pencil. So Fred began.

"I spent my childhood in this very bottle, in the woods, totally alone. When I was eleventy-one, it was time for me to move along in the world. This was not hard, for I had schooling aplenty. I lived in a library for a time and read all that I could get. After about a week, I left to go to serve as an executive in the Co. Co.. The Co. Co., or Coincidence Company, was a group of genies who supervised strange happenings the world over. For example, I know why after every time your nephew came over, you never had quite as many spoons as before, and why a rat ate a hole through your speech the same day the Grand Duke came over for tea. Yes, those were fun days. But, eventually, I left the Co. Co., taking to the road.

"My path led me to a large mountain, where I took my bottle into a small cave and slept for about a week. When I woke up, I found that I couldn't get out of my bottle! There were some sort of metal scales blocking the opening. I tried teleporting out of the bottle. To my surprise, it worked.

"There, lying in the large cavern room on a large pile of crushed and pounded gold, I saw a medium-sized dragon. It was looking at the ruby bottle that was my home very happily, since the pile of treasure it was on contained nothing but gold.

"It began lumbering off, holding it's thumb over the top of the bottle. I quietly followed, crawled up on the dragon's left horn and waited until it came to the great gem room. I am not even going to describe the gem room in detail, because you, being human, would go crazy with greed. You must just imagine a great heap of jewels that half-way filled a cavern as big as a castle.

"As soon as he dropped the bottle on the pile, I floated down, grabbed it and got slightly scorched (with dragon-fire) carrying it out of a crack in the roof. I passed through many other rooms and caves on my way to he surface, and I asked a miner gnome how I could get to the surface. He told me to follow the next cavern to the left, so I did.

"I found myself on a hill above a seaport. It seemed to be used as a dump, and in an old glass bottle I found the little smoggy that I now keep as a pet. It took some time to tame him, but he calmed down at the sight of food.

"Later, I went down to the seaport, where I stowed away on a ship bound for the islands. It sunk, and everything rotted on board except my bottle. Since then, I have been waiting for a chance to adventure again. I did tricks for visitors to a nearby island, and kept the ship from rotting, so I wouldn't sink into the mud and never be found.

"And That Was That, until you came, found me and brought me here. Here now! Stop that!" This to the wispy blue fog, which was growling at the Professor's notepad.

"Nice little smoggy," said the Professor nervously.

"Thank you for your story," said the king. "And now, good night."

Lackey agreed with the latter statement, for he had gone to sleep as soon as the story was ended.

The next morning, as the sun rose, so did the adventurers. They flew in a northwesterly direction, soon coming on a large island. On the western side of the island, there was a wasteland of pits and digging machinery. On the east side of the island, there was a city which had a large pillar in the center. Flying down, they saw a lookout standing on the pillar, scanning the sea. Suddenly, the lookout pointed at the horizon and yelled. They quickly flew closer to see what he was pointing at.

It was a large, black ship that flew a skull and crossbones flag. "Pirates!" shouted the professor.

At that moment, the pirate ship let out a small puff of smoke. They quickly scattered as a cannonball whizzed past them and plopped in the city, doing small damage to a steel-walled bank–like structure.

The pirate ship continued to shoot at the steel bank, finally knocking a large hole in one of the walls. Then the pirates began to sail up to the city. The friends decided that they should try to stop "Those robbers and brigands" as the professor called them.

Therefore, they flew quickly down to the bank, getting there before the pirates. When the pirates came through the hole they had blown in the bank, one by one they were knocked on the head and laid aside, tied by magic cords.

However, the last one in line was the captain, and the smartest of them all. So he waited for his men to signal him, telling him that it was safe, that there were no guards over the money. But, since the signal did not come, he drew his sword and leaped through the door.

His sudden arrival startled the defenders, for they thought that there were no more pirates. He waved his sword at them and told them to untie his men and lie face down on the floor.

Lackey made an act of untying the first, and when the pirate was distracted, Fred turned him into a statue.

Some time later, several scared townsfolk peeked through the door. They were overjoyed that the pirates had not stolen their treasure.

"Treasure?" said the king.

"Yes," said the town spokesman. "Those crates and boxes contain the treasure of the many pirates who once lived on this island, died on this island and buried their treasure on the island. Those pirates..." and here the spokesman kicked one of the bound buccaneers. "Those pirates were trying to steal the treasure and use this island as a base to rob the whole world."

"Thank you!" said all of the grateful townsfolk.

Fred then presented to them the statue of a certain pirate captain, to be put in the town square for the pigeons to sit on. The rest of the pirates were used as laborers in digging up the rest of the old treasure.

The next day, with the thanks of the townspeople, they lifted off and left for the west once more.

As they flew along, they could hardly keep their eyes open, they were so tired. Once in a while, one of them would fall asleep and start falling. So, the others, who were slightly more awake than the one who was asleep, would dive down and wake them up before they hit the water.

They took turns at this in strict rotation, three awake and one asleep. The professor, observant as ever, noticed that "It seems some of us are slightly drowsy," and went to sleep out of turn.

After waking him up, Lackey, as practical as ever, made the suggestion to his friends that they stop and rest a while. Therefore, they (meaning the ones that were awake) started looking for a place to spend the night.

As they looked around, the king spotted a large rock, oval in shape and slightly domed. They decided to stop there and rest, it being the only dry land about. They landed, and as their feet touched the rock, they collapsed snoring.

In the middle of the night, at the awful hour of 4:00, they woke up in a panic. Only those who have been wakened from a sound sleep by being splashed into the cold saltwater on a large rock in the middle of the ocean which suddenly turned into a seamonster can possibly imagine such panic.

Reacting swiftly, Lackey yelled "spugrfgupug!blub" as the sea monster bent over them, licking its teeth.

Fred, a genie of instant (if strange) action, turned them all into whales except himself. HE leaped down the monster's throat, bottle and all, causing it to have a sudden fit of coughing, which still continued as Fred leaped out and yelled "dive!"

So, needing no further urging, they dove quickly and deeply. Now, it happened that the place where they were diving was the deepest hole in the sea, which has yet to be rediscovered. They dove down, down, down, down, until Fred said "End of the line!" It was the bottom of the ocean. There were many large sea creatures swimming about, of which the professor said, "They are mainly of the undiscovered and legendary type, in short, myths." Then he smiled in a self-satisfied manner, immensely pleased that he had refuted the existence of these creatures.

They stayed down for about an hour, then slowly raised up to the surface, only to find that the sea monster had coughed up Fred's bottle and left for parts unknown. Fred reclaimed his bottle, turned the others back into humans, and having had a long day, went to sleep. The others, however, lifted slowly out of the water, and continued, (rather damply) on their way to the west.

As the sun rose on the three hundredth day of their adventure, the four friends could be seen flying over the ocean, in a westward direction, towards the unknown. It was not unknown for long, because as they neared yet another very large island, Fred exclaimed, "That island was where I grew up at! The seaport I left from was right over there, and the dragon's cave was underground to the left, and there is the old forest!"

The king, however, only heard the part about the dragon's cave. "Do you mean the dragon's cave with the piles of gold and jewels?" he asked excitedly.

"Yes," replied Fred cautiously, "but the dragon is probably still guarding it. They live thousands of years." But the professor and Lackey had also caught the gold fever, and so they all dove down towards the entrance to the dragons cave.

When they arrived, they found that there was a sound of loud breathing and a smell of sulfur in the cave. They disputed whether to go in or not, and whether they thought that the sound was of snoring or not. They finally decided to go in and have a peek at the treasure, and if the dragon was awake, to run out of the cave and fly as far away as possible.

They went in. The smell of sulfur increased as they went. The sound of rushing breath increased, until it was a strong wind. They climbed between rows of stalactites and stalagmites, and found that the cave grew moist. The cave had moisture on the walls and floor, and still the smell of sulfur increased. At that moment, the dragon, awakened by four small itches marching down his throat, woke up and began coughing.

The itches flew out of his throat and hovered in the air in front of the dragon. The small purple itch said nervously, "He seems to have grown slightly."

The large itch with the notebook said, "Animals of this size are not possible, in short, they are strictly fictional."

And the other two itches simply said "Flee! Fly! HELP!"

So they flew quickly out of the cave, just ahead of a large hot flame which the dragon idly puffed at them.

He settled back down to sleep, this time with his mouth shut. And the itches flew away westward.

The next day, four slightly singed itches landed on a small island that was completely deserted and a truly wonderful vacation spot. So, feeling in need of a rest, they stopped there for a couple of months, feeling that too much adventure may be harmful to one's health.

The king made many speeches, announcing them a week ahead so as to give the others fair warning. They all talked about the adventures they had had, and Lackey even asked,

"Where do we go from here?" but the others told him to be quiet; they were on vacation, and they didn't want to have to think right now.

After some time, they began to want to go on, so they lifted off and flew west for four days. As you may have guessed, a whole year had passed since they flew out of Dreadnought retirement home...

They flew further west on the 364th day of their travels, and as the sun set, they saw a large island or continent, which the professor could not identify, nor the others.

They set down in the courtyard of a large castle. "Deja vue," said the professor.

"I don't know where we are at all," said the king.

"I know," said Lackey quietly. They turned around and saw him standing with two rats sitting on his shoulders. As their eyes widened, the rats took off and circled up into the night sky, passing on the way a large sign which said: "Dreadnought retirement home."

"We have circumnavigated the globe," declared the professor solemnly.

"No we haven't!" said Lackey. "We've gone around the world."

"Come on and let's go take a look around town" said Fred, who had never been there before.

They all agreed, and so they walked out into a neighborhood of vile slums and decrepit old stores.

"This place is awful," said the king.

"Not much like it used to be," agreed Lackey.

"Who is ruling this place now?" asked Fred.

"I'm not sure," said the king.

"Why do we not go and inspect the monarch of this, our former home?" said the professor.

"Because he would probably throw us in jail," grumbled Lackey.

But they went anyway. The castle was looking almost as bad as the rest of the town, so the king asked an old man what had happened to the town.

"Overlord took all the money," said the old man with a venomous look towards the castle.

They approached the fortress, and when they got there they knocked on the great oak door: *Boom, Boom, Boom.* soon the door opened and a squat, powerful guard popped out, grabbed them and pulled them inside.

He carried them to what had once been the throne room, and dropped them on the floor. There in front of them was the tyrannical Overlord. He had once been the king's Vice Minister, but he subverted the army and made false charges against the king, and the people helped him take power.

The Overlord grinned nastily. "Travelers I see. Find out if they have any money," he said.

The guard turned them upside down and shook them. Out of the king's pocket fell the ruby bottle, the home of Fred. The guard handed the bottle to the overlord, and while his attention was diverted, the three rose into the air, kicked the guard on the head, and grabbed the overlord.

They flew him downstairs, flying out of reach of the guards, and locked him in the deepest dungeon. They then went to the armory and took three pikes. With these, they herded the overlord's soldiers out into a ship that Fred made appear, and Fred sent them off to join the dragon on his island. The overlord they sent too, first taking the keys of the castle and Fred's bottle.

All was well. They had distributed the contents of the treasury among the people, and the people had begun to rebuild the city and castle. The three friends were appointed a triumvirate, and Fred was their advisor. The inauguration speech by the king lasted three hours and a half, but nobody minded.

The professor decided to write books when he was not helping govern the country, and his works include *Mythical Animals I Have Seen*, *Been Thrown Into the Ocean By, and Swallowed By*, and *Dictators I Have Overthrown*.

Lackey just took it easy, and Fred did whatever he wanted to. So peace came to the island and the people settled down under the TRIUMVIRATE.

Triumvirate: (Trai–umm–virat) Government by triumvirs, any of three men in authority.

Resources

These are just a few of the amazing number of fine books available now on writing and learning with children. The numbers following the books are the numbers that I have paired with the catalogs. Most of the catalogs can be obtained free just by writing away for them.

Catalogs worth writing for:

1. *Dale Seymour Publications*, P.O. Box 10888, Palo Alto, CA 94303.

2. *Education Services*, 6410 Raleigh Street, Arvada, CO 80003.

3. *Heinemann Boynton/Cook*, 70 Court Street, Portsmouth, NH 03801.

4. *Homeschool Book Shelf*, Home Education Magazine, P.O. Box 1083, Tonasket, WA 98855.

5. *Incentive Publications*, the Kids' Stuff People, 3835 Cleghorn Avenue, Dept. 989, Nashville, TN 37215.

6. *John Holt's Book and Music Store*, 2269 Massachusetts Avenue, Cambridge, MA 02140.

7. *Landmark Editions*, P.O. Box 4469, 1420 Kansas Avenue, Kansas City, MO 64127.

8. *Learning at Home*, P.O. Box 270, Honaunau, Hawaii 96726.

9. *National Council of Teachers of English*, 1111 Kenyon Road, Urbana, IL 61801.

10. *Pennsylvania Homeschoolers*, R.D. 2, Box 117, Kittanning, PA 16201.

11. *Teachers and Writers Collaborative*, 5 Union Square West, New York, NY 10003.

12. *Zephyr Press*, 430 S. Essex Lane, Tucson, AZ 85711.

General Books on Writing and Learning with Children:

Any Child Can Write, by Harvey S. Weiner. Reviewer Mary Pride says this is her very favorite book on writing.

The Art of Teaching Writing, by Lucy McCormick Calkins. Detailed look at the conference writing approach, with good description of different stages of writing at various ages. (3, 11)

Better Than School: One Family's Declaration of Independence, by Nancy Wallace. A wonderful inside look at one family's homeschooling, with much insight into writing and thinking at home. (4, 6)

Books are by People, Lee Bennett Hopkins. Citation Press. Short articles based on interviews with well–known children's authors and illustrators.

Coming to Know: Writing to Learn in the Intermediate Grades, by Nancie Atwell. Using writing to help students think more clearly in all subjects. (3)

Experiment with Fiction, by Donald Graves. Helps for moving into creating fiction, encouraging the adult to try all ideas along with the children. (3)

Families Writing, by Peter Stillman. Good look at how families can write together, save special family memories, and grow closer in the process. (6)

Free to Write: A Journalist Teaches Young Writers, by Roy Peter Clark. Great practical look at helping children in middle grades develop a journalist's outlook on writing, including many examples of articles by children. (3)

If You're Trying to Teach Kids how to Write, You've Got to Have this Book! by Marjorie Frank. A smorgasboard of suggestions for writing, may be especially useful for writing groups and clubs. (5)

Making Connections with Writing: An Expressive Writing Model in Japanese Schools, by Mary and Chisato Kitagawa. Two teachers visit Japanese schools and share the delightful, insightful and detailed writing of students; lots of samples of children's work. (3)

More than Stories: The Range of Children's Work, by Thomas Newkirk. Helping us get beyond thinking that writing, especially for children, is only official "story writing." (3)

On Writing Well, by William Zinsser. Wealth of ideas on how to improve your writing abilities. (6)

Plain Talk about Learning and Writing across the Curriculum, VA Dept. of Education. Collection of personal essays by teachers working in schools about how they are using writing in all subject areas, even in mathematics; engaging and concrete. (9)

Responding to Children's Writing: Becoming an Active Reader of Your Child's Work, by Susannah Sheffer. Good basic booklet to help you understand how adults can be a help to young writers without taking ownership of the writing task away from the child. (4, 6)

Roots in the Sawdust: Writing to Learn across the Disciplines, edited by Anne Gere. Thoughts from working teachers about using writing in all subject areas, helping students to become more active learners. (9)

The Three R's At Home, by Howard and Susan Richman. In depth discussion of writing process, among many other things, especially how beginning writers use inventive spelling and feel in charge of their own writing. (4, 6, 8, 10)

Write from the Start, by Donald Graves and Virginia Stuart. A must! Insightful look at how writing is usually taught in schools, why this doesn't work, and what parents and teachers can do instead. (6)

Writing the Natural Way: Using Right–Brain Techniques to Release Your Expressive Powers, by Gabriele Russo. Concrete ways to help turn off the critical side of your mind and let your real ideas flow with ease; especially good for high school students. (1)

Written and Illustrated by... A Revolutionary Two Brain Approach for Teaching Students how to Write and Illustrate Amazing Books, by David Melton. Very motivating book giving step by step plans for helping students create original books; lots of student illustrations and writing throughout. (7)

You CAN Teach Your Child Successfully: Grades 4–8, by Ruth Beechick. Good, commonsense ideas for homeschooling parents on how to teach writing, and all other subjects, without resorting to dull and repetitive textbooks. (2)

Poetry Helps:

Children Write Poetry: a Creative Approach, by Flora J. Arnstein. Dover Reprint, 1967. Includes wonderful examples of student poems, sharing how these children grew as writers over time.

For the Good of the Earth and Sun: Teaching Poetry, by Georgia Heard. Insights on poetry appreciation and writing; includes anthology of student poems. (3)

Miracles, by Richard Lewis. Simon and Schuster, 1966. A beautiful anthology of children's poems from all over the world, illustrated with children's artwork.

Sunrises and Songs: Reading and Writing Poetry in an Elementary Classroom, by Amy McClure. How to help middle elementary age students come to enjoy poetry and learn to produce sensitive and evocative poems of their own. (3)

Magazines that publish children's work:

Magazines marked with a * are solely made of up of childrens' work, while the others either publish selected children's articles or letters or run contests or have a special children's section.

*Children's Express: The News Service by Children for Everyone. Children's Express, Dept. P, 245 Seventh Avenue, New York, NY 10001.

*Creative Kids, P.O. Box 637, 100 Pine Avenue, Holmes, PA 19043.

Cobblestone: The History Magazine for Kids, 20 Grove Street, Peterborough, NH 03458

Cricket Magazine P.O.Box 300, Peru, IL 61354

Growing Without Schooling 2269 Massachusetts Avenue, Cambridge, MA 02140.

Highlights 803 Church Street, Honesdale, PA 18431

National Geographic World, Dept. 1706, 17th and M Street, NW Washington, DC 20036.

*Prism Magazine 1040 Bayview Drive, Suite 223, Ft. Lauderdale, FL 33304.

Ranger Rick Nature Magazine National Wildlife Federation, 8925 Leesburg Pike, Vienna, VA 22184-0001

*Shoe Tree, P.O. Box 452, Belvidere, NJ 07823.

*Skipping Stones: A Multi-Ethnic Children's Forum, 80574 Hazelton Road, Cottage Grove, OR 97424

*Stone Soup, Children's Art Foundation, P.O. Box 83, Santa Cruz, CA 95063.

*Young Writer's Challenge, 2255 N. University Parkway, Suite 15, Provo, Utah 84604. 800-678-8607.

Major Writing Contests for Children:

Contests can indeed be inspiring at times, especially once a writer gets going and feels his own voice and wants the challenge of trying for a wider audience. The focus of an official contest is often accepted more readily than the same focus given as an arbitrary "assignment."

Adlyn M. Keffer Memorial Short Story Writing Contest is an annual contest for kids ages 10-18. Write for more info to: National Story League Contest Chairman, Mrs. Edgar Hertzler, 561 Old Orchard Lane, Camp Hill, PA 17011.

All the Best Contests for Kids, by Joan Bergstrom and Craig Bergstrom. A terrific resource on contests of all sorts, with a lengthy section on both writing contests and specific magazines that children might write for along with good writing tips. (12)

Landmark Editions runs the annual "Written and Illustrated By...Contest," and chooses three books each year to professionally publish. As of 1990 they had published eleven high quality books, all of which my children love! (7)

Mott's Apple Awards hosts an annual book review contest for ages 5 to 12. Write to: The Mott's Apple Awards, c/o The International Reading Association, 800 Barksdale Road, Newark, DE 19714.

Raintree Publishers runs the annual "Publish–A–Book Contest" for students in grades 4–6, on selected topics or themes. Publishes one new book a year. Raintree Publishers Inc., 310 W. Wisconsin Ave., Milwaukee, WI 53203.

Shoe Tree Competition for Young Writers sponsors a writing contest in three categories: fiction, poetry, and nonfiction, for kids ages 6–14. Write to: The National Association for Young Writers, P.O. Box 452, Belvidere, NJ 07823.

Young Writer's Contest is an annual contest for grades 1–8 that publishes the winning entries in an anthology of children's work. Write to: Young Writer's Contest Foundation, P.O.Box 6092, McLean VA 22106

Editing and Writing Helps for Children:

BARE BOOKS Treetop Publishing, 220 Virginia Street, Racine, Wisconsin 53405. Publish blank books at affordable prices for children to write in; good for journals or finished and illustrated stories.

Learning Grammar Through Writing, by Sandra Bell and James Wheeler. Shows you how to use your child's own writing errors to teach grammar and usage, letting you by–pass a language drill textbook. (10)

Quick–Word Handbook for Everyday Writers, by Robert Forest and Rebecca Sitton. An easy to use personal spelling dictionary with 1020 high use words, and space for your child to fill in many more; a useful spelling tool for the younger writer. (10)

Keyboarding Skills: All Grades, by Diana Hanbury King. Jacob learned to touch type very easily with this manual which sensibly presents the letters in alphabetical order. (10)

Index

Pennsylvania Homeschoolers
Publishers

The Three R's At Home

Howard & Susan Richman

Gifted Children Monthly: *The Three R's at Home* by Howard and Susan Richman is packed full of anecdotes and practical advice gleaned from these two educators' experience homeschooling their four children.

Home Education Magazine: A warm personal look about how the Richmans homeschool their four children.

Mary Pride: Veteran home schoolers Susan and Howard Richman share their earthy educational philosophy along with tons of stories about how they and their friends "did it." ... A really fun book to read.

Subscribe to *PA Homeschoolers*

If you want to find out the latest in the lives of the Richman family, and read personal writing by other homeschoolers, you might consider subscribing to *PA Homeschoolers,* our 32 page newsletter that comes out four times a year. It is full of articles by homeschooling parents, reviews of homeschooling materials, book reviews by homeschooled children, a "BackPack" full of children's writing, and news about homeschooling in Pennsylvania.

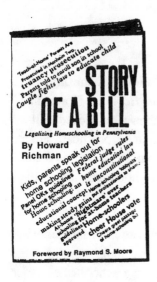

Lana Waldrop: Because Howard and Susan Richman's first book, *The Three R's at Home* was so good, I had no hesitation setting aside time to read another Richman publication. Still, I was surprised to find such gripping suspense in a book about a group of home schoolers getting a home schooling law.

Raymond Moore: In *Story of a Bill* ... you watch in awe as the drama unfolds.

Mary Pride: You will gain an education in how bills become law in a state capitol as well as be entertained by what is really a very gripping story, full of human interest.... The fast pace of a novel, the tension of a whodunit, and a happy ending!

Order Form
__ *The Three R's at Home*—$7.95 paperback (228 pages)
__ *Story of a Bill*—$6.95 paperback (152 pages)
__ *Writing from Home*—$8.95 paperback, $16.95 hardback
__ 6% **PA Sales Tax** on above items (Pennsylvania Residents Only)
__ *PA Homeschoolers* newsletter $10/year (call for rates after '91)
(We pay postage on pre–paid orders)

Make Checks payable to *PA Homeschoolers*
R.D. 2 -- Box 117
Kittanning, PA 16201
(412) 783-6512